# Old Songs in the Timeless Land:
## Medievalism in Australian Literature 1840–1910

by

Louise D'Arcens

BREPOLS

British Library Cataloguing in Publication Data

D'Arcens, Louise.
Old songs in the timeless land : medievalism in Australian
literature 1840-1910. -- (Making the Middle Ages ; v. 10)
1. Medievalism in literature. 2. Australian literature--
19th century--History and criticism.
I. Title II. Series
820.9'994'09034-dc23

ISBN-13: 9782503535661



D/2011/0095/204
ISBN 978-2-503-53566-1
Printed in the USA on acid-free paper

For Eva and Mimi

# Contents

# Illustrations

# Preface and Acknowledgements

This book emerges as a delayed response to a throw-away remark made by a European colleague in 1999 at the major international medieval studies conference held in England each year. The tenor of the remark was one of mystification at why I, an Australian, would be interested in the Middle Ages. Taking umbrage at what seemed to me to be a Europeanist claim to ownership of the medieval past, I responded by arguing that this period was available for study by scholars everywhere, and that excellent work on the Middle Ages could be produced beyond Europe, including in Australia — hardly a controversial argument, given the wealth of world-class scholarship produced by my Australian medievalist colleagues. Nevertheless, the question had gotten under my skin: what *was* the foundation of my interest in the Middle Ages as an Australian? Childhood reading habits? Catholic upbringing? This then gave rise to less navel-gazing versions of the question, such as: what have the Middle Ages 'meant' within Australian culture? Have there been forms of interest in, or ways of understanding, the medieval period that can be identified as 'Australian'? What cultural forces have shaped these local responses? These and other, related questions have led me to write this book. So, although I do not think this was her intention, I am grateful to this colleague for the provocation of her question.

My first entry point into Australian medievalism was academic, as I began to investigate the role of medieval studies in the formation of Australian humanities curricula, and the medieval interests of Australia's first professors. But the indefatigable efforts of the early colonial professors to educate the general public meant that my area of investigation kept widening beyond the universities — first to the public lectures the professors gave, then to the literary (and sometimes political) circles they frequented, and then ever wider, as I became increasingly aware of the need to understand the broader cultural scene into which they were lecturing. This has led me to explore, with some surprise and much pleasure, the large body of literature and theatre between 1840 and 1910 that drew on the Middle Ages both to entertain Australian audiences and, more seriously, to delineate a whole range of concerns particular to Australian society at the time.

It is not possible to capture in a single book the very great riches of nineteenth-century Australian medievalism. Some of the texts discussed in this book warrant detailed analysis in article-length studies, while some of the authors are, like their more famous British counterparts, deserving of their own book-length treatments as medievalists. Furthermore, the complex intersection of literary, theatrical, material, architectural, and pictorial medievalism is only sketched here, but would make a wonderful study. It is my hope that this book can provide a snapshot of what literature is available from the colonial and early Federal period in Australia, in order to inspire others to continue with the excavation.

Some of the chapters in this book draw on material previously published elsewhere. I would like to thank the editors of the following publications for their kind permission to use material from the following articles and chapters: 'From Holy War to Border Skirmish: The Colonial Chivalry of Sydney's First Professors', *Journal of Medieval and Early Modern Studies*, 30 (2000), 519–45; 'Antipodean Idylls: An Early Australian Translation of Tennyson's Medievalism', in *Postcolonial Moves in Medieval, Early Modern, and Baroque Studies*, ed. by Patricia Ingham and Michelle R. Warren (Basingstoke and New York: Palgrave, 2003), pp. 237–56; 'Inverse Invasions: Medievalism and Colonialism in Rolf Boldrewood's A Sydney-Side Saxon', in *Parergon: Journal of the Australian and New Zealand Association for Medieval and Early Modern Studies*, 22 (2005), 159–82; '"The Last Thing One Might Expect": The Mediaeval Court at the 1866 Intercolonial Exhibition', *The La Trobe Journal*, 81 (2008), 26–39; and 'The Past is Another Country: Forms of Australian Medievalism', *Medievalismo/s: De la disciplina y otros espacios imaginados*, Special Issue, *Revista de poética medieval*, 21 (2008), 319–56.

I owe a debt of gratitude to many:

Research for this book has been carried out with financial support from the Australian Research Council (ARC), the University of Melbourne (for an ARC near-miss grant in 2008 that allowed archival work to progress), and the University of Wollongong's wonderful post-maternity leave support scheme, which provided crucial research-assistance funding at a time when I was unable to get to the archives. Finally, the tremendously supportive ARC Network for Early European Research (NEER) has provided financial assistance that has allowed me to meet with colleagues and develop a number of research projects and proposals over the last five years in conjunction with colleagues in the Australasian Medievalisms research cluster.

I offer my heartfelt gratitude to my main fellow-travellers in Australian medievalism, my ARC research partners Professor Stephanie Trigg, Professor Andrew Lynch, and Professor John Ganim. I wish to thank them for many thought-provoking conversations, their comments on my research, for allowing me to hear and read their very inspiring work, and for many other generosities of a more personal kind. They are a joy to know and to work with. So too are my colleagues in the English Literatures Program at the University of Wollongong, whose collegial, friendly, and ethical approach to working together has earned my deepest respect and trust. I am also grateful to other medievalist and 'medievalism-ist' colleagues and friends for many helpful discussions. These include Chris Jones, David Matthews, Anke Bernau, Helen Dell, David Lawton, Nadia Altschul, Kathleen Davis, Richard Utz, Jenna Mead, Clare Monagle, Lawrence Warner, and Melanie Duckworth. My thanks also to the many talented scholars who, over the past decade or so, have turned medievalism studies into such a vibrant field.

For a medievalist, broaching the complex and fascinating public culture of nineteenth-century Australia has been truly daunting, but also exhilarating. I am grateful to the many scholars of Australian literature, theatre, history, and cultural studies whose work helped me to navigate my way across these deep waters, which proved far less familiar than they first seemed. Of my Australianist colleagues, I must single out Leigh Dale and Nicholas Birns for guidance and for reading sections of the manuscript. Those kind enough to have read or listened to earlier versions of the research in this book, and to have offered salutary suggestions, have also included Michael Ackland, Peter Otto, Veronica Kelly, and Robert Dixon.

I have been very fortunate to have had wonderful research and digitization assistants. Many thanks to Sarah Ailwood at the University of Wollongong (now at the University of Canberra) and Anne McKendry at the University of Melbourne for their assistance in archival gathering, and to Jane Sisley at the Australian National University for assistance with digitizing materials. I have been also been gathering materials myself toward this project for a number of years, and need to thank the staff of the Mitchell Library and New South Wales State Library, the State Library of Victoria, the Baillieu Library at the University of Melbourne, The Archives Department of the University of Sydney, New South Wales State Records, and the University Archives and Fryer Library at the University of Queensland.

Geraldine Barnes and Margaret Clunies Ross, my Brepols series editors, have again combined rigour with generosity in their reading of the full manuscript, and I am very grateful for their time and dedication. I would like to offer thanks also to the team at Brepols, especially Claire Mabey, Simon Forde, and Juleen Eichinger, for professional and pleasant dealings throughout the publication process. My thanks go also to Terri-ann White at the University of Western Australia Press for her support of the project from the very beginning, and for the cooperative spirit with which she approached the publication of this book. Thanks also to Chris Tiffin for his thorough and efficient indexing work.

I wish to thank my family, and especially my parents, Brian and Paulina, whose combination of practical assistance (especially babysitting) and quiet encouragement has sustained me over many years. I have also been blessed to have many invaluable friendships, old and new, from which I have drawn sustenance, goodwill, and much-needed distraction. Love and thanks especially to Helen Curic, Antoinette Chan, Cynthia Parr, Sharon Hancock, Peter Looker, Emily Ballou, Julia Bell, Irene Lucchitti, Barbara Curtis, and Emma Griffiths.

My husband Robert Sinnerbrink has been unfailingly supportive throughout this project, and has responded with grace, generosity, and fortitude when prevailed upon to discuss everything from central concepts to the minutiae of phraseology, usually at horrible hours and when he had his own writing to do. I thank him from the bottom of my heart. Finally, I wish to thank my beautiful daughters Eva and Mimi, who were born into their mother's preoccupation with Australian medievalism, and who have endured (mostly) patiently many visits to libraries, archives, galleries, and churches from their youngest days. I will never forget their indulgence of me on days when they would rather have been playing. It is to them, with love, that I dedicate this book.

Introduction

# Warring Elements? Medievalism and Australian Identity in Nineteenth-Century Australian Literature

In the *Fremantle Herald*, 14 May 1881, the local poet 'Gerontius' defended his column 'Legends of the King' against readers' complaints about its regular inclusion of medieval legends. The complaints, which we can only guess at through Gerontius's response to them, seem not to have been directed at the author's highly idiosyncratic reworking of these legends, but aimed deeper, pointing to a troubling un-Australianness at the very heart of his literary endeavour. He was not, we infer, seen to be producing Australian writing for Australian audiences. Gerontius hit back at his critics by demanding why medievalism and a sense of Australian modernity need be regarded as literary antagonists:

> Cannot a man have a cool Australian tone in him and a 'well chewed over' relish [...] for 'mediæval brac a brac' and ancient story? The answer is yours reader to make [...] we may have occasion to show you that the two warring elements may exist peaceably together.[1]

Gerontius's readers were not completely misguided in their perception that the author's dogged (and frequently long-winded) exploration of 'old world notions' sat somewhat at odds both with the up-to-date agenda of the news publication in which it appeared, and with their own desire for a literature that reflected their contemporary Australian environs. As opposed to, say, France, Germany, or the British Isles, where modernity rubbed shoulders physically with the remnants of the medieval past, a preoccupation with the Middle Ages can seem fundamentally counter-intuitive in a collection of colonies whose European settlement commenced

[1] 'Gerontius', *Fremantle Herald*, 14 May 1881, p. 6.

at the High Enlightenment date of 1788. Indeed, Australian historians such as John Gascoigne have pointed persuasively to the formative role of Enlightenment ideals in the development of colonial (and modern) Australia's political, intellectual, economic, and sectarian complexion.[2] But the Enlightenment was not the only European cultural legacy to make a powerful impact on colonial Australia's public life or to shape the self-perceptions of its settler society. Taking Gerontius's lead, this book aims to show that far from being 'warring elements', for many writers in the Australian colonies, a deep cultural and personal attachment to the European Middle Ages coexisted with a determined identification with Australian modernity. A surprising number of writers reached to the Middle Ages for motifs, narrative models, myths, characters, and historical events to express a sense not just of the European past but also the Australian present and future. This is not to say that this literary coexistence was always, as Gerontius claimed, peaceable: indeed in many texts it was divided and strained, with medievalism struggling for air amidst the mélange of cultural allusions surrounding it — classical, oriental, Renaissance, and even, in some cases, indigenous Australian. In other cases Australian writers' medievalism was laced with hostility or irony toward, and exasperation with, the Middle Ages. But even when the medieval period was being explicitly rejected as feudal, hidebound, and barbaric, or alternatively as absurdly romantic and effete, it nevertheless loomed large within the consciousness of those writers trying to understand their own, and Australia's, place within the world at large.

To anyone familiar with the phenomenon of medievalism — the post-medieval imaginative recovery and recreation of the Middle Ages — the proposition of a particularly Australian return to the Middle Ages seems far from counter-intuitive or absurd. The fundamentally creative nature of medievalism means that the absence of the Middle Ages, far from being an obstacle to their transhistorical survival, is a condition that in fact guarantees their abiding presence in the modern cultural imaginary. In places such as Australia, where the archaeological and material traces of an *in situ* medieval past are necessarily absent, this absence, and the sense of historical discontinuity that accompanies it, are the conditions on which all medievalist practice is predicated.[3]

[2] See John Gascoigne, *The Enlightenment and the Origins of European Australia* (Cambridge: Cambridge University Press, 2002).

[3] For a comparable argument about the role played by distance in the study of the Middle Ages in the United States, see Paul Freedman and Gabrielle Spiegel, 'Medievalisms Old and New: The Rediscovery of Alterity in North American Medieval Studies', *American Historical Review*, 103 (1998), 677–704.

The opening stanza of a poem by 'Veni' published in the *Sydney Morning Herald* on 25 October 1882 captures beautifully how the absence of a local medieval past worked as a paradoxical incitement to dwell on this era. Written in response to the destruction by fire of the Garden Palace, the venue that had housed the 1879 Sydney International Exhibition, the poem also contains a meditation on the young colony's lack of picturesque historical traces:

> Ruins! Alas! We have been wont to say
> With half-regretful tone, that in the grace
> And glory of our country's youthful day
> The mystic charm of ruins had no place —
> We lack'd the eerie magic of the Past.
> The moss-grown battlements, and chronic page —
> Did our presumptuous folly think to cast
> On form so fair, the rusty garb of age?

In talking about the colony's bemoaned lack of 'the mystic charm of ruins' and 'the eerie magic of the Past', the writer cannot but call up these very things and imagine them into existence for his/her audience. The concluding lines of the stanza 'Ah Fate, more keen than Time, has shewn us how / One hour sufficed to trace a wrinkle on her [Australia's] brow!' suggest that while Australia lacks authentic medieval presence, her recent acquaintance with Fate's fiery misfortunes, which decimates human civilization with greater speed and savagery than slow-working time, has vaulted her toward a cultural maturity echoing that of more venerable, ruin-strewn societies.[4] As I will go on to argue, these conditions of absence and distance, whether wistfully acknowledged (as in the above poem) or wilfully embraced, granted Australian medievalism throughout the colonial and early Federated period a significant interpretive freedom, paving the way for a wide-ranging and fertile engagement with a world that was, for many, in the strictest sense the product of memory and imagination.

Yet to focus alone on absence, geographical distance and historical discontinuity would be disingenuous. For as a local cultural discourse, Australian medievalism emerged in part as a legacy of British colonialism, and as such also reflects the extent to which this nation has, its physical remoteness and avowed modernity notwithstanding, maintained a sense of proximity to, and continuity with, the medieval European heritage of its settler culture. Its literature, architecture, parliamentary rituals, and material and performance culture all attest to colonial

[4] This poem is also discussed in Andrew Montana, *The Art Movement in Australia: Design, Taste and Society 1875–1900* (Carlton, Vic.: Miegunyah, 2000), p. 176.

Australia's desire to situate itself within deep European and English tradition. This forceful, indeed often urgent, assertion of proximity to illustrious European tradition was motivated not only by a simple desire to overcome geographical isolation but, more murkily, by a denial of the shame of its origins as a British penal colony — and, more problematically still, by a wilful disavowal of the long aboriginal past that was treated with such disregard in the wake of British colonialism. It is for this reason that this book bears the title 'Old Songs in the Timeless Land': it is a key responsibility of any scholarship on medievalism within settler societies such as Australia to recognize the extent to which colonial evocations of continuity with European and English antique tradition were implicated in the refusal and displacement of local traditions that were as sophisticated, and even more ancient. Of course, the notion of pre-colonial and indigenous Australia as a 'timeless land' is, as many have noted, troubling in its misattribution of primitive, ahistorical changelessness to non-European cultures — a misattribution, moreover, that has mandated the imposition of European culture and *chronos* over indigenous 'nature' and its apparently limitless *eion.* This phrase (which Australian readers will recognize as quoting the title of Eleanor Dark's 1941 novel of settlement, *The Timeless Land*), is not, then, evoked uncritically here. Rather, it is used as a reminder of the context of cultural and historical contestation in which Australian colonial medievalist writing was produced. The vast majority of the colonial texts examined in this book do not engage with the indigenous cultures and traditions they are serenely and often only half-consciously displacing, and as such this narrative of historical contestation does not figure overtly in much of the discussion to follow. But it is necessary to frame this relative silence within a prefatory acknowledgement that many of the practices of colonial Australian medievalism can be seen to reflect Australian historian Tom Griffiths's assertion that 'the Great Australian Silence' on indigenous dispossession has been less a silence than a 'white noise' which has '[...] consisted of an obscuring and overlaying din of history-making'.[5]

A prime instance of this gesture of historical displacement is the Mediaeval Court featured at the 1866 Melbourne Intercolonial Exhibition (Figure 1), which showcased the wares of local construction and decoration firms within the charming oddity of an ersatz 'Old English' cathedral interior.

[5] Tom Griffiths, *Hunters and Collectors: The Antiquarian Imagination in Australia* (Cambridge: Cambridge University Press, 1996), p. 4.

Figure 1. Albert Charles Cooke, 'The Mediaeval Court, Intercolonial Exhibition, engraving. *The Australian News for Home Readers*, 20 December 1866. Image courtesy of the State Library of Victoria.

The Court's quietly triumphal engagement with imperialist historicism was evident in the choice of a medieval aesthetic, which embodied a benign, 'universal' English Christian past that had apparently been transplanted effortlessly, and rightfully, in colonial soil. The Court epitomized what Peter Hoffenberg has called the 'imperial nostalgia' of nineteenth-century exhibition culture, its 'cultural policy to create and preserve [...] historical fantasies' in order to create 'an historical Australia' in this case via an evocation of modern Australia's connection to English antiquity.[6] Through its integrated recreation of ancient Christianity and Englishness, the Court also aimed to mark the triumph of this cultural heritage over the 'primitive' indigenous cultures of Australasia and the Pacific, which were represented at the Exhibition in a desultory and fragmented fashion. The scattering of aboriginal artefacts throughout several locales in the exhibition had the cumulative effect of representing indigenous culture as a dispersed and piecemeal culture, with its decontextualized artefacts approaching the status of bric-a-brac, in contrast with the Mediaeval Court, whose richly intact chamber reflected the intactness of the culture it embodied. Here, European antiquarianism and indigenous ethnology were competing discourses for understanding the colony's past.[7] In featuring and fêting the Mediaeval Court as it did, colonial Melbourne nominated unmistakably the cultural infancy that it believed would best fit its ideal image of metropolitan maturity.

It is the charged, complex dialectic of proximity and distance, continuity and rupture, and the ways it has shaped Australian medievalism, that will be the focus of much of this book. Focusing for the most part on literary and theatrical examples from Australia's colonial era, with some discussion of the physical and material culture surrounding their production, this study aims to demonstrate that this dialectic has long been the distinguishing principle of Australian medievalism, encompassing even its most stylistically and ideologically divergent articulations. In a number of cases it has manifested itself through sophisticated, sustained, and self-consciously 'Australian' engagements with medieval characters, events, and motifs. As will be discussed in the final two chapters, however, it is equally, though more obliquely, detectible in what can be described as early Australia's 'throwaway' medievalism: that is the more voluminous body of texts in which the presence of medievalist tropes is incidental, fleeting, and historically undiscriminating. While the study of the former category of texts is undeniably more exegetically satisfying, and yields more obviously rich material for cultural diagnosis, it is also possible to make a case for the importance of examining throwaway medievalism for what it can tell us about the dominant tastes and ideological concerns that have shaped popular Australian medievalism. Emphasizing the largely diffuse, promiscuous

[6] Peter H. Hoffenberg, *An Empire on Display: English, Indian, and Australian Exhibitions from the Crystal Palace to the Great War* (Berkeley: University of California Press, 2001), p. 273.

[7] For a masterful account of these competing views of the past in colonial Victoria, and the relationship between time and timelessness in white perceptions of Aboriginal culture, see Griffiths, *Hunters and Collectors*.

quality of nineteenth-century medievalism is also important as a counter-narrative to the dominant story in which Eurocentric, magisterial Victorian medievalism held sway until its decline under high modernism, after which a fragmented or ironic postmodern reanimation of the Middle Ages took place. Instead, we see that in colonial Australia an ironic, parodic engagement began virtually simultaneously with the more reverent forms of medievalism.

The more sophisticated and developed texts, which will be discussed in Chapters 1 to 3, are most commonly novels and poetry collections from the later colonial period — that is, the final three decades of the nineteenth century — through to the years immediately following Federation. Despite their often complex and ideologically revealing engagement with the Middle Ages and with nineteenth-century practices of medievalism, these texts are only just beginning to be examined for their medievalist content. Although there is no shortage of high quality work on them by Australianists, it is the exception rather than the rule to find this work taking into account their medievalism, except very occasionally (and very briefly) under the rubric of colonial literature's responses to European romanticism and Gothic literature. The last few years have, however, witnessed a growing tendency to treat medievalism in Australian literature and culture as a subject worth analysing in its own right. This shift began fairly unobtrusively about a decade ago with a small number of individual scholars, virtually all of them medievalists working in the discipline of English literature, producing isolated studies either of medievalism or of the development of medieval studies in Australia.[8] Inspired in part by the increasing stream of recent work within medieval studies, particularly that which has analysed medievalism as an instrument of European nationalism, Australian scholars were nevertheless quick to discern that this work's neglect of colonialism as the complement and obverse of European nationalism meant that medievalism's complex intersection with colonial and postcolonial cultures was being overlooked.[9] While one approach to Australian

[8] The main figures in this regard have been Stephanie Trigg, Andrew Lynch, Louise D'Arcens, Jenna Mead (who produced the earliest work in this area), David Matthews, and Geraldine Barnes. For summaries of the development of academic studies of the Middle Ages in Australia, see Louise D'Arcens, 'Europe in the Antipodes: Australian Medieval Studies', in *Studies in Medievalism X, Medievalism and the Academy II*, ed. by David Metzger (Cambridge: Brewer, 1998), pp. 13–40; and Helen Fulton, 'Medieval Studies in Australia', *AUMLA: Journal of the Australasian Universities Language and Literature Association*, 100 (2003), 1–12.

[9] See, for instance, Louise D'Arcens's comments in 'Europe in the Antipodes', 'From Holy War to Border Skirmish: The Colonial Chivalry of Sydney's First Professors', *Journal of Medieval and Early Modern Studies*, 30 (2000), 519–45, and 'Antipodean Idylls: An Early Australian

medievalism has been oriented toward correcting this bias by writing about the important but occluded role of medievalism in Australian social, political, and material culture, other work has additionally used the conceptual and ideological framework offered by postcolonial studies to challenge explicitly the omission of Australia from the received narratives of medievalism. Postcolonial theory, particularly Homi K. Bhabha's extrapolation of Sigmund Freud in his discussion of the post/colonial uncanny (*unheimlich*), has proven especially valuable, as its emphasis on the notion of repressed, estranged familiarity captures perfectly the unexpected iterations of the medieval in the antipodean environment.[10] Less conspicuously theoretical, but equally valuable, has been the excellent body of work produced on imperial culture and on white settler culture, which has provided a nuanced vocabulary for elucidating the complex and divided cultural allegiances reflected in the medievalism produced in societies such as colonial Australia.[11]

A rapid increase in momentum over the past few years has seen this formerly solitary pursuit transformed into a collective concern, as scholars of Australian medievalism have not only grown in their ranks but have also, more importantly, begun to form a range of vital research collaborations. One especially significant and valuable development was the publication in 2005 of the volume of essays *Medievalism and the Gothic in Australian Culture*, edited by Stephanie Trigg. The aim of that volume is, in Trigg's words, to 're-examin[e] the various historical and mythological deployments of the medieval and Gothic past across a range of social cultural fields [...] in the Australian context'.[12] Co-published through Brepols's *Making the Middle Ages* series and the University of Melbourne Press, this volume

Translation of Tennyson's Medievalism', in *Postcolonial Moves in Medieval, Early Modern, and Baroque Studies*, ed. by Patricia Ingham and Michelle R. Warren (Basingstoke and New York: Palgrave, 2003), pp. 237–56.

[10] See Homi K. Bhabha, *The Location of Culture* (London and New York: Routledge, 1994), especially pp. 136–37.

[11] See, for instance, Anna Johnston and Alan Lawson, 'Settler Colonies', in *A Companion to Postcolonial Studies*, ed. by Sangeeta Ray (Maldon, MA, and Oxford: Blackwell, 2000), pp. 360–76. Johnston and Lawson articulate Australian settlers' self-understanding as British yet not-British. They argue that the settlers' sense of alienation from their parent culture was shot through with an internalized hegemonic notion of themselves as 'second class' or 'feral' English subjects. For another useful discussion of the mixture of allegiance and resistance in settler subjects, see Stephen Slemon, 'Unsettling the Empire: Resistance Theory for the Second World', in *Contemporary Postcolonial Theory: A Reader*, ed. by Padmini Mongia (London: Arnold, 1996), pp. 72–83.

[12] *Medievalism and the Gothic in Australian Culture*, ed. by Stephanie Trigg (Turnhout: Brepols, 2005), p. xiii.

aims simultaneously to introduce Australian medievalism to the international field and to initiate Australian readers into the rich but under-recognized phenomenon of local medievalism. It is wide-ranging in its scope, spanning from colonial to twenty-first-century Australian culture, and examining the traces of the medieval, and the active evocation of the medieval, in Australian literature, architecture, popular culture, secular and religious communities, and political institutions and rituals. It is also significant for bringing together the work of medievalists and Australianists. That this broad survey volume is far from exhaustive in its coverage is less a shortcoming than a reflection of the relative infancy of research into this area, and an indication of the large-scale recovery project that lies ahead. This will be a two-fold project involving both exhuming neglected materials and looking at well-known elements of Australian culture with new eyes trained to detect their medievalist substratum. It is to this project that this book aims to make a contribution.

## *Colonial Gothics and the Challenge of Locating Australian Medievalism*

While to nineteenth-century English and European eyes the Australian landscape cannot have borne the signs of a medieval past, this did not prevent its inhabitants or visitors from medievalizing it. One of the most concrete and conspicuous means of achieving this was, as historians such as Brian Andrew have documented, architectural.[13] The colonial civic centres, especially Sydney and Melbourne, were transformed from the middle decades of the nineteenth century by the construction of a number of impressive and ambitious buildings in the then-fashionable Gothic Revival style. The continuing visual dominance of these landmark structures, with their evocations of premodern grandeur, ritual, and piety, prompts Trigg to argue that 'Australia conceives the historical past primarily under the sign of late eighteenth- and nineteenth-century Gothic'.[14] Just two of the most famous examples in Sydney are the main building of the University of Sydney, designed in the 1850s by Sir Edmund Blacket, and St Mary's Catholic Cathedral, designed in the 1860s by William Wilkinson Wardell, Australia's foremost disciple of the English architectural revivalist Augustus Welby Pugin. Among Melbourne's best-known (and, today, best-loved) Gothic Revival buildings is the English,

[13] See Brian Andrew, *Australian Gothic: The Gothic Revival in Australian Architecture from the 1840s to the 1950s* (Carlton, Vic.: Miegunyah, 2001).

[14] 'Introduction', in *Medievalism and the Gothic in Australian Culture*, ed. by Trigg, p. xiii.

Scottish, and Australian (ES&A) Bank, also designed in Venetian Gothic style by William Wardell and built between 1883 and 1887.[15] Nor was this limited to urban centres: among the more striking rural examples was what historian Michael Sharland has called the 'fowl castle', an eccentric Gothic tower-shaped dovecote, which is one of two battlemented towers built at mid-century by the landholder Joseph Archer on his properties in the Tasmanian Midlands.[16] Most famous, perhaps, and entirely singular in the Australian context, was the monastic township of New Norcia, located on the Victoria Plains north of Perth in Western Australia, which grew up around the isolated aboriginal mission that had been founded in 1846 by displaced Spanish Benedictines.[17] Although its distinctive and eclectic blend of Gothic Revival, Spanish Mission, and Italian Renaissance-influenced buildings was to come some decades after the initial settlement, the foundational act of naming it after Benedict's birthplace is a clear evocation of the ancient monastic tradition of which it continues today to be a living artefact.

And yet the name *New* Norcia is more complex than this, for it is suggestive of continuity but also of rupture, implying that the establishment of this community was also the foundational moment of a new tradition belonging to the red soil of the New World. It is true that as a Spanish and Catholic settlement, New Norcia was somewhat anomalous within Australia's dominant British Protestant *translatio imperii*; nevertheless, its historical ambiguity was typical, underlining the extent to which medievalizing the land- and streetscapes of colonial Australia was an undertaking fraught with ambivalence. On the one hand these buildings, especially

[15] See Sarah Randles, 'Rebuilding the Middle Ages: Medievalism in Australian Architecture', in *Medievalism and the Gothic in Australian Culture*, ed. by Trigg, pp. 147–69. For a more comprehensive discussion of Australia's Gothic Revival Architecture, see Andrew, *Australian Gothic*. For a more theoretically sophisticated analysis of Gothic style and imperial and post/colonial ideologies, see the essays in *Empire and the Gothic: The Politics of Genre*, ed. by Andrew Smith and William Hughes (New York: Palgrave Macmillan, 2003).

[16] Sharland's description, from his *Stones of a Century* (1957), is quoted by Jenna Mead in 'Medievalism and Memory Work: Archer's Folly and the Gothic Revival Pile', in *Medievalism and the Gothic in Australian Culture*, ed. by Trigg, pp. 99–118 (pp. 105–06).

[17] The history and recent developments of New Norcia are outlined in a number of publications, one of which is *A Place Like No Other: The Living Tradition of New Norcia*, ed. by David Hutchison (South Fremantle: Fremantle Arts Centre, 1995). See the settlement's website <http://www.newnorcia.wa.edu.au/> for information about its history and its current activities. A more recent foundation, the Cistercian abbey of Tarrawarra in Yarra Glen, East of Melbourne, is discussed by Megan Cassidy-Welch in '"A Place of Horror and Vast Solitude": Medieval Monasticism and the Australian Landscape', in *Medievalism and the Gothic in Australian Culture*, ed. by Trigg, pp. 189–204.

the earlier ones, were highly visible assertions of the colonies' links with the imperial centre — Archer's towers, for instance, functioned, in Jenna Mead's apt phrase, as 'a synecdoche for Englishness'[18] — and as evocations of a venerable past surviving into the present. This pursuit of cultural continuity is epitomized in Edmund Blacket's statement that '[i]t is impossible for an Englishman to think of an University without thinking of Mediaeval Architecture', a conviction that underpinned his Gothic Revival design for the University of Sydney.[19] On the other hand, they embodied the proud beginnings of a distinct local settler culture. First of all, they came to differ from their English and European counterparts, both medieval and medievalist, at a material level, in that they were partly built from local raw products such as Pyrmont sandstone and Australian blackwood, mingled local motifs among the traditional symbolism of their heraldic carvings and stained glass windows, and altered their dimensions to accommodate the greater heat and harsher light of the antipodean environs. Secondly, and more importantly, they made tangible the prosperous colonies' aspirations to challenge the primacy of their imperial parent culture, and to shed some of its ideological baggage. While the design of University of Sydney's main buildings might have purposely evoked the great medieval English universities, the notable absence of religious iconography on their windows and stonework reflects the colonists' determination to avoid the sectarian divisions that plagued the British university system. Similarly, as Sarah Randles perceptively notes, the Neo-Gothic grandeur of St Mary's cathedral, like the Melbourne Mediaeval Court discussed earlier, 'evoked the sense of an unbroken religious tradition' between Old and New Worlds, but also advertised a different sectarian complexion for the colony, 'help[ing] to give Catholicism a position in the mainstream of Australian society very different from that which it had occupied in Britain'.[20]

The impulse to medievalize the Australian landscape continued into the literature which is the focus of this book. Here too the Gothic proved to be a serviceable literary idiom for those attempting to render the forbidding and, to European eyes, perverse grandeur and desolation of the Australian natural scene. Unlike ecclesiastical architecture, in literature the Gothic was not the only, or even the dominant, medievalist representation favoured by Australians; as the chapters of this book show, chivalric and heroic images of the past also loomed large within

[18] Mead, 'Medievalism and Memory Work', p. 104.

[19] Quoted in Randles, 'Rebuilding the Middle Ages', p. 155.

[20] Randles, 'Rebuilding the Middle Ages', p. 153.

the colonial medievalist imaginary, along with the nostalgic notions of preindustrial medieval harmony popularized by John Ruskin, William Morris, and the aesthetic movement that emerged in their wake. But it deserves an honourable mention here for methodological reasons, as it throws into relief the complexities involved in identifying certain forms of medievalism in Australian literature. As the unruly opposite of the resplendent architecture that bore the same name, the Australian literary Gothic described the local natural scene in terms that strongly aligned this landscape with the gloomy medieval architectural spaces of Gothic fiction; but it did so without making direct mention of the Middle Ages. This period was, rather, evoked obliquely as a literary construction, via a series of tropes and adjectives associated with modern fantasies of dark and brutal premodernity. But it is vital that this indirect mode of allusion does not lead us to disqualify these texts as examples of medievalism. For, as will be discussed later into this chapter and throughout the book, the heavily mediated relationship to the medieval past in these and other works is a distinguishing feature of Australian medievalism — and, indeed, of medievalism itself.

One of the best-known literary articulations of the Gothic landscape in nineteenth-century Australia, by Marcus Clarke, demonstrates this well. Clarke does not Gothicize this landscape by dotting it nostalgically with baronial ruins or deserted churches; rather, he ingeniously presents it as a haunting (and haunted) but aesthetically generative space in which the Australian poet can learn to sing, using the land's sublime Gothic vocabulary: 'whispered to by the myriad tongues of the wilderness, [the poet] learns the language of the barren and the uncouth; he can read the hieroglyphics of haggard gum trees [...] [t]he phantasmagoria of that wild dreamland called the Bush interprets itself'.[21] This Gothicizing of the landscape was, moreover, not limited to literature: it is strongly evident in paintings such as Eugene von Guérard's *South End of Tasman's Island* (1867), in which the image of the fluted, Jurassic South East coast of Tasmania is painted to resemble the imposing ruin of a medieval castle or cathedral and the towering pipes of a great ecclesiastical organ. The fact that the rock formations on this coast have attracted such names as Cathedral Rock, while other cliffs in the Tasmanian interior are called the Organ Pipes, suggests that von Guérard was not alone in reading the Tasmanian landscape through a Gothic architectural vocabulary.

Late nineteenth-century writers also reached for familiar Gothic tropes when contemplating the violence at the heart of Australia's colonial history, from the

[21] Marcus Clarke, 'Preface' to Adam Lindsay Gordon, *Sea Spray and Smoke Drift*, in Gordon, *Poems* (1893; London and Melbourne: Thompson, Massina, 1920), pp. v–xiv.

enforced banishment and institutional brutality endured by convicts in the years of penal settlement to the cruelty and degradation meted out by white settlers to the dispossessed indigenous Australians. Again Marcus Clarke figures, with his representation of the barbarity of Australia's then recently defunct convict system in his 'realist' historical romance *His Natural Life* (serialized 1870–71; book publication 1874), which is ranked among the most important Australian novels of the nineteenth century. With its accounts of convicts descending into savagery, murder, and even cannibalism, Clarke's gruesome account of penal servitude in the colony of Van Diemen's Land (now Tasmania) confronts us with a purgatorial world of tortured souls alienated from their humanity.[22] Clarke's recourse to these Gothic images presents convictism as, to use David Matthews's incisive phrase, 'Australia's own equivalent to castellated culture'[23] — that is, a ghastly punitive past that echoes the Gothicized medieval past, and within whose contours lurk the spectral presences of the abused and their tormentors. Matthews's notion of equivalence is corroborated by Henry Kingsley's eponymous narrator in the 1859 novel *The Recollections of Geoffry Hamlyn*, who says that the horrors of 'penal servitude for life' in Van Diemen's Land convey to modern Australians the 'idea of what it used to be in old times'.[24] Kingsley's allusions to convict life also evoke bleak images of violence, lunacy, and cannibalism — the latter strongly indicating (as with Clarke's novel) the influence of the notorious case of Alexander Pearce, the Irish convict who in 1822 confessed to cannibalizing fellow escapees while on the run from the Macquarie Harbour penal settlement. Elsewhere, as is exemplified by J. M. Marsh's poem 'At Sandy Crossing', the primeval horror of the land colludes with the nightmarish isolation of frontier life, leading to madness, alcoholism, moral decay, and a cycle of violent retribution between settlers and aborigines. Marsh's bleak image of a deserted outback station reads like a veritable sampler of Gothic commonplaces. To quote from the second stanza only:

> Swift the filing years have flitted o'er the stage of hoary time
> Since the house of 'Sandy Crossing' flourished in its baleful prime
> ... Now the prowling fearsome dingo howls his monody of woe,
> And the hooting mopehawk answers when the moon is very low —

[22] Marcus Clarke, *His Natural Life*, ed. by Graham Tulloch, intro. by Michael Meehan (Oxford and New York: Oxford University Press, 1997).

[23] David Matthews, 'Marcus Clarke, Gothic, Romance', in *Medievalism and the Gothic in Australian Culture*, ed. by Trigg, pp. 3–17 (p. 9).

[24] Henry Kingsley, *The Recollections of Geoffry Hamlyn* (Cambridge: Macmillan, 1859), p. 295.

> Like to sprites of evil omen o'er the forest harpy's lair
> For the blood of many victims ever cries for vengeance there.[25]

Again, there is no direct evocation of the Middle Ages as a historical period or even as a source of ancient legends. But the ubiquitous Gothic evocation of medieval barbarity, decay, and gloom haunts the poem's image of this colonial scene, lurking unmistakably at one remove, recognizable yet mutated by its contact with a new, non-European society.

## *The Colonial Medievalist Trace: Structure and Rationale of this Study*

The dialectic of historical fidelity and imaginative departure outlined in this introduction is not unique to Australia, but is, rather, reflective of medievalism as an intellectual and cultural practice in general, whether Old or New World. Studies of Victorian England, for instance, frequently remind us that the recuperative and creative impulses of Victorian medievalism emerged out of the perception that industrialization and mass urbanization — in short, modernity — had alienated the English from their own history and left them, in the words of Richard Schoch, 'dememorialized in their own time'.[26] But if we think of medievalism as flourishing in this gap of dememorialization, oscillating between departure from and return to the medieval past, then Australian medievalism, which responds to a double dispossession from European history across time and space, can arguably be seen to be one of the most potent and complex expressions — indeed, even a quintessential example — of medievalist practice.[27]

Thinking about Australian medievalism as quintessential medievalism is useful because it enables us to understand Australian appropriations of the Middle Ages without resorting to pejorative notions of them as derivative of British forms, which are then erroneously elevated to the status of models, despite themselves

[25] J. M. Marsh, 'At Sandy Crossing', in *A Golden Shanty: Australian Stories and Sketches in Prose and Verse* (Sydney: Bulletin Newspaper, Series No. 1, 1890), pp. 53–54.

[26] Richard Schoch, *Shakespeare's Victorian Stage: Performing History in the Theatre of Charles Kean* (Cambridge: Cambridge University Press, 1998), p. 12.

[27] A comparable claim about the 'exemplary' nature of Australian medievalism is made by Trigg, although she is evaluating the particular phenomenon of medieval revival: 'there can be no pretence of medieval survival [...] In this regard, Australian medievalism is actually exemplary. Unable to mask the very real differences between the medieval and the modern through an implied physical continuity, it foregrounds the acts of recuperation that I argue condition and structure all [acts of revival]'. *Medievalism and the Gothic in Australian Culture*, ed. by Trigg, p. xvi.

being appropriations. If we accept the idea that British and Australian medievalist texts are all part of the continuum of representations of the medieval past, the fact that a number of the British texts were prior to the Australian ones does not place them in a more 'originary' position vis-à-vis the Middle Ages. Many of the examples that will be discussed in this book were responding to British (and in some cases, American) medievalism, but we should not thus be led to dismiss them as merely simulacral. For this reason, this book is not a reception study, but orients its discussion more positively toward how Australian writers developed a body of medievalist literature that was responsive to, and formative of, the cultural landscape of colonial and early Federal Australia. Naturally such an account would be incomplete without offering appropriate consideration of the antipodean reception of the major British and American medievalist works; but if our understanding of medievalism as an international phenomenon is to be advanced, reception should not be featured at the expense of exploring the many fascinating and highly varied ways in which literary medievalism came to be localized and vernacularized.

In taking this approach, this book argues that it is Australian texts which expose most nakedly something fundamental to medievalism itself: that its appropriative logic is one in which the Middle Ages can be understood not simply as an originary historical moment to be represented or reanimated but, rather, borrowing a term from the French philosopher Jacques Derrida, as a *trace* that is differentially interpreted across time and space, enduring yet also changing across the medievalist representations we study. The notion of the trace as it is elaborated by Derrida is complex and undergoes different iterations throughout his work, but one of the clearest articulations can be found in the statement that '[t]he trace is not a presence but is rather the simulacrum of a presence that dislocates, displaces, and refers beyond itself'.[28] In this sense of the trace, the Middle Ages are thus not immediately and straightforwardly present in the Australian texts discussed here: the Norman conquest and chivalric culture, for instance, become sites for a whole array of differing socio-historical fantasies. But neither do the various mediations of this event render it completely absent, as though it were only its representations. And yet medievalism is a hermeneutic rather than a forensic practice; for while it acknowledges the historical existence of the medieval period, it does not seek to reconstruct and thereby recover the original 'presence' of the Middle Ages. In order

[28] Jacques Derrida, 'Différance', in *Speech and Phenomena: And Other Essays on Husserl's Theory of Signs*, trans. by David B. Allison (Evanston: Northwestern University Press, 1973), pp. 129–60 (p. 156).

not to fall into relativistic platitude, we need to acknowledge that the modern (and colonial) traces we study gesture back beyond themselves; but they do not point to a pure origin but to a complex, internally divided origin, to which we cannot have unmediated access and of which we cannot take full possession through historical knowledge. As the very different texts in this book demonstrate in their own individual ways, it is in its very adaptation of medieval traces to local conditions that Australian medievalism best expresses not only the colonial condition but the medievalist condition as well.

The chosen timeframe of 1840–1910 warrants some explanation; after all, literary and theatrical medievalism in Australia preceded and postdated this period. Some of the colonies' very earliest convict ballads, for instance, written soon after arrival in 1788, evoked Dante's *Divine Comedy* in their purgatorial visions of penal servitude, while the journals of early explorers and naturalists clearly scrutinized the 'new' vistas and peoples before them through the lens of Old World civilizations, as well as with a 'quasi-medieval mindset' influenced by premodern travel writing, as Geraldine Barnes and Adrian Mitchell have said of William Dampier's *A Voyage to New Holland* (1703/09).[29] This body of early scientific and non-fictional writings is not treated within this study, which focuses on later fictional representations; but these texts were formative of both international and local views of natural and human existence in the colonies, and as such merit future study of their distinctive uptake of medievalism. Furthermore, medievalism also thrived in Australia beyond 1910, with the horrors of the Great War inspiring, as Andrew Lynch has expertly shown, the densely allusive medievalist war poetry of writers such as Christopher Brennan.[30] Later forms of Australian medievalism have also been taken up in Trigg's *Medievalism and the Gothic in Australian Culture*, and without doubt much work is still to be done on the mass of twentieth- and twenty-first-century iterations. But what marks out the seventy-year period nominated in this study is not only the sheer concentration of medievalist work produced at this time (which coincides with the international high point in medievalist literature, art, and architecture), but, more interestingly, the way it returned so strikingly to the Middle Ages as a means of engaging with the particularities of colonial life. Despite its dizzying aesthetic and ideological diversity, and its engagement with

[29] Geraldine Barnes and Adrian Mitchell, '"Passing through Customes": William Dampier's Medieval Baggage', in *Medievalism and the Gothic in Australian Culture*, ed. by Trigg, pp. 131–45 (p. 145).

[30] Andrew Lynch, 'C. J. Brennan's *A Chant of Doom*: Australia's Medieval War', *Australian Literary Studies*, 23 (2007), 49–62.

international trends, the literary medievalism produced between 1840 and 1910 shared a powerfully local orientation that reflects an increased momentum in the local quest to understand Australia's emerging society, and thus merits inclusion in a single study. The decision to stray into the first decade of the twentieth century does not reflect an uncritical subscription to the 'long nineteenth century' thesis of cultural history: after all, in Australia 1901 did mark the beginning of a new political and cultural epoch with the transition from colonialism to Federal nationhood, and this is reflected in some of its literary medievalism. But given the magnitude of this political transfiguration at the century's cusp, and its potential to alter Australia's cultural and geopolitical relationship with Britain and Europe, there is a surprising level of thematic, stylistic, and ideological continuity between much of the Australian medievalism of the nineteenth century and that of the early twentieth, and it is this continuity that is acknowledged here.

This book does not attempt to organize its material into an evolutionary narrative that tracks the development of 'stages' of creative medievalism in Australia, for to do so would straighten unduly the meandering and often recursive paths it traced through the literature and theatre of colonial and newly federated Australia. There are some identifiable strains, such as the predilection for satirizing colonial politics via the discourses of medieval chivalry, discussed in Chapter Four, or the use of Viking and Anglo-Saxonist tropes to describe the British colonization of Australia, discussed in Chapter 1; but these cannot readily be called stages because their appearance, though frequent, is piecemeal and discontinuous, with instances scattered across several decades. Nor is there any attempt to categorize the 'types' of medievalism found within Australian works, although there is some identification of shared themes, styles, and forms when these can be seen genuinely to emerge. The unbridled eclecticism of the literary medievalism of this period means that it resists tidy taxonomizing: in some cases, a single text can be seen to skate vertiginously across heroic, Gothic, and feudal portrayals of the Middle Ages in the space of a few lines, while elsewhere we find the unembarrassed introduction of the vocabulary and *dramatis personae* of faëry folklore into representations of the Australian bush. The inclusion of such examples in this study discloses the avowedly anti-purist approach it embraces. Rather than setting out to isolate the medievalism found in Australian literature, in (vain) pursuit of the most unadulterated instances, this book is more concerned with emphasizing this medievalism's distinctive, even definitive, multi-valency — its capacity to combine with an array of separate seemingly incongruous discourses in the service of offering aesthetic and ideological commentary on colonial modernity. Finally, this book's definition of medievalism also encompasses texts, images, and material objects that others might describe as 'anti-medievalist'. 'Medievalist' is not taken here only to signify unproblematic nostalgic longing for medieval social, cultural, and aesthetic forms, or simple ideological partisanship (whether progressive or conservative) with medieval forms of political and social organization. Rather, insofar as Australian cultural practices can be seen to engage actively with the Middle Ages in a way that is not only inflected by the modern and the colonial, but indeed is aimed at interpreting or even 'creating' the modern and the colonial, even those iterations that are anti-medievalist in sentiment fall under the investigative rubric of medievalism.

The chapters that follow range across a myriad of medievalist representations, with the aim of bringing to light the breadth and richness of Australia's fictive engagement with the medieval in the nineteenth and early twentieth centuries. The first three chapters take the form of more intensive studies of selected canonical Australian works and authors, reconsidered through their relationship to the history of medievalist literature, in which they are anything but canonical. With the exception of Adam Lindsay Gordon, these writers have never before been discussed as medievalists, and none of them has ever been included in any of the many accounts written on nineteenth-century medievalism. Chapters 4 and 5 turn their attention to the almost viral phenomena of medievalist poetry and plays that emerged in the contexts of the periodical press and the colonial theatre. The distinction between these two sections is not a hard-and-fast one; with the possible exceptions of Joseph Furphy's novels and some of Adam Lindsay Gordon's poems, most of the texts examined were directed at a wide readership, including the novels, many of which were serialized in the popular press before being published as volumes. Taken together, these chapters present us with a society in which medievalism, far from being a submerged or minor cultural interest, or the jealous preserve of exalted Laureates and learned antiquarian scholars, was a vibrant and very public phenomenon, surviving and even thriving in the mainstream of the literary and theatrical marketplaces.

Chapter 1, 'Life on the Murrumbidgee: Anglo-Saxonism in the Work of Rolf Boldrewood and Joseph Furphy', explores the transmission, via these authors' work, of international Anglo-Saxonist discourses on race, labour, and national destiny to the Australian colonial environment. While Boldrewood's work is contextualized within the colonial fetishizing of ancient bloodlines and pedigrees, Furphy's very singular (and hostile) engagement with Anglo-Saxonism is read as a sympathetic response to Mark Twain's rejection of the race- and class-fetishes of Southern American medievalism. Through a comparative analysis of Boldrewood's adaptation of Anglo-Saxonist racial typologies to settler Australia and Furphy's resistance to Anglo-Saxon England as a founding myth for Australia's independent nationhood, the chapter explores the ideological elasticity of this medievalist discourse in late colonial and newly Federated Australia.

Chapter 2, '"Backwards and Forwards in the Strangest Way": Medievalism, Modernity, and the "Australian Girl" in Novels by Australian Women', looks at the paradoxical presence of medievalism in a number of novels written by Australian women in the late nineteenth century, in particular novels by Catherine Martin, Miles Franklin, Ada Cambridge, Rosa Praed, and 'Tasma' (Jessie Couvreur). Its focus is on what can be called these writers' 'meta-medievalism', that is, their often deeply critical explorations of their fellow Australians' imbibing of popular fantasies of the Middle Ages. In particular, it examines how these writers expose the pretensions and hypocrisies underpinning both the colonial fascination with medieval pedigrees and the colonial uptake of the late nineteenth-century Aestheticist craze for medieval beauty and preindustrial artisan culture. The chapter shows how their narratives of women's lives in rural and metropolitan Australia offer insightful, nuanced, yet mordant critiques of the impact of contemporary medievalism on the formation of tastes, social distinctions, and gender roles in the colonies.

Chapter 3, 'Bush Idylls and Galloping Romances: Medievalism in the Poetry of Adam Lindsay Gordon', is the book's only single-author study. Offering a number of close readings of Gordon's medievalist poems, the chapter argues for his development of both a distinctive Gothic idiom and a painfully unredemptive medievalist existentialism that links these poems to his more famous representations of life in the Australian bush. This discussion of Gordon's work is framed within an analysis of his posthumous status and the complex legacy that has led to him being anointed as Australia's quintessential medievalist poet. His work and legacy are, furthermore, examined in the context of the late nineteenth-century desire to identify an originary Australian bard, a quest that, the chapter argues, should be understood as equivalent to, and influenced by, the European and British philological quest for originary 'medieval' poesy.

Chapter 4, 'The Drivel of our Fathers: Medievalism in Popular Australian Poetry', moves away from the more rarefied example of Gordon's verse to examine the large but scattered body of medievalist verse produced both in published volumes and, especially, in the daily and periodical press. While some of this verse was sophisticated and well versed in the canons of nineteenth-century medievalism, as is the case with the poems produced by Fidelia Hill and Ada Cambridge, much of it was not only determinedly populist and disposable but also extremely cursory in its medievalism, ransacking the popular imaginary indiscriminately for tropes and terms that signified instantaneously and superficially as 'medieval'. This body of more historically promiscuous verse includes works by a range of better-known poets such as Henry Lawson, Victor Daley, and E. J. Brady, but also many verses produced by a host of obscure and anonymous poets. The chapter argues that it is, in fact, the very promiscuity of this poetry that makes it a highly valuable resource for understanding both how medievalism was brought into the service of current-affairs commentary and how perceptions of the Middle Ages were disseminated through the popular print culture of colonial Australia. This chapter also considers medievalist representations in the political cartoons that frequently accompanied this popular verse, and looks at how these cartoons played on a general 'knowing' perception of the Middle Ages to lampoon the foibles of prominent figures in colonial public life.

Finally, Chapter 5, 'The Round Table and Other Furniture: Medievalism on the Colonial Australian Stage', continues to look at the more ephemeral populist representations by examining medievalism in nineteenth-century Australian theatre. It differs from the previous chapter insofar as it does offer a survey of the impact of international medievalist trends on the Australian stage; but alongside this survey, a strong emphasis is placed on locally authored medievalist drama, in particular the melodramatic plays of Edward Geoghegan, Conrad Knowles, and others, and the historical burlesques written by William Mower Akhurst and Marcus Clarke. Emphasis is also placed on the vital creative input of local scenic artists, who were instrumental in creating theatrical medievalism's distinctive, and highly praised, antiquarian aesthetic. Arguing for theatre's unique physical immediacy as a mode of medievalist representation, this chapter also seeks to dismantle the 'realist/escapist' paradigm that has conventionally regarded theatre with non-contemporary and non-local themes as disengaged from the Australian scene; it does this by examining a number of Australian medievalist plays that used their historically and geographically distant settings to comment on matters of intimate, even uncomfortable, proximity to the lives of their colonial audiences.

As a work directed at a mixed audience of medievalists and Australianists, this book aims to avoid framing its discussions too exclusively within discipline-specific debates and to avoid over-using terminology that is exclusive to theoretical work on medievalism, colonialism, postcolonialism, and textual dissemination. But it would be disingenuous to suggest it does not owe a deep debt to theorists in all these fields. As such, theoretical and disciplinary concepts and terms, particularly those which have passed into more generalized academic and non-academic usage, are evoked frequently, though sometimes obliquely, and theoretical work is discussed when necessary. In general, however, the aim throughout has been to theorize on the relationship between medievalism and colonialism through discussion of the texts themselves; for without their keen witness to the nuances of medievalist Australia, this study would not have been possible.

Chapter 1

# LIFE ON THE MURRUMBIDGEE: ANGLO-SAXONISM IN THE WORK OF ROLF BOLDREWOOD AND JOSEPH FURPHY

On 25 June 1887, in an issue largely devoted to examining Queen Victoria's Golden Jubilee, the Sydney-based weekly journal *The Bulletin* published a cartoon entitled 'The Australian Jubilee Peerage: A Detailed Scheme for the Institution of Various Long-Needed Australian Orders of Nobility'. In keeping with that journal's robust anti-imperial iconoclasm, the cartoon lampooned the jubilee peerages that had been bestowed upon colonials by depicting a dozen mock coats-of-arms with mottoes and crudely drawn devices befitting the events, conditions, and history of life in the Australian colonies (Figure 2).[1]

A number of the heraldic devices depicted are closely topical in their allusions: One cheekier instance of this, in which recent events are amalgamated with playful medievalism, can be seen in the coat-of-arms of 'The Order of C.B. (Colonial Beer)', designed 'to be conferred upon the survivors of the NSW "Brewers Holy War"'. The irreverence of the comparison of a local trade war with the Crusades is visually supplemented by the juxtaposing of the motto 'Ich Dien' (I serve) — a motto most closely associated with the Prince of Wales but claiming an origin dating to Edward the Black Prince's 1346 victory at Crécy — with the image of a barmaid serving a brew to a leering customer.

Less directly topical, but no less mordant in its assault on the mores of colonial society, is the coat-of-arms representing 'The Order of P.G. (Pinchgut)', which is to be conferred 'only upon old and true colonial aristocracy' (Figure 3).

[1] *The Bulletin*, 25 June 1887, p. 18.

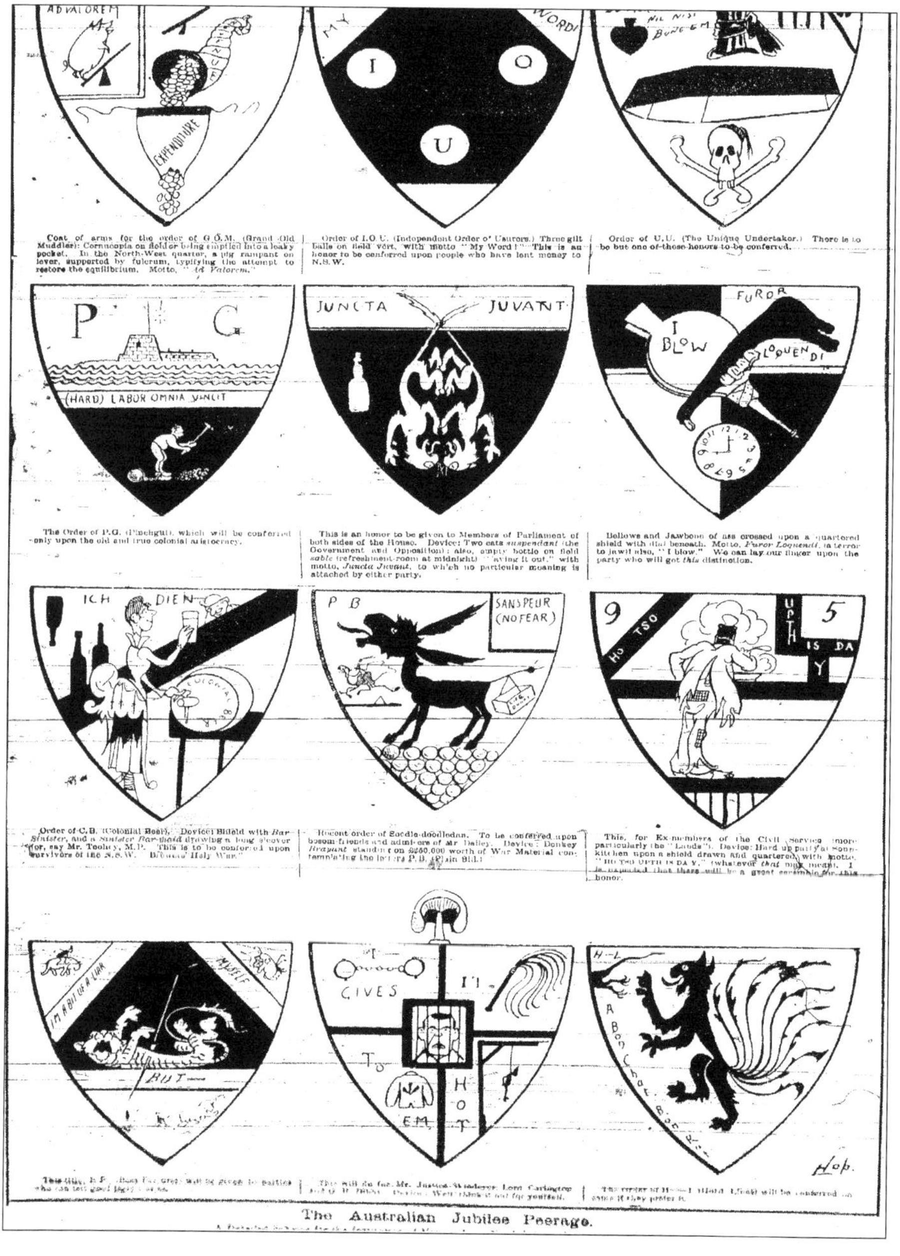


Figure 2. Livingston York Hopkins ('Hop'), 'The Australian Jubilee Peerage: A Detailed Scheme for the Institution of Various Long-Needed Australian Orders of Nobility', *The Bulletin*, 25 June 1887.

The Order of P.G. (Pinchgut), which will be conferred only upon the old and true colonial aristocracy.

Figure 3. Livingston York Hopkins ('Hop'), 'The Order of P.G. (Pinchgut)', detail from 'The Australian Jubilee Peerage', *The Bulletin*, 25 June 1887.

The attribution of ancient nobility to the convict inmates of Pinchgut, the notoriously punitive prison-island in Sydney Cove (better known today as Fort Denison), serves as an ironic reminder of the decidedly ignoble origins of Australia's longest-dwelling Europeans, a fact which is visually reinforced in the accompanying image of a laterally divided shield in which devices of Pinchgut and of a convict breaking rocks are divided by the centrally placed motto '(Hard) Labor Omnia Vincit'. Despite the motto's topicality — *labor omnia vincit* (work conquers all) was the motto of the recently formed American Federation of Labor — it is precisely because this armorial satire is broader in its reach that it is arguably the most subversive of the dozen created by the *Bulletin* cartoonist 'Hop' (Livingston York Hopkins). Not limited to current affairs, it offers trenchant commentary on the peerage system itself and, more pointedly, on the role such honours played in colonial public life.

What was this role? In *Pounds and Pedigrees*, the historian Paul de Serville offers a lengthy and often amusing account of ambitious Melbournians' 'craze for honours'[2] either in the form of hotly pursued individual knighthoods or in

[2] Paul de Serville, *Pounds and Pedigrees: The Upper Class in Victoria 1850–80* (Melbourne: Oxford University Press, 1991), p. 206.

pedigrees linking them to ancient English families and their ancestral lands. Indeed, the colonial pursuit of pedigrees, and the accompanying entitlement to bear a coat-of-arms, was persistent enough to eventually compel Sir John Bernard Burke to offer a colonial extension to his genealogical guide *Burke's Peerage*, so that in 1891 and 1895 there appeared the two volumes of the compendious (and often highly dubious) *Colonial Gentry*, with its many Australian entries. According to de Serville, 'by the third quarter of the century tastes in genealogy had reached bloated proportions', with colonists going to extravagant lengths to trace their families back to illustrious antecedents. One such colonist was the Melbourne town clerk Edmund Gerald Fitzgibbon, whose (disputed) assumption of the medieval title of White Knight of Derry offered irresistible fodder for the *Bulletin*'s cartoonists, who repeatedly portrayed him as a pompous undersized figure, absurd in his full suit of armour (Figure 4).[3]

Another was William Arthur Callendar à Beckett, whose indefatigable searches uncovered a range of desirable medieval ancestors, including a Saxon king, a brother of St Thomas Beckett, and a series of medieval mayors and members of parliament. Unfortunately for à Beckett, the dazzling pedigree remained elusive, stubbornly refusing to be linked definitively to the present. Sir George Verdon (who would later build the splendid medievalist ES&A bank building in Collins Street, Melbourne) was luckier, as Burke's *Colonial Gentry* furnished him somewhat speciously with a Norman patriarch, Bertram de Verdun, as an early ancestor.[4]

These pedigree hunters, according to de Serville, sought to raise themselves above the worthy but undistinguished *nouveaux riches* surrounding them. But this motive is itself suggestive of more complex and profound ideological anxieties than simple snobbery; for underlying the quest for genealogical distinction we can detect a desire to ward off the spectre of shame — a strenuous refusal of any loss of caste in the colonies, and, perhaps even more urgently, a dissociation from the ignominious 'convict taint' tarnishing the fortunes of a number of the colonies' rising families. Ironically, in the case of à Beckett, it was the money made by his ex-convict father-in-law John Mills that allowed him to indulge his quest for an aristocratic medieval heritage, culminating in the purchase of an ancestral property in Wiltshire. The *Bulletin* cartoon, then, by bestowing mock honours on Australia's 'convict aristocracy', humorously but powerfully exposes the layers of denial at the base of

[3] Bernard Barrett, 'FitzGibbon, Edmund Gerald (1825–1905)', *Australian Dictionary of Biography*, 18 vols (Carlton: Melbourne University Press, 1966–2007), IV (1972), 181–82.

[4] On à Beckett and Verdon, see de Serville, *Pounds and Pedigrees*, pp. 195–98 and p. 203 respectively.

Figure 4. Tom Durkin, image of Edmund Gerald Fitzgibbon, detail from 'Melbourniana', *The Bulletin*, 23 February 1895.

the colonial yearning for nobility, while its doctored Labor motto deftly recalls the inhumane conditions of convict transportation and forced labour that underpinned the Eastern colonies' foundation, the vestiges of which were still very present in the living memory and indeed the living population of New South Wales, Victoria, Tasmania, Queensland, and Western Australia.

The actions of these colonists show, as de Serville argues, that many had a deeply personal stake in the idea of a storied genealogical continuity between the Australian colonies and Britain: 'An interest in genealogy was a declaration of love for the home country [...] its popularity suggests the desire to maintain one's links and roots, to preserve one's identity of background and inheritance as much cultural as familial'.[5] It is important, however, to acknowledge the extent to which this personal invocation of medieval English ancestry was a reflection of these colonial Australians' subscription to the larger-scale imperial ideal that Sir Charles

[5] De Serville, *Pounds and Pedigrees*, p. 192.

Dilke in 1868 dubbed 'Greater Britain' a complex cultural-political entity whose will to unity was an expression of the powerful and ancient genetic ties that bound it together.[6] As Duncan Bell argues, while the political form this entity should take was disputed, with ideas ranging from the centralized model of Imperial Federation to the looser model of confederation between quasi-independent states (something more akin to colonial nationalism), it was nevertheless generally agreed that it was 'a community bound by shared norms, values, and purpose', because it was, at base, a 'racial polity', bound together by a shared English heritage.[7] The notion of English ethnic continuity, so frequently invoked by later nineteenth-century imperial thinkers as to be regarded as a commonplace, is epitomized by John Seeley's formulation, in *The Expansion of England* (1883), of 'ethnological unity' as the racial-cultural *sine qua non* of Greater Britain's political development.[8]

In offering one among the many Australian examples from this period it is difficult to surpass, for sheer rhetorical force and economy, Henry Parkes's now-legendary invocation at the 1890 Melbourne Federation Conference of the 'crimson thread of kinship [that] runs through us all'.[9] Coming from the man widely proclaimed to be 'the Father of Australian Federation', Parkes's metaphor reveals that English ethnocentrism was, in Russell McGregor's apt phrase, 'neither inimical nor incidental to Australian nationalism',[10] and that Australia's move toward political autonomy did not signify even for its main advocates a rupture from what Parkes had in 1884 described the 'consanguineous political organism' of the Empire.[11]

Parkes's phrase is, of course, also noted for its ethnocentric exclusion of a whole swathe of internal populations, from indigenous Australians to non-European immigrants and non-English Europeans, in particular Irish Catholics. Many commentators, especially since the emergence of Critical Whiteness studies with its welcome dissection and de-naturalization of Anglo-Saxonist racial and ethnic

[6] Charles Dilke, *Greater Britain: A Record of Travel in the English-Speaking Countries During 1866 and 1867*, 2 vols (London: Macmillan, 1868).

[7] Duncan Bell, *The Idea of Greater Britain* (Princeton: Princeton University Press, 2007), pp. 113, 10.

[8] John Robert Seeley, *The Expansion of England: Two Courses of Lectures* (London: Macmillan, 1883), p. 50.

[9] See Henry Parkes, *The Federal Government of Australasia: Speeches Delivered on Various Occasions (November 1889–May 1890)* (Sydney: Turner and Henderson, 1890), p. 75.

[10] Russell McGregor, 'The Necessity of Britishness: Ethno-Cultural Roots of Australian Nationalism', *Nations and Nationalism*, 12 (2006), 493–511 (p. 494).

[11] Henry Parkes, 'Australia and the Imperial Connection', *Nineteenth Century*, 15 (1884), 869.

norms, have discussed the far-reaching, and in some cases devastating, impact the notion of English 'blood' had in late nineteenth-century Australia and beyond. These critics emphasize its role in underwriting white racial supremacy as a mandate for imperial power and its attendant abuses, from indigenous dispossession to enforced Pacific Islander labour ('black-birding'). Douglas Cole's statement that 'haematic ideas were a significant force behind the desire for a White Australia' is an early instance of the critical examination of how the notion of blood Parkes's 'crimson thread' was increasingly utilized not simply as a metaphor but as a physiological justification for the geopolitical and cultural dominance of England over much of the globe.[12] This can certainly be seen in William Gay's extended use of this conceit in the sonnet 'To the People of the United States', written in Australia in 1896. Notwithstanding its questionable poetic merit, it is significant for its tethering of shared Anglo-American and Anglo-Australian kinship within an historical arc that sweeps from the 'dear source' of a shared medieval past forward to a unified triumphal destiny:

> Men of our blood and speech! O let us be
> Brothers once more as in the former time
> When Chaucer shaped for us his sturdy rhyme
> Or Howard swept the Armada from the sea:
> Men of our blood and speech! If ye did flee
> For God and freedom to an alien clime,
> Forget not them who, resolute, sublime,
> Grappling with kings at home, made England free;
> And if in your red blood, and if in theirs,
> Yea, even in ours, who wax in Southern peace,
> There runs a redder strain that brooks no wrong,
> But hot, unquenchable, the veins along,
> Burns for the right until its pulses cease,
> From one dear source we are alike its heirs.[13]

[12] See, for instance, Warwick Anderson, *The Cultivation of Whiteness: Science, Health, and Racial Destiny in Australia* (Carlton: Melbourne University Press, 2005); Susanne Schech and Jane Haggis, 'Migrancy, Whiteness, and the Settler Self in Contemporary Australia', in *Race, Colour, and Identity in Australia and New Zealand*, ed. by John Docker and Gerhard Fischer (Sydney: University of New South Wales Press, 2000), pp. 231–39; and *Historicising Whiteness: Transnational Perspectives on the Construction of an Identity*, ed. by Leigh Boucher, Jane Carey, and Katherine Ellinghaus (Melbourne: RMIT Publishing, in association with the School of Historical Studies, University of Melbourne, 2006).

[13] William Gay, *The Complete Poetical Works of William Gay* (Melbourne: Lothian, 1911), pp. 66–67.

Gay's reference to Chaucer's 'sturdy rhyme' supplements the pan-Anglo sanguinary link by making a specifically medievalist appeal to a shared linguistic heritage founded on the later fourteenth-century 'Chaucerian moment', when the English tongue became a vehicle of emergent ethnic-political ambition. Nevertheless, it is the crimson thread, or in this case, the 'red strain', that bears the sonnet's central ideological weight.

A majority of commentators have for some time stressed the link between notions of racial kinship and the increasingly widespread influence of scientific and anthropological racial theories in the second half of the nineteenth century, in particular the popular doctrine of polygenesis, which espoused the belief that there were a number of different human species in which ability, intellect, and potency were unequally distributed.[14] Importantly, as Timothy L. Carens, among others, has discussed, polygenesis was inherently scientific in that it contradicted the biblically grounded belief that all extant humans were descended from Noah's three sons.[15] This emphasis has been corroborated in the sphere of the public imaginary, where the eugenic nightmares of the twentieth century have done much to consolidate popular perceptions of the link between racism and science. Undeniably, there is something compellingly horrific in the scenario of colonial gentlemen-anthropologists justifying the dispossession of a people, or prognosticating the inevitable decline of an indigenous civilization, based on the set of a jaw or the circumference of a skull. Additionally, as Tom Griffiths and others have demonstrated, there is no denying the impact of evolutionary thought, and the darker social theories it spawned, on how racial destiny came to be understood in colonial Australia and elsewhere.[16] But the power of this narrative should not lead us to neglect the profound and troubling debt popular racial theory in Australia owed to nineteenth-century historicism in general, and to medievalism in particular, especially in the form of one of its most influential, and ideologically serviceable, discourses: Anglo-Saxonism. For when nineteenth-century commentators used the term 'Anglo-Saxon', they were not just invoking a scientific racial category

[14] Early commentaries condemning the use of Social Darwinist truisms to rationalize, and indeed naturalize, imperialist *Realpolitik* include C. O. Ovington's 1900 article 'War and Evolution' and George Peabody Gooch's 1901 essay 'Imperialism', in C. F. G. Masterman's collection *The Heart of the Empire* (London: Unwin, 1901).

[15] See Timothy L. Carens, *Outlandish English Subjects in the Victorian Domestic Novel* (New York: Palgrave, 2005).

[16] Griffiths, *Hunters and Collectors*. For the superficial nature of imperialist invocations of Darwinian theory, see Paul Crook, 'Historical Monkey Business: The Myth of a Darwinized British Imperial Discourse', *History*, 84 (1999), 633–57.

but, importantly, an *historicized* conception of the English people, who were retrofitted with a range of qualities that had purportedly characterized them since 'the Anglo-Saxon period', a time loosely construed as stretching from the first Anglo-Saxon settlements in the fifth century to the period approaching, or even immediately following, the Norman invasion in the mid-eleventh century. So although the term 'Anglo-Saxon' might seem to be no different from terms such as 'English' or its more broadly defined cognate 'British' or, more broadly still, 'white' it was in fact distinguished by its medievalist resonance, which, Peter Cochrane has perceptively argued, 'anchored all sorts of claims to virtue, achievement and destiny deep in history'.[17] Without denying the active engagement with scientific and anthropological theories of race in colonial Australia, it is worth recalling the extent to which these doctrines were in many cases ultimately dependent on history, rather than on current scientific data, for evidence of the English race's superiority over others.

In the myriad of ideological uses to which Saxon England was put in Victorian England and nineteenth-century America, two dominant strains can be isolated that came to be of particular relevance for Australia. First, there was the racially inflected version which celebrated the energizing impetus of the introduction into medieval England of various Teutonic peoples including Angles, Saxons, Vikings, and finally Normans (who were frequently referred to as 'Norsemen' as part of the determined English negation of their troubling Frenchness), all of whom were believed to have deposited their sea-faring drive and their will to conquest into the English blood-bank, thereby fitting the English for imperial expansion. In particular the Norman invasion, according to Clare A. Simmons, was believed by a number of nineteenth-century commentators to have injected the lost 'race vitalism' into the degenerate English Teutons and helped them to realize their manifest destiny of cultural and political domination over the globe. The second major ideological use of Anglo-Saxon England, sometimes referred to as 'Whig' Anglo-Saxonism, was the rather different, more politically oriented version that insisted on the pre-conquest freedoms enjoyed by the Saxons, and on the egalitarianism of their social and political institutions, which, the argument went, were destroyed by the descent of the 'Norman Yoke' upon the Saxons. Anglo-Saxonism's multiple ideological valences make it an invidious task to describe Whig Anglo-Saxonism straightforwardly as 'the democratic version' of this phenomenon;

[17] Peter Cochrane, 'Anglo-Saxonness: Ancestors and Identity', *Communal/Plural*, 4 (1994), 1–16 (p. 7). Cochrane's short but astute account stands out for being so far the most sustained examination of the historical complexion of the term 'Anglo-Saxon' in colonial Australia.

add to this the difficulty of hiving off the use of this discourse by so-called 'conservative' nineteenth-century ideologues from those of their 'progressive' contemporaries.[18] Nevertheless, it can be said that this version of Anglo-Saxonism was generally more serviceable to those who, from Chartists to democrats to abolitionists, were interested in the restoration of what they believed to be ancient freedoms that had been lost under a usurping feudal social order.

Exploring how these strains of Anglo-Saxonism were manifested in late nineteenth- and early twentieth-century Australia is valuable both because it gives us insight into Australian literary medievalism and its intersection with race and class politics, and because it adds a much-needed antipodean dimension to what is already known about nineteenth-century creative Anglo-Saxonism. Much has been said not only about the role of Anglo-Saxonist visions of early medieval England in the development of both conservative and democratic models of Victorian English nationalism,[19] but also about the centrality of Anglo-Saxonist discourse to the formation of national consciousness and political institutions in North America, the most comprehensive study being Reginald Horsman's 1981 book *Race and Manifest Destiny.*[20] Far less, however, has been said about the transmission of Anglo-Saxonist discourses on race, labour, and national destiny to the Australian colonial environment, or about the role of this discourse in the formation of notions of Australian literary nationalism. This chapter will be examining this by focusing first of all on a number of texts by Thomas Alexander Browne, a.k.a. Rolf Boldrewood (1826–1915). Boldrewood is to known to many for his most famous work, *Robbery Under Arms*, a bushranger tale in the tradition of the historical romance, which was enjoyed by English royalty and adapted repeatedly for stage presentation in the nineteenth century. Far less attention has been given to Boldrewood's other works, but they are extremely pertinent for examining Anglo-Saxonism in colonial Australia. After discussing Boldrewood, the chapter will examine *Rigby's Romance*, the novel-cum-symposium written by turn-of-the-

[18] A similar point is made by Billie Melman in 'Claiming the Nation's Past: The Invention of an Anglo-Saxon Tradition', *Journal of Contemporary History*, 26 (1991), 575–95.

[19] *Anglo-Saxonism and the Construction of Social Identity*, ed. by Allen J. Frantzen and John D. Niles (Gainesville: University Press of Florida, 1997), Asa Briggs, 'Saxons, Normans and Victorians', in *The Collected Essays of Asa Briggs*, 3 vols (Urbana: University of Illinois Press, 1985–91), II, 215–35; and Clare A. Simmons, *Reversing the Conquest: History and Myth in Nineteenth-Century British Literature* (New Brunswick: Rutgers University Press, 1990).

[20] Reginald Horsman, *Race and Manifest Destiny: The Origins of American Racial Anglo-Saxonism* (Cambridge, MA: Harvard University Press, 1981).

century writer Joseph Furphy (1843–1912), who is best known for his association with and contributions to the then-nationalist journal *The Bulletin*, and especially for his sprawling, comic bush epic *Such is Life*, the character of which was described by its author with the now-legendary phrase: 'temper democratic, bias offensively Australian'.[21] Furphy, in whom Socialist and anti-imperialist sympathies were combined with loyalty to the white English race, offers a vision of Anglo-Saxon England that is radically different not just from Boldrewood's but even from most left-leaning articulations in England. The very divergent interpretations of the early English Middle Ages in the work of these two authors reflects the ideological elasticity of Anglo-Saxonism as a medievalist discourse in colonial and newly federated Australia.

Anglo-Saxonism brought a distinctive, deep historical complexion to racially inflected English triumphalism in Australia. The victories of recent English history, especially the expansionism of the imperial age, figured prominently as historical proofs of English greatness; but these triumphs were also repeatedly presented as expressions of the qualities inherited from Australia's Anglo-Saxon forbears. Thomas Livingstone Mitchell, for instance, opened his 1848 *Journal of an Expedition in the Interior of Tropical Australia* with the claim that the Australian explorer's desire to explore the continent's northern tropics was 'impelled by the wayward fortunes of the Anglo-Saxon race already rooted at the southern extremity of the land whose name had previously been "Terra Australis incognita"'.[22] Use of this conventional motif continued to gain momentum and historical depth across the decades: to pluck just one from many late nineteenth- and early twentieth-century examples, a 1907 article in *The Lone Hand*, a Sydney monthly journal that was a supplement to *The Bulletin*, attributed the English occupation of Australia not to political or economic ambition, nor to penal expediency, but rather to 'that roving instinct which bespeaks the unconquerable Norse element in the British blood'.[23] As with English Anglo-Saxonist discourse, the notion of sea-faring English 'Norseness' or Teutonism was subject to a range of inflections in Australian

[21] Letter from Furphy to J. F. Archibald, editor of *The Bulletin*, 4 April 1897, printed in *Bushman and Bookworm: Letters of Joseph Furphy*, ed. by J. Barnes and L. Hoffman (Melbourne: Oxford University Press, 1995), p. 28.

[22] Thomas Livingstone Mitchell, *Journal of an Expedition in the Interior of Tropical Australia in Search of a Route from Sydney to the Gulf of Carpentaria* (London: Longman, Brown, Green, and Longmans, 1848), p. 2.

[23] Anon. (Frank Renar), 'Prolific Australia: The Continent of the British Race', *The Lone Hand*, 1 (1907), 68.

literature and social commentaries: it could refer to the purported Scandinavian origins of the pre-conquest Anglo-Saxons who sailed to English shores; or to the alleged Nordic heritage of the invading Normans who came to dominate England; or, finally, to the felicitous mixture of indigenous and invading Nordic strains in the wake of 1066. But whatever it was taken to mean, all instances of English greatness across the centuries were understood to have emerged as a result of it. To quote Peter Cochrane's eloquent summation:

> the line of descent [to Australia] was lamp-lit by the bright points of ancestral affinity. Where these points belonged on the time line was open to various opinions. But there was more agreement about the point of origin, the beginning of the line. That was the Anglo-Saxons.[24]

The medieval past, then, regarded as the crucible of essential Englishness, was an indispensable stage-set in the story of English supremacist and imperialist thought in colonial and early federal Australia.

What, if anything, did Australians do with this cultural legacy that was different from the English and Americans? Donald Cole has argued that Victorian and Edwardian explorations of Anglo-Australian kinship 'lapsed easily into Anglo-Saxonism with scarcely a local twist'.[25] Looking at the bulk of non-fictional uses of Anglo-Saxonist discourse in Australia, there is some basis to Cole's claims, for in them we encounter frequent tepid (though undoubtedly also heartfelt) repetitions of the 'Saxon/Norse seafaring blood' trope that appeared in British and American texts as an all-purpose historico-racial vindication of Anglo-dominance. Charles Edwin Woodrow Bean's *Flagships Three* (1913), with its claim that 'wild strains of Viking [and kindred] blood that poured into England in the dark ages [...] is the blood [...] that made Australia',[26] is testament to the persistence of this commonplace in twentieth-century commentaries on Australian national destiny. Cole's criticism can also be directed at many of the verse forays into Australian Anglo-Saxonism, most of which appeared in periodicals and newspapers throughout metropolitan and regional Australia. While these carry significance as indices of the popular transmission of historical Anglo-Saxonism, they yield almost nothing that is distinctively local in their treatment of their historical theme. Rather, their conventional celebrations of restless Anglo-Saxon forebears are

[24] Cochrane, 'Anglo-Saxonness: Ancestors, and Identity', p. 16.

[25] Douglas Cole, '"The Crimson Thread of Kinship": Ethnic Ideas in Australia, 1870–1914', *Historical Studies*, 14 (1971), 511–25 (p. 522).

[26] C. E. W. Bean, *Flagships Three* (London: Alston Rivers, 1913), p. 68.

simulacral to the point of being evacuated of virtually anything that might be described as antipodean in observation or interpretation. A poem appearing in *The Fremantle Herald* on 7 September 1867 anticipating Prince Alfred's visit to Australia (though Western Australia was not, alas, to play host to the royal guest on this trip) epitomizes this facile reiteration in the stanza where it exhorts:

> Arise ye sons of England, born on Australia's coasts
> Bring forth the young progenitors of Anglo-Saxon hosts.
> 'Neath the open vault of heaven, loud let their voices ring,
> The anthem of your ancestors, let your children sing.

Not even its explicit reference to Australia mitigates the sense that this stanza could have been penned anywhere in the English-speaking world. The final line rounds off the poem's conformist medievalism by twinning the visiting Prince with Alfred the Great, whom the Victorians commemorated as the quintessential Anglo-Saxon leader: 'May the *second* English Alfred be remembered like the first'.[27]

Occasionally one does find examples that are a little more idiosyncratic in their deployment of the conventional tropes. One example of this is Adam Lindsay Gordon's poem 'Ye Wearie Wayfarer: Hys Ballad in Eight Fyttes', the pseudo-medieval title of which belies its bluff equestrian tone. In Fytte VII it is not the colonizing impulse but the skilled horsemanship of the Australian bushman that is directly imputed to an Anglo-Norman heritage:

> if once we efface the joys of the race
> From the land, and outroot the Stud,
> GOOD-BYE TO THE ANGLO-SAXON RACE!
> FAREWELL TO THE NORMAN BLOOD![28]

But Cole's assertion of unalloyed colonial imitation is most clearly challenged when we examine the work of Boldrewood; for in his novels, many of which first appeared serialized in journals, we see that Anglo-Saxon England provided fertile soil for extensive and original elaborations of Australia's racial and political future. It is not so much that Boldrewood's general position on race was remarkable for his time: indeed, a number of his works recycle a conventional interpretation of the medieval English past as offering a racial-historical mandate for British imperialism. In his semi-fictional travel memoir *My Run Home* (1897), for instance, he claims that it is 'the old Norse recklessness' that leads young Englishmen to 'set up for

[27] Anon., 'A Welcome to Prince Alfred', *The Fremantle Herald*, 7 September 1867.

[28] 'Ye Wearie Wayfarer: Hys Ballad in Eight Fyttes', in Gordon, *Poems*, p. 28.

themselves at Bunderabulla Crossing-place, the red River, or snow-capped Hokanui',[29] a sentiment that is even more pronounced in *The Miner's Right: A Tale of the Australian Goldfields* (1890), where Sydney cove is described as 'that picturesque city which the sea-roving Anglo-Saxon has reared on the strand of the peerless Haven of the South',[30] while the sailors who bring settlers out are 'those gallant offshoots of the old Norse brood, whom the Motherland sends out yearly on the decks of her still increasing fleet to plant her standard and win new empires on the furthest bounds of the round world' (p. 324). Nor was Boldrewood alone among writers of Australian romance adventures in his use of Anglo-Saxonism: his friend and fellow novelist Henry Kingsley, for instance, described his fair-complexioned heroine Alice Brentwood in *The Recollections of Geoffry Hamlyn* as having 'Norman' beauty, and even his Irish emigrants turn out to be Anglo-Norman Irish overlords. Rather, it is because of the size of Boldrewood's Anglo-Saxonist oeuvre that he was able to move beyond the brief Anglo-Saxonist commonplaces of many of his peers and engage in an elaborate, indeed, at times rather tortuous, mapping of an ancient English identity onto the propertied classes of the Australian colonies. His prolific output, and especially the lengthy narratives of some of his fictions, allowed him not just to remark on Australia's potential to be a space of renewal for the ancient English race, but also to show through story how this could be achieved.

Unlike those who subscribed to the ideal of a pure and free Saxon England before the imposition of the 'Norman Yoke', Boldrewood was among those who believed that it was, to use de Serville's phrase, 'the combination of Saxon tenacity and Norman enterprise' that 'defined the English national character'.[31] His entire *oeuvre* reveals a fixation with the Norman conquest and its aftermath, and especially with Sir Walter Scott's version of post-conquest England in *Ivanhoe* (1819), a novel Boldrewood numbered among his life-long favourites.[32] Despite its sympathetic portrayal of the oppressed post-conquest Saxons, *Ivanhoe*'s conclusion projects a future of happy cohabitation and miscegenation between Saxons and Normans, out of which emerges not only a more harmonious society but also a

[29] Rolf Boldrewood, *My Run Home* (London: Macmillan, 1897), p. 55. All future references are to this edition.

[30] Rolf Boldrewood, *The Miner's Right: A Tale of the Australian Goldfields* (London: Macmillan, 1890), p. 316. All future references are to this edition.

[31] Paul de Serville, *Rolf Boldrewood: A Life* (Carlton, Vic.: Melbourne University Press, 2000), p. 19.

[32] Sir Walter Scott, *Ivanhoe*, ed. by Graham Tulloch (Edinburgh: Edinburgh University Press, 1998).

higher English type, embodied in its hero, Wilfred of Ivanhoe. Under the influence of Scott's profoundly influential ethnic allegory, many characterized this higher type as humble yet commanding, home-loving yet pioneering, plain yet civilized; and, with their blend of Teutonic bloods, hybrid and yet fully English.

This notion of mixed Englishness is vital to grasp as it is central to the Australianized Anglo-Saxonism that is evident throughout Boldrewood's writings. It is perhaps most bluntly stated in his memoir 'Portland Bay' where, discussing a distinguished colonial family, he says 'the longer I live, the stronger becomes my conviction that the genuine Englishman, compacted as he is of many and diverse races, holding so many of the strong points of each, is the best 'all-round man' the earth affords'.[33] We see this blended perfection embodied in the protagonist-narrator of *The Miner's Right.* By describing himself as 'Hereward Pole, a cadet of the ancient house of Shute, in honour and antiquity second to none of the companions of the Norman conqueror' (p. 162), this narrator evokes a joint Saxon-Norman lineage: his ancestors were Norman, but he is named after the famous Saxon resistance leader Hereward, whose legend had been revived by numerous Victorian Anglo-Saxonists, including Charles Kingsley in his 1865 *Hereward the Wake*, and after whom Scott had named characters both in *Ivanhoe* and in his Crusades tale *Count Robert of Paris* (1832). This mixed lineage equips Boldrewood's hero with the pioneering spirit that brings him to Australia's South-East goldfields, and the perseverance that sustains him through the harsh conditions. This Norman energy, and accompanying hauteur, reappears in other descriptions of powerful squatters. In 'Le Chevalier Bayard', Boldrewood's pen-portrait of the Victorian landholders of his youth, Evelyn Sturt, brother of the explorer Charles Sturt and 'veritable *fine fleur* of the squatter type', is described as possessing

> the features, the bold aristocratic regard with which the earlier romance writers were wont to depict the Norman Baron, whose part I make no doubt he would have acted most creditably, had Fate but arranged his existence synchronically.[34]

Similarly, in the novelette 'Our New Cook: A Tale of the Times' (1898), the hardy and unyielding gentleman squatter Ralph Ratcliffe is likened by another character

[33] Rolf Boldrewood, 'Portland Bay', in *Old Melbourne Memories* (London and New York: Macmillan, 1896), p. 93. All future references to *OMM* are to this edition. For an ingenious discussion of how the same notions of interbreeding emerged in the context of colonial discourses on sheep-farming, see Leigh Dale, 'Empire's Proxy: Sheep and the Colonial Environment', in *Five Emus to the King of Siam: Environment and Empire*, ed. by Helen Tiffin (Amsterdam: Rodopi, 2007), pp. 1–14.

[34] 'Le Chevalier Bayard', in *Old Melbourne Memories*, p. 171.

to *Ivanhoe*'s burly Norman baron, Reginald Front-de-Boeuf.[35] The extent of the author's commitment to this fused racial paradigm is also clear in his fantasizing of an Anglo-Norman ancestry both for himself and for his *nom de plume* Boldrewood, for whom he claimed descent from the world of *Ivanhoe*, saying of his ancestral lands, 'here stood the mighty oaks, the lofty elms, which might have been saplings when Gurth and Wamba sang their roundelay'.[36] By taking this pen name, which is poached from Walter Scott's poem *Marmion*, Boldrewood bestowed upon himself an ancient fused English lineage in which his ancestor Rolf, despite being a Norseman, fought with Harold at the Battle of Hastings and then went on to marry Edelgitha, the Saxon heiress of Boldrewood Chase.[37] Although the Galway-born Browne does not appear to have engaged in the assiduous pedigree hunting of some of his fellow colonists,[38] the failed squatter-turned-writer was preoccupied with his own racial heritage, adding the final 'e' to his surname to reflect his claim of descent from the Anglo-Norman overlords of medieval Ireland.

The influence of *Ivanhoe*'s Normanized England is most nakedly evident, and most sustained, in that involved discussion of Scott's swineherd Gurth which appears in Boldrewood's strikingly titled novel *A Sydney-Side Saxon*, which had been serialized in 1888–89 and published as a novel in 1894. Despite his own failure as a landowner and the abiding financial debt that dogged him, the majority of Boldrewood's novels channel the voice of privileged, landholding (what is locally called 'squattocratic') Australia, and *A Sydney-Side Saxon* is no exception to this. It should be noted, however, that squattocratic aspirations notwithstanding, Boldrewood did not pass over Gurth's enslavement to Cedric, the Saxon thane. The narrator of *A Sydney-Side Saxon*, the impoverished English farm labourer-

[35] Rolf Boldrewood, 'Our New Cook: A Sign of the Times', in *A Romance of Canvas Town and Other Stories* (London: Macmillan, 1901), p. 166.

[36] Boldrewood, *My Run Home*, p. 60. The adoption of Boldrewood as a *nom-de-plume*, as well as the author's transformation of his birth-surname 'Brown' to the more Anglo-Norman 'Browne' on the death of his Irish father in 1864, reflects his conformity to what Sophie Gilmartin has described as a tendency, from 1830 on, to present English pedigrees as 'an ancient mixture of the Anglo-Saxon and the Norman'. See Gilmartin, *Ancestry and Narrative in Nineteenth-Century British Literature: Blood Relations from Edgeworth to Hardy* (Cambridge: Cambridge University Press, 1998), p. 5.

[37] Boldrewood, *My Run Home*, pp. 63–64.

[38] De Serville (*Pounds and Pedigrees*, pp. 194–95) mentions that it was Boldrewood/Browne's brother Sylvester Brown who delved into the family's history. It was during this search that Boldrewood/Browne's illegitimacy was discovered.

turned-wealthy Australian landholder Jesse Claythorpe, self-consciously defines himself against the example of the swineherd, of whom he says the following:

> Here was a white man born a slave, and made to work whether he liked it or not [...] [o]f course, it was a long time ago, when King Richard, the Lion-hearted, was alive. There couldn't be anything like that now. But when I began to study things a bit, it didn't seem as if there was a mighty deal changed in the present day. Wasn't father a thrall? A slave, if you like it better, though he hadn't a collar round his neck — leastways none you could see.[39]

Here Gurth, with his collar of thraldom, is taken to be a prototype of the oppressed manual labourers of nineteenth-century England, which leads Jesse to seek a life for himself in Australia, where he will be 'more like Gurth's master than the poor swineherd himself' (p. 22). Here Boldrewood participates in what Cole describes as a popular mythology in which 'an effete, poverty-stricken, and caste-ridden England' is opposed to Australia as 'a new continent free from class distinctions, overbearing aristocracy, sweated pauperism, and oppressive militarism'.[40] In drawing such a direct parallel between Gurth and contemporary labourers, Boldrewood echoes but also, interestingly, differs from Thomas Carlyle's famous argument in Book III of *Past and Present* (1843) that Gurth, by virtue of his integration into the feudal order, was 'happy in comparison with many a Lancashire and Buckinghamshire man of these days not born thrall of anybody!'[41] But Boldrewood's anti-feudalist image of England does not sit easily with his overriding infatuation with old nobility, and he soon leaves off from this form of social criticism and goes on to racialize the story rather than dwell on it as a class allegory. He attributes Gurth's enslavement not to class oppression but to a disempowerment, but that is attributable to his Saxon apathy — he is a 'son of Beowulf (p. 19)' — a racial quality which Boldrewood suggests has continued in the even more degenerated English lower classes and which can be overcome not by class activism but by populating the colonies, thereby activating their dormant colonizing tendencies bequeathed to them by their Norman forebears. Out of this he develops an imaginative racial allegory in which the Australian colonies are populated by mixed Anglo-Norman types who embody an ideal combination in which unpretentious Saxon endurance and love of freedom are enhanced by the Norman

[39] Rolf Boldrewood, *A Sydney-Side Saxon* (London: Macmillan, 1894; Sydney: Cornstalk, 1925), pp. 20–21. All future references will be to this edition.

[40] Cole, '"The Crimson Thread of Kinship"', p. 518.

[41] Thomas Carlyle, *Past and Present*, intro. by Ralph Waldo Emerson (Boston: Little, Brown, 1843), p. 211.

flair for colonization; thus they atavistically reanimate the best qualities of their combined racial stock.

Boldrewood's novels sustain this racial-historical allegory, it must be said, by way of two troubling evasions. The first is the herding of all white Australian settlers under the Anglo-Saxon or Anglo-Norman banner. It is true that Boldrewood draws many affectionate portraits of Celtic Australians, from the massive Cornish miners of *The Miner's Right* to the Irish mother of the hero Dick Marston in *Robbery Under Arms* and the Highland clansmen described as 'desirable colonists' in *Old Melbourne Memories* (p. 19). But when it comes to anatomizing the Australian racial type, this Celtic lineage is subsumed into the English. This is particularly pointed in *Shearing in the Riverina* (1871), where the impressive specimens of white Australian manhood whom he describes as 'of Anglo-Saxon or Anglo-Celtic descent' are, by the end of the same paragraph, gathered into the category of 'the Anglo-Australian labourer' for the purposes of a disquisition on the superiority of Australian men as 'the finest [...] the race [note the singular] is capable of producing'.[42] Thus Boldrewood side-steps any untoward racial hybridity — and more urgently, any inconvenient admission that these Celts were historically not intrepid colonists but, in fact, were themselves colonized in the Old World by the English.

Second, Boldrewood's racial allegory rests on a studious refusal to acknowledge that colonial Australia's beginnings were not as a lucrative paradise for free settlers but, rather, as a forsaken convict settlement founded on the enforced transportation of England's poor, urban criminal underclass (not to mention Irish political prisoners). The image of 'new Norman' intrepid seafarers might serve as a representation, however romantic, of English merchants, explorers, or pastoralists; but the analogy comes somewhat unstuck when applied to those English men and women who arrived in the colonies in chains and who were, recalling Jesse's formulation, essentially white slaves.

It is nevertheless surprising that Boldrewood could not find some space for convicts within his ethno-historical allegory of Australian society. Indeed, their non-volitional passage to the colonies could have offered a transplanted example of the English rural underclass whom Jesse believed to be the descendents of Gurth, and thus could have reinforced the novel's preoccupation with the trait of Saxon apathy and the necessity of race renewal under the antipodean sun. Any pure Saxons encountered in the novel, such as the alcoholic and indigent former gentleman Jack Leighton, whose family had lived in the same region of England

[42] Rolf Boldrewood, *Shearing in the Riverina, New South Wales* (London: Smith, Elder, 1873) p. 75. First published in *Cornhill Magazine* (1865).

'since King Harold's time [...] before the battle of Hastings' (p. 134), are presented as fallen types, in the likeness of Scott's degenerate post-Conquest Saxon Athelstane the Unready. These Saxon types can only be redeemed by intermarriage with 'perfected' mixed-English (that is, Anglo-Norman) types, in order to produce Australian offspring of perfected, composite racial stock. Leighton is redeemed by marriage to Jesse's sister, who, despite being her husband's social inferior, offers him much-needed racial regeneration. According to the Social Darwinist logic that lurks beneath the surface of the text, it is the very composite nature of this new Anglo-Norman-Australian racial type that renders it infinitely reproducible without degeneracy; so no intermarriage with other racial groups (particularly indigenous Australians) is required, or indeed desirable. In 1909, the New South Wales politician and Federationist B. R. Wise would aver that the new Australian type had 'preserved the ancient and inbred integrity' of the Anglo-Saxon race;[43] but Boldrewood had already developed the paradoxical but ingenious alternative of *inter*bred integrity: the 'Coming Australian', to invoke the much-used phrase, was in fact the 'Returning Anglo-Norman'. This establishing of a paradoxical 'mixed purity' allows Boldrewood to come up with an elaborate medievalist solution to what Robert Dixon has called the 'impossible condition' of English racial renewal: 'that Britons should somehow renew themselves while preserving their 'racial' and cultural integrity on the frontier'.[44]

However, Boldrewood's preoccupation with the racial aftermath of the Norman occupation of England throws into stark relief the novel's avoidance of the more pressing and immediate situation created by British colonial occupation: that is, the enslavement and dispossession of indigenous Australians.[45] While Boldrewood's narrator Jesse recounts his horror at the thought of Gurth's enslavement, he quickly takes the opportunity, upon arriving in the outback, to purchase an aboriginal man Talgai, and remains completely untroubled by any notion that Talgai's racial destiny might lie anywhere but in servitude. This contradiction is underwritten by the novel's twofold notion of the English character. First, Boldrewood naturalizes Anglo-Australian settlers' dispossession of indigenous lands, and their subjugation

[43] B. R. Wise, *The Commonwealth of Australia* (Boston: Little, Brown, 1909), p. 21. Cited in Cole, '"The Crimson Thread of Kinship"', p. 519.

[44] Robert Dixon, *Writing the Colonial Adventure: Gender, Race, and Nation in Anglo-Australian Popular Fiction 1875–1914* (Cambridge: Cambridge University Press, 1995), p. 129.

[45] See Louise D'Arcens, 'Inverse Invasions: Medievalism and Colonialism in Rolf Boldrewood's *A Sydney-Side Saxon*', *Parergon: Journal of the Australian and New Zealand Association for Medieval and Early Modern Studies*, 22.2 (2005), 159–82.

of indigenous people, by suggesting that their emigration to Australia is an atavistic repetition of William's victory at Hastings. They are presented as simply responding to a racial compulsion to impose themselves on those whom they vanquish. Second, and more surprisingly, the Saxon racial memory of oppression under the Normans — the so-called 'Norman Yoke thesis[46] — functions in the novel to reinforce the white settlers' moral mandate to control the indigenous population. Jesse's racial identification with Scott's fictional 'white man born a slave', with his symbolic collar, shifts our attention away from the real black slaves, with very real collars, whom he would have encountered repeatedly in the course of his decades in the colony. The English as colonizers can thus retain the moral righteousness reserved for the injured, as well as asserting their right to regain their historical destiny through conquest.

Despite its sometimes rickety ideological edifice, Boldrewood's Scottian 'solution' for colonial Australia reveals that he was not simply an imitator of Scott's *Ivanhoe* but an original adaptor of *Ivanhoe*'s paradigm of Anglo-Norman perfected Englishness to his Australian surroundings. The deeply local nature of Boldrewood's Anglo-Saxonist fiction is especially apparent when it is compared to other *Ivanhoe*-esque serialized stories published in Australian periodicals in the middle decades of the nineteenth century, none of which engage in any way with contemporary Australia. 'Atholbane: A Romance of Kenmore Castle', for instance, which was serialized in *The Queenslander* in early 1870, is a hybrid Scottian effort in which Anglo-Norman elements reminiscent of *Ivanhoe* (post-conquest setting; one hero is a Normanized Saxon knight) rub shoulders with the Scottish border setting of the *Waverley* novels. Even more derivative of *Ivanhoe* and also of Scott's *Count Robert of Paris* is 'Adolphe de Crevecouer: A Tale of the Crusades', by 'Ervoli', which appeared in 1869 in *The Fremantle Herald*, a publication surprisingly rich in Anglo-Saxonist verse and short fiction. Set in Jerusalem, and featuring 'paynim' hordes pitted against a set menu of sturdy Saxons — Hereward, Cedric, Leofric, Beowolf [sic] — this Scottian cocktail shadows *Ivanhoe* so closely that it even includes a Saxon chieftain Redglaive, who, like Scott's hero Wilfred, adopts the moniker *desdichado* (disinherited) until his identity is restored by Richard Coeur de Lion. Although, like a number of *Ivanhoe*

[46] The 'Norman yoke' thesis, which argued that the constitutional freedoms enjoyed in Anglo-Saxon England had been stripped away post-Conquest and replaced by an oppressive occupying rule, was especially significant for those arguing for parliamentary and suffrage reform in late eighteenth- and nineteenth-century Britain. For a summary of this phenomenon, see Christopher Hill's famous essay 'The Norman Yoke', in *Democracy and the Labour Movement: Essays in Honour of Dona Torr*, ed. by J. Saville (London: Lawrence and Wishart, 1954), pp. 11–66.

continuations, most famously William Makepeace Thackeray's *Rebecca and Rowena* (1850), 'Adolphe' flirts with miscegenation by concluding with a declaration of (doomed) love between the hero and a peerless 'Oriental maiden', in every other respect it is unadulterated faux-Scott.[47] Finally, James Skipp Borlase's 'Galfried of Arlington: A Historical Nouvelette', which ran in *The Australian Journal* in September 1865, is another instance of undigested Scott. Set in 1095 in a post-conquest border country (this time the Welsh border, a setting probably derived from Scott's 1825 Crusader novel *The Betrothed*), its *dramatis personae* includes a haughty Norman baron, a defiant Saxon thane, and a blonde heroine whose name, Rovena, is almost comically derivative of *Ivanhoe*, being but one letter away from that of Scott's famously bland Saxon heroine Rowena. Certainly, the publication of these serial tales attests to a strong taste for ersatz Scott in the popular literary diet of the Australian colonies, but their contents, unlike those of Boldrewood's novels, are slavishly close to Scott's and could have been written anywhere. Indeed, in the case of 'Atholbane', its attribution to 'S. Cobb, Esq' suggests that it was the work of the popular American writer Sylvanus Cobb Jr, and so not locally produced. The derivative nature of these tales throws into relief the fact that Boldrewood's Saxonist medievalism, far from simply capitalizing on a popular taste for Scottian themes and characters, was, for all its blind spots, developed ultimately in the service of his vision of Australia's future.

If Boldrewood's work is to find a more fitting counterpart, it is surely the work of Southern American plantation novelists such as William Gilmore Simms (1806–70). The parallels between the two, as men and as writers, are arresting. First of all, according to Horsman, Simms was of Scotch-Irish and English ancestry, but 'was able to submerge himself into an all-powerful Anglo-Norman or Anglo-Saxon race'. Like Boldrewood, his self-image and novelistic practice owed much to Walter Scott: when, some way into his career, he evolved into 'a defender of southern institutions and a promoter of southern nationalism', he referred to himself using Scott's romantic term 'Southron'.[48] As a novelist and a commentator on American

[47] As will be discussed in Chapter 4, this fetishizing of 'Oriental maidens' also reflects the nineteenth-century fascination with the motif of interfaith attraction in the thirteenth-century tale *Aucassin and Nicolette*. The cross-dressing heroine of 'Adolphe', who accompanies her husband to the Crusades, might also be reminiscent of Elizabeth Barrett Browning's early medievalist effort, 'The Romaunt of the Page'.

[48] Horsman, *Race and Manifest Destiny*, pp. 165–66. Among the many articles on Simms's use of 'Walter-scottismo' to formulate local models of Southern American heroism, see Michael Kreyling, 'The Hero in Antebellum Southern Narrative', *Southern Literary Journal*, 16 (1984), 3–21.

and especially Southern racial destiny, Simms's promotion of ancient Englishness was inspired, like Boldrewood's, by a love for *Ivanhoe*, which in turn led him, like Boldrewood, to emphasize the blended Anglo-Norman nature of English ethnicity. In particular, he drew on the legacy of the Norman invasion to offer a racially determinist account of Anglo-American expansionism and conquest, whether over Mexico or over its own African slave population. This rhetorical highlighting of the 'good old Norman stock', as he called it in an 1846 poem, dovetailed with his desire to emphasize the feudal, aristocratic origins of 'the chivalry', the Southern property-owning classes, which, combined with their racial superiority, offered a knockdown historical mandate for Southern slave ownership. Simms was by no means the only Southern writer who drew on the Anglo-Norman legacy as historical grist for the mill of American manifest destiny; but he is worth singling out because his Anglo-Saxonism, by servicing his apologias for plantation slavery, arguably offers a striking American parallel to Boldrewood's Anglo-Saxonist naturalization of indigenous enforced labour in *A Sydney-Side Saxon*. This becomes even more pronounced in light of the sentiment expressed by Boldrewood's prosperous squatter Mr Steadman in 'Our New Cook'. Having, after much ado, secured a cook for his rural homestead, and guarding her closely on the journey home, he says 'here let me remark that I at least never for a moment wondered why the Southerners fought so desperately for their slaves. Could I not enter into their feelings? [...] Don't tell me! Human nature is the same everywhere'.[49] While the tone is facetious, it is also thoroughly unreflective; and Steadman is, moreover, presented as an affable and sensible narrator-protagonist whose views remain unchallenged throughout the tale. Taken together the works of Boldrewood and Simms bear testimony to some of the darker purposes of racialized Anglo-Saxonism, as well as to the influence throughout current and former British colonies of Sir Walter Scott's story of post-conquest England, and to its force as a vehicle to deal with unique local preoccupations with race and national destiny. Simms's work has long been recognized as symptomatic of what Mark Twain diagnosed as the 'Sir Walter disease' that swept through the American South; Boldrewood's work reveals that the Australian colonies carried their own distinctive, if less virulent, strain of the disease. Despite Twain's polite inclusion of

[49] Boldrewood, 'Our New Cook', p. 144. The contrast Steadman draws between himself and the unvigilant slave dealer whose cargo escaped in *Uncle Tom's Cabin* more obliquely suggests Boldrewood's opinion on the subject.

Boldrewood's work in colonial Australia's 'brilliant and vigorous' literary output,[50] one can only wonder whether a closer perusal of novels like *Sydney-Side Saxon* would have changed the great satirist's mind.

Twain's legendary denunciation of 'Sir Walter disease' in *Life on the Mississippi* sheets home 'measureless harm' to Scott: indeed, his pernicious influence on 'the making of Southern character' makes him, in Twain's view, responsible for the American Civil War. According to Twain, 'it was [Scott] that created rank and caste [in the South], and also reverence for rank and caste, and pride and pleasure in them';[51] an attitude which, Twain believed, not only fuelled parochial snobbery toward the mercantile Yankees but was also central to the feudal mentality that underpinned the continuation of Southern slavery. Commentators and historians of the American South have taken issue with the scope of Twain's invective, but not with its central insight, and many have confirmed the ubiquity of Scott-influenced racialized Anglo-Saxonism in this region before and after the war.[52] In Australia a comparable, though less thunderous, judgement on the dangers of Anglo-Saxonism can be found in the 1885 essay 'Melbourne and Her Civilization, as They Strike an Englishman', by the Socialist writer Francis Adams, who lived in Australia between 1884 and 1890. In this essay Adams does revisit the truism that 'the civilization of Australia, of Melbourne, is an Anglo-Saxon civilization, a civilization of the Norman blood'; but he does so as part of a rumination on Adam Lindsay Gordon's exuberant tribute to 'THE ANGLO-SAXON RACE!' and 'THE NORMAN BLOOD!' in 'Ye Wearie Wayfarer'. His qualified admiration of Gordon's art goes hand-in-hand with his sceptical exposure of the racial supremacism underlying its Anglo-Saxonism:

> Well, if there is one quality which distinguishes this race, this blood, it is its determined strength. Wherever we have gone, whatever we have done, we have gone and we have

[50] Twain speaks of his time in Melbourne as part of his record of his speaking tour through Australia in *Following the Equator: A Journey around the World* (Mineola, NY: Dover, 1989), Part 3, Chapter 22, p. 214. An article in *The Sketch* (27 November 1895, p. 245) mentioned that while there he was called on by Boldrewood, who seems not to have recognized the irony of his visiting the most virulent critic of his hero Scott.

[51] Mark Twain, *Life on the Mississippi* (Boston: Osgood, 1883), p. 469.

[52] See, for instance, the account of Scott's influence in Rollin G. Osterweis, *Romanticism and Nationalism in the Old South* (New Haven: Yale University Press, 1949). Peter Schmidt argues that this influence continued beyond the Civil War, saying 'Scott arguably provides the most influential narrative paradigms for both the white South's understanding of its defeat and subjugation, and for its rebirth'. See Schmidt, 'Walter Scott, Postcolonial Theory, and New South Literature', *Mississippi Quarterly*, 56 (2003), 545–54 (p. 548).

> done with all our heart and soul. We have made small, if any, attempt to conciliate others. Either they have had to give way before, or adapt themselves to us. India, America, Australia, they all bear witness to our determined, our pitiless strength. What is the state of the weaker nations that opposed us there? In America and Australia they are perishing off the face of the earth; even in New Zealand, where the aborigines are a really fine and noble race, we are, it seems, swiftly destroying them [...] [d]o we want any further testimony than this to the pitiless strength of 'the Anglo-Saxon race [...] the Norman blood'?[53]

The invocation of English 'pitiless strength' is much more wry and ambiguous than Twain's take-no-prisoners style; but this should not blind us to the force of Adams's decoupling of social progress from Teutonic virtue or to his anti-imperial critique, a critique which appeared again in his popular 1888 verse collection, *Songs of the Army of the Night*, where England is depicted as brandishing 'Bible in one hand, bludgeon in the other'.[54] By counting the human cost of British imperialism, exposing unequivocally its implication in the destruction of local indigenous populations, he punctures the self-flattering celebration of Anglo-Saxon/Anglo-Norman colonizing energy favoured by so many prominent colonists.

Despite its dominance in Australia, imperialist Anglo-Saxonism did not hold a total monopoly over the political field. A number of those who promoted the ideal of political separation from Britain seized on the mythology of Saxon 'free institutions' — epitomized by traditions such as the folkmoot and the *witenagemot* or tribal general assembly — to argue that it was, in fact, more truly English to become an independent polity. Again, the influence of American writers on Australian political thought is in strong evidence. According to Horsman, America's separation from England was understood by some to be expressing her people's atavistic Anglo-Saxon urge to preserve their own freedom: 'in the very act of revolution the Revolutionary generation believed they were reinforcing their links with their Anglo-Saxon ancestors while separating from the government of Great Britain'.[55] So too, in Australia, colonial nationalists in particular argued that the Australian pursuit of separate national sovereignty was precisely an expression of an inherited ancient English respect for freedom, and hence was an act of ethnic loyalty. According to George Arnold Wood, writing in 1920, 'Australia became independent because Australians were British, and because being British they made

[53] Francis Adams, 'Melbourne and Her Civilization, as They Strike an Englishman', in Adams, *Australian Essays* (Melbourne: Inglis, 1886), pp. 2–3.

[54] Francis Adams, 'To England' in *Songs of the Army of the Night and Mass of Christ* (London: Fifield, 1910), p. 67.

[55] Horsman, *Race and Manifest Destiny*, p. 23.

Australia not a part of Britain, but another Britain. Australia independent is far more British than was Australia dependent'.[56] McGregor and others have argued that a British identity continued to be 'integral to, even necessary for'[57] Australian nationalism. What Wood's comment demonstrates is that the fetishizing of an essentially English love of freedom offered Anglophilic Australian nationalists a powerful historical precedent to buttress their call for political independence.

A fascinating exception to this celebration of Saxon freedom is the work of early nationalist and modernist writer Joseph Furphy, which includes a commentary on early medieval England that reflects his profound resistance to instrumentalizing pre-conquest governance as a founding myth for Australia's independent nationhood. Writing in the years leading up to, and immediately after, the formation of Australian nationhood in 1901, Furphy had recourse to the same central tropes as the other Australian writers considered here, but used them in a very singular way in his quest to formulate his views on the ideal form of social and political organization for Australia.

There has been an enormous amount of critical attention paid to Furphy's contribution to Australian bush mythology, with its distinctive masculinist ethos of mateship. His work, especially his masterpiece *Such is Life* (written in the 1890s, published 1903), has frequently, though not unanimously, been situated within the practices of literary nationalism because of its development of myths and images that characterized the Australian people. Furphy's writing is also distinctive as nationalist literature in that he attempted, as Australia moved toward and into nationhood, to formulate an ideal vision of an independent Australian polity, a Christian Socialist polity, and under these auspices his literature called for law reform and redistribution of land and wealth. None of the voluminous scholarship on Furphy examines the role of medievalism in his vision of Australian nationhood, despite his repeated references to medieval literature and history, including a significant, highly sceptical discussion of Saxon England in his elaboration of an Australian utopia in the novel *Rigby's Romance.*

*Rigby's Romance* is an enlarged version of a chapter that Furphy had excised from *Such is Life* sometime before 1901. He revised and expanded it, and it was

[56] George Arnold Wood, 'Australia and Imperial Politics', in *Australia: Economic and Political Studies*, ed. by Meredith Atkinson (Melbourne: Macmillan, 1920), pp. 330–415 (p. 397). In *Race and Manifest Destiny*, Horsman notes that a number of American commentators similarly argued that the Anglo-Saxon love of freedom was the underlying impulse for America's War of Independence from Britain.

[57] McGregor, 'The Necessity of Britishness', p. 494.

published over 1905 and 1906 as a serial in the weekly newspaper *Barrier Truth*, produced in the central mining town Broken Hill and read enthusiastically by many of the miners there. It was not published in novel form until 1912, six years after Furphy's death.[58] In *Rigby's Romance* we again see Furphy supplementing his evocation of national character embodied in egalitarian bush mateship with an argument for State Socialism as the ideal form for the future Australian polity. John Docker, puzzling over its curious, dilatory structure and occasionally indeterminate satiric position, has classified it as Menippean Satire.[59] The fact that Furphy opens the novel with a quotation from the General Prologue of Chaucer's *Canterbury Tales* also situates the text within the medieval tradition of Estates Satire, which sets out to critique the various social ranks. Chaucer's text, with its cross-section of fourteenth-century English society, its humorous social critique, and its ironical narrator, is arguably an under-investigated model for the novel, although Croft does mention it briefly. Furphy's centrepiece is a symposium on romance and politics conducted by a motley crew of bullockies and other bush types gathered together on the banks of the Murray River in pursuit of a rumoured thirty-pound cod. Its main narrator is the peripatetic Tom Collins, Furphy's famously unreliable narrator from *Such is Life*, who pits himself as an avowed conservative against the central figure in the symposium, Jefferson Rigby, a North-Eastern American and committed Socialist.

The impact of Scott's vision of twelfth-century England in *Ivanhoe* is clearly apparent in Chapter 17 of the novel, where we encounter a discussion in which Scott's Saxon swineherd Gurth the same figure who embodied Saxon racial enervation in *A Sydney-Side Saxon* is presented as an exemplum of dispossession and alienated consciousness among the working classes. This chapter is devoted to Rigby's lamentation on the abiding historical alienation of the lower classes from their own will and political agency. For Rigby, Saxon England has significance as one instance of a universal history of class inequality. Gurth is emblematic of subjected lower classes everywhere who have forfeited their freedoms 'through ignorant neglect of their own responsibilities and slavish toleration of class

[58] The process leading to the publication of this text is recounted by Julian Croft in his chapter on *Rigby's Romance* in *The Life and Opinions of Tom Collins: A Study of the Works of Joseph Furphy* (St Lucia: University of Queensland Press, 1991), pp. 216–45.

[59] John Docker, *The Nervous Nineties: Australian Cultural Life in the 1890s* (Oxford: Oxford University Press, 1991), pp. 115–21.

encroachment'.[60] While freedom may have once been an egalitarian Saxon birthright, Rigby is more concerned with tracing its erosion:

> My own remote ancestor, the free Saxon barbarian, who voted his chosen leader to the chieftainship, was represented in the time of Ivanhoe by a descendant wearing a brass collar, inscribed: 'Gurth, the son of Beowulf, is the born thrall of Cedric' [...] Cedric's freedom had broadened down till it absorbed not only Gurth's freedom, but Gurth himself. (p. 120)

Scott's Saxon thane Cedric, regarded fondly by Scott's readers either as a generous Master to Gurth or as a noble but doomed resistance leader against the occupying Normans, becomes, in Rigby's system, a self-interested slave-owning landholder whose ethnic affiliations are secondary to his dominant place within an oppressive Saxon social order. This emphasis on lost liberty is in direct (and possibly deliberate) opposition to the image of the free Saxon ancestor sketched in William Lane's 1892 Sydney-set Socialist novel *The Working Man's Paradise*, where we find a nostalgic apostrophe to an idealized Teutonic/Caucasian barbarian past:

> oh for the days when our race was young [...] when the men, trampling a rotten empire down, feared neither God nor man and held each other brothers and hated, each one, the tyrant as the common foe of all! Better days when from the forests and steppes our forefather burst, half-naked and free, communists and conquerors, a fierce avalanche of daring men and lusty women who beat and battered Rome down like Odin's hammer that they were![61]

This passage differs sharply from Rigby's portrait of the Saxon hierarchy. For Lane, as Andrew McCann has perceptively noted, 'the possibility of a socialist future is phrased as a longing for a lost moment of race purity and vitality'.[62] Lane's conventional image of Teutonic egalitarianism throws into relief the contrarian perspective Furphy adopted on the subject, and reveals the extent to which this placed him at odds with those whose opinions he might generally be expected to share, another example being the trade union leader and New South Wales politician Edward William O'Sullivan (1846–1910), who traced the lineage of his own unionism back to the early Saxon and Teutonic frithgilds.[63]

[60] Joseph Furphy, *Rigby's Romance: A 'Made in Australia' Novel* (Melbourne: DeGaris, 1921), p. 95. All future references are to this edition.

[61] William Lane, *The Workingman's Paradise: An Australian Labour Novel* (Sydney, Brisbane, London: Edwards, Dunlop, 1892), p. 130.

[62] Andrew McCann, 'Romanticism, Nationalism and the Myth of the Popular in William Lane's *The Workingman's Paradise*', *Journal of Australian Studies*, 70 (2001), 1–12 (p. 8).

[63] Cited in Cochrane, 'Anglo-Saxonness, Ancestors, and Identity', p. 14.

Significantly, Furphy was familiar with the major strains of British Anglo-Saxonism — he had read Scott, all of Thomas Babington Macaulay's published works, and was an avid reader of Thomas Carlyle — but he also clearly distanced himself from his British precursors. First, his doubt concerning the mythology of Saxon freedom is distinct from the views of the Chartists and other anti-aristocratic agitators in Britain such as Macaulay, who subscribed to the Norman Yoke thesis wherein their ancestors had lived in solidarity and freedom. Secondly, his portrayal of Gurth as an ancestor of the modern exploited labourer eschewed the paternalism of Carlyle's influential exegesis of Gurth in *Past and Present*. Although Rigby's statement that 'the English peasant in Chaucer's time was much better off' (p. 119) than his descendents in later centuries reflects Furphy's genuine admiration of Carlyle, his presentation of the Saxon thane as a cruel slave-owner rather than benevolent Lord took issue with Carlyle's contention that the protected thrall Gurth, who 'lacks not his due parings of the pigs he tends', was better off than the atomized labourers of contemporary England.

It is not surprising that Furphy should have approached the figure of Gurth differently than British writers, considering the strong alternative influence on him of writings from the American Labor movement, American abolitionist tracts, and American utopian novels, especially Socialist utopias such as Edward Bellamy's *Looking Backward* (1888).[64] The chapter on Gurth in *Rigby's Romance* begins with a quotation from James Russell Lowell, the prominent American poet and abolitionist who had admired the Anglo-Saxons as an historical people but was a vehement critic of the spread of Anglo-Saxonist 'claptrap' to support American racism and territorial expansion.[65] Nevertheless, Furphy's American hero Jefferson Rigby differs from American precedents such as Lowell and from his namesake Thomas Jefferson (a great espouser of Saxon liberty) in his clear refusal to found his utopian vision of Socialist Australia on the myth of preconquest Saxon freedom. One of Rigby's interlocutors, who clearly subscribes to the Norman Yoke thesis, attempts to correct Rigby's vision of class alienation in Saxon England, saying 'you're forgetting the Norman Conquest' (p. 120). Rigby's response, which places

[64] The influence of American Socialist thought on Furphy, and especially on *Rigby's Romance*, is sketched in Joseph Jones, *Radical Cousins: Nineteenth Century American & Australian Writers* (St Lucia: University of Queensland Press, 1976), pp. 102–07.

[65] *The Anti-Slavery Papers of James Russell Lowell*, ed. by William Belmont Parker, 2 vols (Boston: Houghton Mifflin, 1902), I, 19–20, 13 February 1845. Cited in Horsman, *Race and Manifest Destiny*, p. 264.

him, and by proxy Furphy, in a tiny minority of nineteenth-century thinkers, contends that the Norman Conquest was:

> a matter of indifference [...] what did it matter to Gurth whether Saxon earl or Norman baron kept him making bricks without straw? [...] By the way, the manual-labour Saxon was hopeless enough and servile enough under the Saxon earl Leofric, a few decades before the Conquest. (pp. 120–21)

He furthermore emphasizes that the workers' loss of freedom was sustained 'without foreign incursion' (p. 119). His portrait of pre-conquest England is of a land mired in social inequality that was only minimally affected by foreign occupation. This attempt to rebut the widespread romantic adaptation of *Ivanhoe* directly aligns Furphy with Twain, a fellow dissenter whom he admired deeply (he refers to him as 'the foremost humorist of our language' in *Such is Life*).[66] Furphy was, without doubt, a highly original thinker; nevertheless, one cannot but be struck by how closely Furphy's anti-romantic view of early England is aligned with that expressed in Twain's 1889 satiric time-travel masterpiece *A Connecticut Yankee in King Arthur's Court.* The episode of Twain's that is most readily called to mind in Rigby's pronouncement — an episode that had also received high praise in a *Bulletin* review[67] — was the much-quoted one in which Twain's Yankee hero Hank Morgan encounters the small farmers and artisans of early medieval England, who '[b]y a sarcasm of law and phrase [...] were freemen' but who were in fact oppressed by the 'gilded minority' of nobility, gentry, and Church.[68] Returning to this theme in a later chapter, Twain's hero, like Furphy's, draws a direct historical link between these servile 'freemen' and the poor Southerners of his own youth:

> It reminded me of a time thirteen centuries away, when the 'poor whites' of our South who were always despised and frequently insulted, by the slave-lords around them, and who owed their base condition simply to the presence of slavery in their midst, were yet pusillanimously ready to side with slave-lords in all political moves for the upholding and

[66] Furphy, *Such is Life: Being Certain Extracts form the Diary of Tom Collins* (Sydney: Bulletin Newspaper, 1903), p. 207.

[67] 'Mark Twain's New Book: A Crusher for Royalty', *The Bulletin*, 8 March 1890. For an account of the novel's influence on nationalist and Socialist thought in Furphy's Australia, see Joseph Jones, 'Mark Twain's Connecticut Yankee and Australian Nationalist Thought', *American Literature*, 40 (1968), 227–31.

[68] Mark Twain, *A Connecticut Yankee in King Arthur's Court*, ed. by Charles Dudley Warner (New York: Harper, 1889), p. 96.

> perpetuating of slavery, and did also finally shoulder their muskets and pour out their lives in an effort to prevent the destruction of that very institution which had degraded them.[69]

More subtly yet unmistakably, *Rigby's Romance* enters into an ironic dialogue with Twain's condemnation of Scott's romantic medievalism in *Life on the Mississippi* (1883). This is most apparent in the various mock-serious honorifics the narrator Tom bestows on Rigby, such as Major, General, Judge, and Colonel. In *Life on the Mississippi*, Twain opines that '[i]t was Sir Walter that made every gentleman in the South a Major or a Colonel, or a General or a Judge, before the war; and it was he, also, that made these gentlemen value these bogus decorations'.[70] Tom's attempted undermining of his adversary is expressed in these honorifics, which playfully liken the realist and Socialist (and implicitly anti-Scottian) Yankee to the feudalist antebellum Southern gentlemen who revered Scott.

It must be said that Furphy was a notorious ironist who frequently included speeches whose satiric intent is often difficult to grasp, as they were delivered 'straight', as it were, without any clear narratorial commentary to signal that the speaker was being satirized. We need to consider that Rigby's vision is not offered as one with which we are meant to agree. Indeed, the failure of Rigby's reunion with his erstwhile beloved Kate Vanderdecken leaves us with the impression of the character as a driven but cold ideologue. There is, however, much in Furphy's correspondence that reveals that his own views were closely aligned with those expressed by Rigby, whom he professes to be an ideal male character;[71] so when discussing Rigby's view of Saxon England, there is good reason to suggest it coincides closely with Furphy's own views. Judging by Furphy's correspondence, and by the fact that *Rigby's Romance* contains a lampoon of Boldrewood's *Robbery Under Arms*, it is clear that Furphy was no admirer of his older contemporary; so there is a strong chance that his account of Saxon England is written in partial reaction against Boldrewood's, as well as in response to Lane, Twain, and others. Furphy's account, especially if we consider the possibility that it might be a reaction against Boldrewood's, is a decisive, though uneasy, attempt to move away from this determinist racialization of historical institutions and social relations.

Furphy's idiosyncratic interpretation of Scott's England is significant for two major reasons. First, by rejecting the significance of the Norman Conquest he eschews the narrative in which the Normans embodied an energizing impulse that was vital to the realization of England's colonial mission. Second, by focusing on

[69] Twain, *A Connecticut Yankee*, p. 287.

[70] Twain, *Life on the Mississippi*, p. 469.

[71] Croft emphasizes this point in *The Life and Opinions of Tom Collins*, pp. 218–20.

the element of class oppression in the Gurth exemplum, Furphy attempts to downplay the racial implication within it. The continued subjection of the lower classes in Saxon England, and their descendants in England and in newly federated Australia, is not a reflection of irreversible racial degeneration, as many readers of Scott contended. Rather, in Rigby's view, English and indeed Australian history has seen a broadening of human rights, however modest, 'between the 11th century and the 19th, between Senlac [here he uses the Normanized name for the English stronghold at Hastings] and [the] Eureka [Stockade]' (p. 121). However, he stresses that this has only been achieved through the human sacrifice involved in agitation and uprising, and can be reversed by apathy. He goes on to chide his fellow bush-workers for their acquiescence to oppression, saying,

> What could my ancestor, the free barbarian Gurth, do? What he did is exactly what you're doing now. He obediently contributed his human birthright to the building up of Cedric's monopoly, and therefore succeeding Gurths were hanged, mutilated, flogged, branded, and slaughtered wholesale, merely for thinking they had any rights at all, and thinking too audibly. (p. 122)

He then goes on to challenge them: 'Let your whole life be a protest against the system which aims at leaving a coming generation the miserable option of serfdom, suicide, or Sicilian Vespers' (p. 123). Only organized resistance can cure the disease of individualism, and break the stranglehold of squattocratic amassing of land and capital, which together threaten his vision of a Christian Socialist Australia. In this respect, Furphy made a highly distinctive Australian contribution to Anglo-Saxonist discourse that expands our sense of the ideological uses to which it could be put in Australia in the long nineteenth century.

While Furphy's scepticism about Norman and Saxon characteristics distanced him from Boldrewood's racist and imperialist Anglo-Saxonism, critics have in recent years pointed to the ethnocentrism inherent not only in his outlook but, more generally, in the ideological platform of the Labor movement in late nineteenth- and early twentieth-century Australia, particularly its support of the White Australia policy.[72] Indeed, Furphy is on record on a number of occasions openly expressing the hope he invested in the future of White Australia.[73] It is thus vital not to fall into

[72] See, for instance, Frances Devlin-Glass, '"Touches of Nature that make the Whole World Kin": Furphy, Race, and Anxiety', *Australian Literary Studies*, 19 (2000), 355–72. Devlin-Glass argues, however, that Furphy was relatively liberal according to the white supremacist standards of his time.

[73] Devlin-Glass singles out his *Bulletin* journalism and sections of *Such is Life* as exemplars; see 'Touches of Nature', p. 356.

facile apologism for Furphy's racial blind-spots, for instance his avowed suspicion of Chinese miners and workers in Australia. Indeed, one of the least assimilable parts of Rigby's argument, and one that resonates with Social Darwinist notions of racial degeneration and perfectibility, is his claim that Gurth's descendants have fought for greater freedoms in accordance with 'the grand law which guarantees the sure recoil of any redeemable race against aggression' (p. 121). Nevertheless, it is important to situate these notions within his historical vision of class conflict and domination. His distrust of the Chinese, for instance, like that expressed by other Labor protectionists, came from his belief that their underselling of their labour was part of a servility that had resulted from having surrendered themselves to despotism — a feature which, going back to our chapter in *Rigby's Romance*, is not unique to them but links them to every race in every time under every political system, including the Saxons. Here we see Furphy subscribing to the thesis of monogenesis, that is the belief in a shared origin for humans, rather than the then-fashionable polygenic theories in which races are separate species. What distinguishes populations, in Rigby/Furphy's view, is not racial difference but their 'progress-potency', that is whether they have fought to win back the freedom that is their universal birthright. The descendants of Gurth have won their (limited) freedom, and must continue to do so, through protest and martyrdom, while conversely the 'Asiatic' races have conceded despotism and hence have degenerated in Rigby's phrase, 'got down to the husks'. These people are not, however, condemned to exclusion from Rigby's vision of 'the coming Australia'. Rather, if they can throw off servility and struggle for the restoration of their primordial liberties, they will take their natural place within this egalitarian polity.

Furphy's novel is a reminder that a close interest in the ethnic 'fallout' from Saxon England was not the exclusive preserve of those who identified with wealth and privilege. Rather, the vital differences between Furphy's and Boldrewood's appropriations of the same events from the Anglo-Saxon past highlight not only the variability of this type of medievalism in Australia's early novels but, crucially, the amenability of Anglo-Saxonism to dissenters and conservatives alike. While the two writers agreed on almost nothing, taken together, they confirm the seemingly unlikely fact that the distant place and time of medieval England offered a vital historical precedent for the gamut of late nineteenth- and early twentieth-century thought about the racial and political future of Australia, whether this future was envisaged to be as a flourishing British colony or as an autonomous nation.

Chapter 2

# 'BACKWARDS AND FORWARDS IN THE STRANGEST WAY': MEDIEVALISM, MODERNITY, AND 'THE AUSTRALIAN GIRL' NOVELS BY AUSTRALIAN WOMEN

In her 1885 memoir *Australian Life, Black and White*, Rosa Praed tells of an encounter in a London drawing room with a man who had, many years earlier, received an evening's hospitality at her family's station in Bungroopim, in what was then northern New South Wales. The son of an Australian magnate who had now 'come into his kingdom in England', this unnamed acquaintance had been, at the time of his visit to Bungroopim, living rough as a drover, camping outdoors 'with his cattle and his black boys'. Reminiscing about the comforts of her Australian drawing room, the man makes a somewhat opaque remark:

> 'Ah!' he said. 'I have never forgotten that evening at Bungroopim — the music, the odds and ends that women put about, the sight of yellow-covered *Cornhill* and dear old *Blackwood* on the table. It all took me backwards and forwards in the strangest way'.[1]

Looking more closely at Praed's description of Bungroopim's drawing room, the man's recollection of its strange multi-temporality, its quality of 'backward-and-forwardness', is well justified. It is a room in which Europhilic nostalgia and Australian futurity contend and yet harmonize in a welcoming way: elegant French windows open into a room in which an original painting by the seventeenth-century Dutch painter David Teniers the Younger hangs on an unvarnished wall

[1] Rosa Praed, *Australian Life, Black and White* (London: Chapman and Hall, 1885), p. 108. All future references will be to this edition.

above 'big squatter's chairs [...] kangaroo skins and opossum rugs' (pp. 106–07). The after-dinner entertainments include a performance of Beethoven's *sonata pathétique*, but also a touching 'little song' composed and sung by Praed's Australian girlhood friend Jennie Mardsen 'to the weird air of one of Chopin's mazurkas' (p. 108). Presiding over this temporally and culturally hybrid scene is, aptly, a large oil painting with the title 'Time', which Praed describes as 'allegorical, and symbolical of the various stages of the human career'. A seventeenth-century Dutch altarpiece, this painting is an example of early pictorial medievalism at its most incongruous and unsettling. Its Netherlandish preoccupation with time and mortality is expressed uneasily in an image wherein a figure of Father Time, Latin-inscribed scroll in hand, oversees with foreboding eyes a scene made up of the Tree of Knowledge and 'groups of fantastically dressed ladies and knights in armour on richly caparisoned horses [...] mummers, and jesters [...] and mediaeval pageants' (p. 39). It is little wonder that a colonial drawing room dominated by such an image could induce a sensation of temporal vertigo in an unsuspecting visitor, for within its allegorical economy Australian future and premodern past collapse: the Coming Man of the New World is one with the medieval revellers in the atemporal pageant that is the vanity of human endeavour.

Praed offers a fascinating meditation on the significance of this painting, which she tells us had also taken pride of place on the bare slab walls of the parlour in her earlier home at Naraigin, where it was flanked by Italian Madonnas, Dutch interiors, and Flemish scriptural paintings. On the one hand, she tells us, her child-self at Naraigin could not reconcile the Dutch altarpiece's fantastic biblico-medievalism with the prosaic details of her own life. And yet her dim comprehension of its allegorical nature engages her imagination, leading her to interpret it through the central moral conundrum plaguing her childhood: that is, the cycle of interracial violence between the local European settlers and indigenous inhabitants. Unable to decipher the biblical message on Time's scroll — very possibly Ecclesiastes 1. 2's *vanitas vanitatum, omnia vanitas* (vanity of vanity; all is vanity), a common sentiment expressed in Northern Renaissance Time allegories — she decides that it must be Latin for 'Thou shalt not kill'. The recollection of her uneasy childhood intuition that Father Time was 'grieving [the] transgression' of the sixth commandment 'in our proceedings' leads Praed to dwell on the role played by European settlers in accelerating the 'atmosphere of murder' of the frontier settlement in which she lived as a child (p. 40).

This medievalist allegory, and the distinctly Australian meditation it prompts, is of special interest in this chapter because the strange 'backwards-forwards' historical sensibility evoked by the painting is emblematic of the paradoxical presence of medievalism in numerous novels written by Australian women in the nineteenth century. For these writers, medievalism offered a range of discourses on which they drew frequently, but also inconsistently. It is this complex and multifarious use of these discourses, and their specific application to Australian womanhood, that will form the focus of the current chapter.

This chapter is situated at the crossroads of a number of critical approaches to medievalism and to Australian women's writing. First, it aims to redress the very significant absence of work on the medievalist texts produced by women writers. Clare Broome Saunders has recently claimed that 'the whole question of female-authored medievalism has received scant attention'; even the very noticeable acceleration of work on medievalism over the past decade 'largely focus[es] on the work of only the celebrated male authors of the nineteenth century'.[2] There have been excellent individual chapters and essays devoted to nineteenth-century English women medievalists such as Charlotte Yonge (whose work is generally analysed under the auspices of nineteenth-century Anglo-Saxonism and Anglo-Catholicism), Mary Eliza Haweis, and others, and their numbers are gradually increasing.[3] There is also a body of important work on female medievalist scholars, from eighteenth-century scholar Elizabeth Elstob to the present.[4] But so far only a tiny handful of studies have devoted any significant space to considering the ways in which women poets and novelists moulded the discourses of medievalism to serve their purposes as commentators on the lives of women. Elizabeth Fay devoted some of her 2002 study *Romantic Medievalism* to women, while Judith Johnston's *George Eliot and the Discourses of Medievalism* (2006) examines this thematic thread throughout Eliot's oeuvre. Most recently, Saunders's *Women Writers and*

[2] Clare Broome Saunders, '"Judge No More What Ladies Do": Elizabeth Barrett Browning's Active Medievalism, the Female Troubadour, and Joan of Arc', *Victorian Poetry*, 44 (2006), 585–97 (p. 585).

[3] See, for instance, Mary Flowers Braswell, 'The Chaucer Scholarship of Mary Eliza Haweis (1582–1898)', *The Chaucer Review*, 39 (2005), 402–19, and Sarah R. Wakefield, 'Charlotte Yonge's Victorian Normans in *The Little Duke*', in *Beyond Arthurian Romances: The Reach of Victorian Medievalism*, ed. by Jennifer Palmgren and Lorretta Holloway (Basingstoke: Palgrave Macmillan, 2005), pp. 53–72.

[4] See, for instance, *Women Medievalists and the Academy*, ed. by Jane Chance (Madison: University of Wisconsin Press, 2005); Barbara A. Hanawalt, 'Golden Ages for the History of Medieval English Women', in *Women in Medieval History and Historiography*, ed. by Susan Mosher Stuard (Philadelphia: University of Pennsylvania Press, 1987) pp. 1–24; and Kathryn Sutherland, 'Elizabeth Elstob', in *Medieval Scholarship: Biographical Studies on the Formation of a Discipline*, ed. by Helen Damico, 2 vols (New York: Garland, 1998), II, 59–74.

*Nineteenth-Century Medievalism* (2009) argues for a 'strong alternative tradition of women using medievalism as a discourse to facilitate a hidden and acceptable means of subversion, transgression, and ultimately empowerment'.[5] This chapter, while concurring with Saunders's point, differs from her study in two key ways. First, unlike most of the women she discusses, the Australian writers examined here were not dedicated medievalists; indeed, in many of their works, with the exception of Catherine Martin, there is little evidence of deep knowledge of premodern literature, art, or history. Rather — and this is the second key difference — they were responding not to the Middle Ages but, rather, to medievalism itself, as a series of tropes, practices, and objects around them that were often only tenuously linked to the Middle Ages and whose presence was more symptomatic of the modernity, or indeed the futurity, of women and Australians alike. In this respect they can be more accurately described as meta-medievalists; but it is for this very reason that they must be included in this study, for their work suggests that it was arguably at one critical remove that medievalism became most serviceable to Australian women novelists.

This chapter also sets out to supplement the wealth of excellent work on the New Woman novel, and in particular the four decades of research on its antipodean iteration, the Australian Girl novel. Teresa Mangum is typical among scholars of the New Woman in emphasizing the political intervention involved in female novelists of the 1880s and 1890s 'creating representations of women that confronted the self-abnegating, submissive, and housebound image of Middle-class Ideal Womanhood' and 'critique[ing] prevailing forms of femininity and its superstructure, marriage, by way of editorial analysis and alternative plots'.[6] Susan Magarey, pointing to the solid body of late nineteenth-century Australian women's writing that featured non-conventional, educated, democratic heroines and plotted anti-conjugal narratives, has argued that the New Woman novel 'acquired a particular resonance in the Australian colonies' because it accorded with the Australian nationalist quest for an iconic female counterpart to the Coming Australian Man: the Australian Girl.[7] As such, these novels, in a way parallel to

[5] Clare Broome Saunders, *Women Writers and Nineteenth-Century Medievalism* (Basingstoke: Palgrave Macmillan, 2009), p. 9.

[6] Teresa Mangum, *Married, Middebrow, and Militant: Sarah Grand and the New Woman Novel* (Ann Arbor: University of Michigan Press, 1998), p. 2.

[7] Susan Magarey, 'History, Cultural Studies, and Another Look at First Wave Feminism in Australia', in *Debutante Nation: Feminism Contests of the 1890s*, ed. by Susan Magarey, Sue Rowley, and Susan Sheridan (St Leonards, NSW: Allen and Unwin, 1993), pp. 96–110 (p. 105).

many of their British equivalents, were bound up with notions of national futurity and cultural critique, as well as with analysis of gender relations. It is this intersection which informs this chapter, but an extra dimension has been added, in that medievalism is used here as a kind of side-window to access the largely submerged engagement with concepts of the premodern that underlay Australian women's otherwise very current depictions of colonial society and women's place within it. Patricia Murphy has argued in *Time is of the Essence: Temporality, Gender, and the New Woman*, that it is vital to register the ways in which New Woman novels' emergence out of the late Victorian period, with its preoccupation with time and progress, led them to 'import temporal discourses, in subtle but revelatory ways, to illuminate heightened gender anxieties wrought by this rebellious anomaly'; indeed, the very concept of 'New' womanhood (along with 'Coming Man') implicates itself within a paradigm of historical typology. Murphy contends that these novels 'occupied a transitional literary moment, one that both continued the Victorian attentiveness to temporal forces and presaged the modernist disillusionment with an inherited temporal burden';[8] and so it is with Australian women's novels, whose engagement with medievalism as a temporal discourse reflects that discourse's unique capacity to probe contemporary gender politics via its oscillation between past and future, and premodernity and modernity.

Like many of the male writers explored elsewhere in this book, some of the women whose work is discussed in this chapter were born in Britain and came to Australia in childhood (Catherine Martin) or adulthood (Ada Cambridge); others were born in Australia but left in early adulthood to live abroad, only returning to Australia late or sporadically (Rosa Praed, Henry Handel Richardson, Miles Franklin, Tasma). But all of them lived in Australia long enough to take abiding inspiration from its people, its landscape, and its culture in their fiction, whether this fiction was written inside or outside of Australia. While some of them, like Miles Franklin's 1901 *My Brilliant Career*, address themselves overtly to an Australian audience, these texts were written for an imperial cosmopolis primarily encompassing British and Australian audiences. As such, their inclusion of medievalist discourses and practices as an index of gender, class, and racial politics in Australia demonstrates medievalism's capacity to function in the late nineteenth century and early twentieth century as both a common imperial currency and a reflection of the minutiae of antipodean colonial environments.

[8] Patricia Murphy, *Time is of the Essence: Temporality, Gender, and the New Woman* (Albany: State University of New York Press, 2001), p. 2.

## *Butchers and Baronets: Genetic Medievalism*

Like Saunders's study, this chapter does not attempt to be a comprehensive analysis of medievalism in Australian women's fiction of the late nineteenth century, which is sprinkled liberally with references to contemporary medievalist literature, particularly Tennyson, as well as to such medieval giants as Dante, whose *Commedia* is probably the most cited medieval text by these writers. It narrows its focus, rather, to a selection of novels that can be identified as treating two distinct but related forms of medievalism: *genetic medievalism* and *material medievalism.* Medievalism features within the racial paradigms underpinning a number of these novels not as a rejection the modern, but as a disclosure of an underlying premodern genetic condition of Australian modernity, and, in particular, of the development of newly formulated gender relations within the coming Australian nation. Although women writers, in their quests to create the New Australian Woman in fiction, differed from Boldrewood in that they did not develop elaborate medievalized racial typologies, they nevertheless frequently relied on a medievalist racial atavism comparable with Boldrewood's — an atavism which, paradoxically, mandates both the modernity and the Australianness of their heroines. Their novels suggest, furthermore, that a number of them shared Boldrewood's mania for the discovery of ancient English pedigrees, if not in life (none of them adopted a medievalist *nom de plume* or confected a medieval Anglo-Celtic pedigree for themselves) then at least as a stock-in-trade literary *deus ex machina.* It is fair to say that their reliance on a 'surprise baronetcy in the mail' to develop the plot or to provide a *dénouement* that removes financial or social obstacles for the central lovers (or, indeed, conveniently dispatches a degenerate aristocratic suitor back to England) appears with a regularity that is amusing to a reader today. This attests in part to a fascination with medieval genealogy but also to the constraints imposed by the romance genre, which relies heavily on this genealogical trope, and the challenges involved in using this genre as a vehicle for moving beyond a preoccupation with aristocracy and formulating new gender roles for a 'new' land. Moving 'backwards and forwards', then, these novels seem to create a singular and intriguing collocation in which the medieval noblewoman and the New Australian Woman fuse 'in the strangest way'. In this respect they can be said to be engaging in a form of medievalism, in which their heroines' status as Australian New Woman is mandated by qualities they possess due to their antique heritage.

Looking through these novels we find a number of examples where outlining the long pedigree of a heroine functions as a shorthand for her intrinsic nobility.

Len Platt has recently given an account of this obsession with racial pedigree in the novels of Rosa Praed, arguing that her Australian novels are 'awash with [...] discourses of breeding and blood in the contexts of race and nation'.[9] Platt offers numerous examples from Praed's novels in which physical superiority and ancient social distinction are given a prominent place within Praed's eugenicist vision of Australia's pastoral future. To take just two examples, the ineffably superior Lady Waverying in *Outlaw and Lawmaker* (1893) is 'the natural product of centuries of civilization', while Lady Bridget in the later novel *Lady Bridget in the Never-Never Land* (1915) is described by her squattocratic suitor Colin McKeith as having 'the blood of fighting ancestors' in her veins. Praed does not match Boldrewood's elaborate post-conquest typology, but his ideal of 'pure mixed Englishness' in Australia is played out as these heroines contribute the refining element of their ancestral breeding to the social and/or physical composition of the Coming Australia.

These discourses can also be found in novels that seemingly have no commitment to this kind of eugenic historicism. In the 1910 novel *The Getting of Wisdom* by Henry Handel Richardson (Ethel Florence Lindesay Richardson), for instance, the young piano prodigy Laura Romsbotham is accepted at her exclusive Melbourne boarding school, despite all her up-country gaucheness and social *faux-pas*, because

> [she] had race in her; in a well-set head, in good hands and feet and ears. Her nose, too, had a very pronounced droop, which could stand only for blue blood, or a Hebraic ancestor — and Jews were not received as boarders in the school. [...] inherited instincts and traditions were not so easily subdued.[10]

Although this is not rigorously pursued in the novel, and is not part of a pronounced racial substratum within its narrative, its aristocratophilic connotations should not be conjured away, especially as the final statement here suggests that Laura's native talent and her ineffable quality of superiority over her richer classmates, not to mention the ambition that takes her beyond the confines of her colonial education, are due to this 'blue blood' of hers. Catherine Martin also offers an antique pedigree for her intelligent and cultured New Woman heroine Stella Courtland in her 1890 novel *An Australian Girl*. Stella's mother was 'descended from an old Highland family, and in face and bearing she bore the unmistakable stamp of high-

[9] Len Platt, '"Altogether Better-bred Looking": Race and Romance in the Australian Novels of Rosa Praed', *JASAL*, 8 (2008), 31–44.

[10] Henry Handel Richardson, *The Getting of Wisdom* (London: Heinemann, 1931), p. 111. All future references will be to this edition.

bred refinement';[11] and so Stella is 'tall and finely formed' with a 'singularly noble' brow that reflects both her strong intellect and her hereditary refinement (p. 9). But Martin's novel is more ambivalent about the allure of the aristocracy. Although Stella's true love Anselm Langdale is aristocratic, many scathing remarks and vignettes throughout the novel are reserved for those colonial socialites who fixate on attaching themselves to the aristocracy, and there is a clear distinction drawn between aristocracy and true gentility. 'Aristocracy', especially as manifested in such ugly characters as Talbot Tareling, becomes a byword for vulgar, haughty self-regard and moral degeneracy, and in this respect it is important that it is the age of Stella's pedigree rather than its rank that confers nobility on her. Despite this, she still qualifies as one of the 'backwards and forwards' medieval New Women of Australian women's fiction.

But for every example where ancient race equals futurity, there are tales that question this equation, and include significant exceptions to this collocation of 'old race' and New Woman. *A Sydney Sovereign* by 'Tasma' (Jessie Couvreur) is one such. In this novelette, Reginald Barrington returns home from his outback station to take up his inheritance as a Squire on the Isle of Wight, only to find his heart claimed by two women: Lucy, the long-faithful love of his youth whom he has now outgrown, and Roberta Marl, an artless Thomas Hardy-esque nymph who is the sister of his station manager in Australia. The narrator underlines Lucy's ancient heritage by telling us her dowry includes

> broad acres, and a rent-roll in keeping with them — a name that may be traced back with honourable directness through a line of sword-bearing ancestors — family plate and old china, in quantity to stock a museum — and with all this the truest, the fondest, most constant of hearts, of a constancy that even the most exacting of Crusaders could hardly have imagined.[12]

But although she is genteel and faithful, she is presented as medieval in a somewhat insipid way, being compared to an 'expressionless' Madonna, and is most assuredly a woman of the past, keeping company with Reginald's ageing mother, while the pert and vivid Robina is a woman of the future. Lucy's pastimes of reading medievalist fiction, playing 'old world chants' (p. 100) on the piano, and her acumen as an 'authority on antiques and heirlooms' (p. 105), all align her with a past which, while venerable, pales against Robina's elemental charms, which are simultaneously more primordial and more modern. It is true that Lucy ultimately succeeds,

[11] Catherine Martin, *An Australian Girl* (London: Richard Bentley and Son, 1891), p. 28.

[12] Tasma (Jessie Couvreur), *A Sydney Sovereign And Other Tales* (London: Trübner, 1890), pp. 62–63. All future references are to this edition.

through passive persistence, to best her young rival and hold Reginald to his diminished devotion to her, but their union is not celebrated by the narrator; rather, the entrapping nature of the historical union is highlighted by a chilling absence of commentary. Robina's futurity is, by contrast, marked by the fact that she ends up in Australia, looking after Reginald's station with her brother. The tale ends with them both, in their opposite corners of the world, wistfully commemorating a blossoming love divided by history and obligation.

The irrepressible Sybilla Melvyn, heroine of Stella 'Miles' Franklin's landmark 1901 novel *My Brilliant Career*, is another character whose status as New Woman is predicated on an overt rejection of medieval pedigree. Described by numerous contemporary critics as the quintessential literary New Australian girl, the poor but ambitious Sybilla famously rejects the velvet manacles of a squattocratic marriage to Harry Beecham and hopes to become a writer, a dream which is not yet realized at the novel's end. Given Sybilla's iconic status as a democratic Australian girl — or, indeed, a radical, according to some of Franklin's disapproving early readers[13] — it comes as a surprise to find her laying claim to an ancient pedigree that includes Norman forebears. Almost (and probably deliberately) in the manner of a character from a Boldrewood story, she begins her tale with a potted genealogy that promisingly combines aristocratic Norman energy and 'tone' with the resourcefulness of new blood:

> My father was a swell in those days — held Bruggabrong, Bin Bin East, and Bin Bin West, which three stations totalled close on 200,000 acres. Father was admitted into swelldom merely by right of his position. His pedigree included nothing beyond a grandfather. My mother, however, was a full-fledged aristocrat. She was one of the Bossiers of Caddagat, who numbered among their ancestry one of the depraved old pirates who pillaged England with William the Conqueror.[14]

Franklin openly declared that '*My Brilliant Career* is not the story of my *own* life'.[15] Still, it is amusing to note the discrepancy between Sybilla's matrilineage and that of Franklin, whose maternal great-great-grandfather Edward Miles had in fact been a convict of the First Fleet, and to wonder at the fun the writer may have been having not just with genealogy but with genre. Such an opening, according to the narrative conventions of Boldrewood and his ilk, should lead us to expect a genteel settler romance in which all ends well and prosperously for this family of Anglo-

[13] Jill Roe, *Stella Miles Franklin* (London: Fourth Estate, 2008), pp. 66–72.

[14] Miles Franklin, *My Brilliant Career / My Career Goes Bung*, intro. by Elizabeth Webby (Sydney: Harper Perennial, 2004), p. 4. All future references are to this edition.

[15] Letter to A. G. Stephens, 10 October 1902; quoted in Roe, *Stella Miles Franklin*, p. 70.

Norman Coming Australians; but in this expectation we are sorely disappointed. Mr Melvyn, both feckless and unlucky, leads his family into penury and shame. Sybilla's mother's Norman background does not manifest itself in any enterprising scheme to recover the family's fortunes, while her father sinks back into the obscurity of his beginnings, broken and addicted to alcohol. Furthermore, while the story later appears to pursue a romance arc that promises to save Sybilla from social death, readmitting her into the respectability first of the English gentle classes and later of the Australian landed classes, this too comes to nothing, at Sybilla's own hands. But we should not be surprised, for we receive an early warning that this genealogy has been introduced only to be disavowed:

> my organ of veneration must be flatter than a pancake, because to venerate a person simply for his position I never did or will. To me the Prince of Wales will be no more than a shearer, unless when I meet him he displays some personality apart from his princeship — otherwise he can go hang. (p. 5)

And so it turns out. She laughs when proposed to by the ludicrous English gentleman Frank Hawden, and evades intimacy with the impoverished gentleman-cum-barrister Everard Grey. Finally, having dispatched Harry Beecham for the last time, she addresses the reader with a declaration that was music to the ears of her *Bulletin* comrades, but a battle-cry against the Boldrewood formula of cross-class perfected Englishness:

> I am thankful I am a peasant, a part of the bone and muscle of my nation, and earn my bread by the sweat of my brow, as man was meant to do. I rejoice I was not born a parasite, one of the blood-suckers who loll on velvet and satin, crushed from the proceeds of human sweat and blood and souls. (p. 257)

And on this note the novel concludes. *My Brilliant Career* has been admirably and exhaustively analysed by others, and this discussion, like that of Furphy in the previous chapter, does not aim to negotiate the complexities of Franklin's engagement with the radical and nationalist thought of the time. But it is clear that on her way to finding a path beyond the formulas of romance to the challenges of realism in *My Brilliant Career*, Franklin found time to identify, and stridently demolish, the medievalist racial paradigms on which the settler romance genre had quietly but definitively rested.

Given Franklin's sympathy with the labour movement, this is not an unexpected position for her to have taken. It is perhaps more surprising to find one of the most sustained critiques of the genealogical fetish in Tasma's 1892 novel *Uncle Piper of Piper's Hill*. In this novel, the Cavendishes, blue-blooded but impoverished, emigrate to Melbourne to live with the enormously wealthy brother of Mrs Cavendish, the eponymous Uncle Piper. In this novel, which is another paean to the dignity of work (though less strident than Franklin's), the Cavendish family is poor because the father will not condescend to find occupation. His low-born but beautiful wife, whom he 'betrayed his race' to marry, is not work-shy herself; but, overawed by her husband's rank, she cannot bear to see him lower himself. By contrast, the plebeian Uncle Piper, now retired and living in his palatial South Yarra mansion, has accrued wealth and power as a result of his entrepreneurial acumen and years of hard work at such undignified occupations as butchery. The Cavendishes, finding themselves dependent on the largesse of this man, whose former occupation is a source of acute embarrassment but whose generosity to them has been unfailing, are confronted with the prospect of living in a city where patricians and plutocrats move in the same circles. While Mrs Cavendish and the older daughter Margaret accept their new circumstances with equanimity and gratitude, Mr Cavendish and his snobbish daughter Sara react with a combination of resentment, haughty denial, and opportunism.

Much fun is had at the expense of Mr Cavendish, as we are invited to enjoy the spectacle of him being humbled by his dependence on one whom he regards as his inferior. Most laughable are his pitiable attempts to invoke his medieval genealogy as a way of holding himself aloof from the 'humiliation' of living in Melbourne. He is not the only character in the novel who has recourse to the Middle Ages to express his self-regard; as we will see later, even Uncle Piper is not averse to appropriating medieval status symbols to announce his success to the world. But Mr Cavendish far exceeds the others, for he actually sees himself as partly medieval, intimately, indeed bodily, linked to the premodern past. On one occasion he declines to dine with his parvenu brother-in-law because he is suffering from what he claims to be one of his 'hereditary headaches'. These headaches purportedly afflict all male members of his line, and are, the narrator wryly reports,

> distinctly traceable [...] to the cleaving of the skull of an ancestral Cavendish, who had a posthumous son, by whom they were transmitted in an unbroken line to the present era. The period of skull-cleaving was coincident with the period of battle-axes, and was in every sense a more glorious and more comfortable age.[16]

It is difficult to tell whether Tasma is genuinely evoking notions of racial degeneration in her characterization of Mr Cavendish as an indolent, feeble and self-pitying man obsessed with 'the fatalities that had attended the House of Cavendish' (p. 55). One the one hand, he would appear to have a number of the most recognizable

[16] Tasma, *Uncle Piper of Piper's Hill* (London: Heinemann, 1892), p. 162. All future references are to this edition.

symptoms of degeneracy: apart from his physical frailty, he also suffers from a total lack of will to self-improvement, a characteristic he shares, we recall, with those other degenerate noblemen, Mr Leighton in *A Sydney-Side Saxon* and Athelstan in *Ivanhoe*. On the other hand, his ridiculous claim to ancestral headaches suggests that he nurtures and broadcasts his physical feebleness as a sign of the antiquity of his blood. A similarly ambiguous use of racial discourse is used in descriptions of Mr Cavendish's younger daughter Sara. Unlike her father, she is statuesquely beautiful and in rude good health (both attributes inherited from her mother); but she shares not only Mr Cavendish's arrogance but his disposition to indolence, which the narrator speculates could be due to her Cavendish lineage. In an interesting twist, however, Sara's is not the degeneracy of overbred purity reaching back to the Middle Ages, but a strain of atavistic orientalism resulting from more recent miscegenistic adventures:

> The House of Devonshire can show, as history has already attested, more than one princely vagrant among its ancestors, whose wanderings among the Moors and Turks three centuries ago may have had a remote share in tingeing Sara's blood with an infusion of the lymph of the Eastern odalisque. (p. 29)

This passage is interesting because it gives the lie to Mr Cavendish's fantasy of his unadulterated ancient Englishness, leaving us to ponder on the two conflicting genealogical accounts for the same disposition. Furthermore, its speculative modality ('may have had a remote share') suggests that its allusions to decadence — Oriental, English, or otherwise — are sceptical and playful. For it is equally clear in the narrative that Sara's languid self-complacency is a result of the indulgence her beauty has always won from others, and of the fact that she, like her father, has wilfully imbibed the mythology surrounding the ancient House of Cavendish, which has convinced her of her prerogative to be waited upon by others. The fact that Margaret, also a Cavendish, has an entirely more humble nature, suggests that it is Mr Cavendish's and Sara's defects of character, including their disdain for rendering service and their insufferable snobbery, that ultimately make them unfit to prosper in the colonies.

Far less ambiguous is the novel's satire of genealogy hunting. Again Mr Cavendish is the main culprit. In order to reconcile himself to the debasement of relying on his brother-in-law's unacceptably recent wealth, he decides that the 'most graceful course' available to him is to medievalize Uncle Piper by hunting down a pedigree that would 'throw a veil over the unfortunate accident of his birth'. Acting on a dim recollection of a Count Piper 'somewhere or other some centuries ago', he sets out to 'reconstruct' Mr Piper's family tree:

> He would spend whole hours in the Melbourne Library, pouring [sic] over books of heraldry. Every chronological or biographical document bearing upon the age in which Count Piper was supposed to have lived was made the subject of long and minute examination. (p. 236)

His fanatical attempt to redeem Uncle Piper also leads Mr Cavendish, like those colonials discussed by Paul de Serville, into voluminous correspondence with English genealogical societies and colleges of heraldry. When Mr Piper questions the value and purpose of this research, the narrator tells us Mr Cavendish, continues, but

> contented himself by deploring the sad effects of low association on the undoubted descendant of a count, and pondering on the possibility of introducing a hog in armour instead of a stag at gaze into the coat-of-arms that he foresaw would be a result of his researches. (p. 237)

The humour in this episode turns on its combination of broadly drawn caricature and subtly ambiguous phrasing. One the one hand we have the exaggerated sketch of Mr Cavendish's desperate search for authenticating evidence, and on the other we have phrases such as '*reconstructing* a family tree' and '*introducing* a hog in armour', which suggest slyly that pedigree hunting involves as much self-interested invention as it does historical research.

## *Consuming the Past: Material Medievalism*

Tasma's satirizing of Mr Cavendish's fetish for medieval ancestry points us to a distinguishing feature of the work of Australian women writers, who seem to have been far less interested in Australians as atavistically *medieval*, and more interested in Australians as *medievalists*. In particular, the novels written by women around the late 1880s and early 1890s reflect a fascination with colonial Australians' imaginative engagement with popular fantasies of the Middle Ages as a paradise of preindustrial beauty. But when presented as a series of cultural and material practices, this medievalism fares highly ambivalently at the hands of these women writers. Characters evincing a desire to revisit or recreate the Middle Ages in literary, aesthetic, or architectural form are frequently associated with such negative qualities as affectation, dilettantism, immaturity, ostentation, and artifice; and, seemingly paradoxically, with conspicuous consumption and mercenary materialism of a particularly decadent cast. In such cases, attraction to the premodern threatens to compromise either the characters' gender propriety, or the integrity of their Australian identity, or both. Elsewhere, however, an imaginative relationship to the medieval past, embracing typical Victorian notions of this period's romance and purity, provides an alternative to the uniformity and perceived cynicism of modern metropolitan femininity, forging a path to cosmopolitanism, erudition and, more importantly, to individuality. Within the complex terrain of the 'Australian Girl' novel, the sacrificial spirituality of medieval Catholicism is also canvassed as an alternative to self-interest and cynicism as the emergent founding principles of the marital economy of late colonial Australia.

The interior scene from Praed's *Australian Life* with which this chapter opened is, for all its idiosyncratic detail, part of a pronounced preoccupation among nineteenth-century Australian women writers with what we might call 'spatialized medievalism'; that is, medievalism as it is located and articulated physically within colonial domestic life. Scattered throughout these novels are a number of vividly drawn portraits of the medievalist domestic architecture constructed and owned by Australia's emergent mercantile ruling classes, as well as a range of closely observed depictions of the medievalist interiors and 'atmospherics' created by Australian women in both urban and rural domestic environments. As the Praed passage demonstrates, and a number of other texts to be discussed here corroborate, the main reference point for these explorations is the medievalism produced out of the prolific material culture of the late nineteenth century, in particular that of the Arts and Crafts and Aesthetic movements that emerged in response to the mid-century work and philosophy of John Ruskin and the Pre-Raphaelite movement, and of the Decadent movement that emerged as Aestheticism's amoral sibling. It is true, as we will see, that these writers are clearly familiar not only with Scottian, Tennysonian, and other literary strains of popular Anglo-medievalism, but also, in the case of Catherine Martin, with the medievalist canons of German Romanticism. But what sets their writing apart is its insightful and nuanced understanding of the impact of contemporary material medievalism on the formation of colonial taste and social distinctions. In these novels, medievalism is found not just in books but also in houses, rooms, furniture, decorations, clothes, and bodies.

A complex set of responses to colonial medievalist desire emerge in those texts where we see Australian characters actually creating medieval environments for themselves at home. One such text is Tasma's *Uncle Piper*. In this novel, Uncle Piper has built a 'crenellated tower with four plate-glass windows, a Persian rug, and painted panelling' onto his modern mansion (p. 69). Our knowledge of the man after whom the novel is named is framed by our introduction to his crude architectural attempt at medieval grandiosity, with its muddle-headed mélange of baronial cliché and modern convenience, lightly seasoned with orientalism. The portrait of Uncle Piper's mansion, with its eclectic 'backwards and forwards' historical allusions, could have been modelled on a number of the boom-time piles erected around Toorak and South Yarra in the 1870s and 1880s, the extreme eclecticism of which, Andrew Montana tells us, conveyed the 'trappings of ancestry [...] but with an emphasis on the self-conscious artistic effect rather than on authenticity'.[17] One such mansion was Bracknell, the home of politician and plutocrat Sir Matthew Davies. While Bracknell has now been demolished, according to *The Australasian* of 2 July 1892 it had a tower which was a 'great attraction', a report borne out in a drawing of the house. And while we are not told what Uncle Piper's 'painted panelling' involves, there is every reason to think it might have boasted something like the scenes from Chaucer's *Clerk's Tale* that adorned Bracknell's panelled ceiling, or some such evocation of antique Englishness.[18]

It is easy, our narrator admits, to mock this as a bloated monument to colonial pretension. But we are then swiftly cautioned against such a reaction. As the tale proceeds, the portrait we receive of Uncle Piper is sympathetic, and so his desire for a self-constructed medieval edifice is not held against him. In fact, the narrator describes as 'touching' his anxiety that his newly planted trees might not flourish enough before he dies to produce the shaded effect of an ancestral Chase. While he is not spared a critical portrayal for his brusque manner or his autocratic stubbornness, his unpretentious and generous character and his spirit of enterprise stand as strong foils to the novel's authentic but degenerate aristocrat, Mr Cavendish. As such his tower assumes the more disarming status of a folly, rather than a parvenu's paradise. In some ways it bears comparison, despite its larger size, with the endearing suburban castle of the legal clerk Mr Wemmick in Charles Dickens's *Great Expectations* (1861). In both cases, the domestic medieval space marks a respite from the tough necessities of the characters' work lives, a soothing retreat into a suburban manorial 'good life'. Uncle Piper's tower is, moreover, the expression of the newfound dignity and largesse of a once dirt-poor English boy who has made good in the Australian colonies.

In *Uncle Piper*, architectural medievalism is surely in part an expression of naïve colonial nostalgia: although Uncle Piper unabashedly prefers Australia, where he has made his fortune, the architectural idiom he falls back on to declare this colonial fortune is ancestral rather than modern. But the novel exposes the extent to which this nostalgia in nineteenth-century society is heavily implicated within *nouveau riche* aspiration and is, therefore, absolutely modern. Montana's comment that medievalist effects in domestic architecture were 'the hallmarks of status in

[17] Montana, *The Art Movement*, p. 88.

[18] Montana, *The Art Movement*, p. 76.

which both notions of British ancestral privilege and independent colonial success could be flaunted'[19] applies perfectly to the tower at Piper's Hill, which bears witness to the ironic and inextricable relationship in Australian architecture between feudal trappings and capitalist success. For all their gestures toward the simplicity of the past, such medievalist possessions were, in fact, ambiguous symbols of the triumph of modern conspicuous consumption.

The forgivable innocence of Uncle Piper's medievalism is thrown further into relief when compared to the more suspect forms practiced by his indolent son George and George's beloved, the clever but brittle and hedonistic Laura. The two are united in their love of medievalist verse. Located among the detritus of their many abandoned pastimes (French horn, half-finished oil painting, a suspended course of study of Auguste Comte) lies a 'well-used edition of Swinburne' (p. 150), implying that their only sustained activity has been consumption of the poet's work. It is true that Swinburne's oeuvre was eclectic, and so the reference to him need not necessarily imply a predilection for medievalism; but the fact that he, the author of widely known Arthurian and medievalist verse, is later paired in the novel with 'Dante Rossetti' suggests George and Laura's devotion to medievalism in what was, for many in the 1890s, its most fatuous form: Aestheticism.

The later nineteenth-century Aesthetic movement inherited its love of medieval forms predominantly from the artworks of the Pre-Raphaelites, including Dante Gabriel Rossetti, Edward Burne-Jones, and, especially, William Morris, whose paintings, furnishings, wallpapers, and books, with their fusion of medieval design and modern manufacture, generated the international Arts and Crafts movement. The Arts and Crafts movement had, in turn, taken its lead from John Ruskin's toweringly influential writings in praise of medieval Gothic architecture and of the organic artisanal ethic of the Middle Ages in which, he argued, objects that combined beauty and utility were produced under the harmonious communal conditions of the medieval guilds.[20] While the Aesthetic movement retained Ruskin's and Morris's appreciation of medieval beauty, which it frequently

[19] Montana, *The Art Movement*, p. 62.

[20] Arguably the most important of Ruskin's works in this respect was *The Stones of Venice* (3 vols, 1851–53), with its famous and much-praised essay on 'The Nature of Gothic' (vol. 2). I have used the 1981 edition, ed. and intro. by Jan Morris (London: Faber, 1981). Morris famously followed Ruskin's ideals in Morris and Co.'s artisanal modes of production, and in his promotion of the fusion of art and utility, which is concisely expressed in his 1880 lecture, 'The Beauty of Life': 'have nothing in your houses that you do not know to be useful, or believe to be useful'. See *Hopes and Fears for Art: Five Lectures Delivered in Birmingham, London, and Nottingham, 1878–1881* (London: Ellis & White, 1882), p. 108.

combined with classical and oriental forms, there was little concern for their ideal of medieval objects as balanced expressions of beauty, utility, and morality. Andrew Montana is right to point out that this movement in Australia was not coherent in ethos or appearance,[21] but if one is to identify an overarching quality of Australian literary Aestheticism, it is a general embracing of medieval visual and verbal 'effects' without any accompanying anti-industrial impetus; indeed, as will be elaborated throughout this chapter, for many in colonial Australia Aestheticism was far more strongly associated with commerce than with art.

Returning to *Uncle Piper*, Tasma clearly wrote with the assumption that her audiences would have been *au fait* with the nuances of Aestheticism, many of which were subject to widespread satire. In the allusion to Swinburne, many readers, both British and Australian, would also have spied the ghost of Reginald Bunthorne, the absurd faux-medievalist 'fleshly poet' in *Patience*, Gilbert and Sullivan's 1881 satire on Aestheticism, who is widely believed to have been modelled on Swinburne. Given the vast popularity of this satire in both Britain and Australia, Swinburne is hardly an innocent reference; unlike the more naïve medievalism expressed in Uncle Piper's tower, reading him is a sign of George's ne'er-do-well, over-privileged immaturity. In Laura's case, her medievalist literary proclivities are of a piece with the unsettling whisper of artifice that clings to her youthful and fashionable figure — she is likened in rapid (and somewhat incongruous) succession to a Watteau on porcelain, a Dresden vase, and a Turner landscape. It is only when she and George are removed from their medievalist environment and habits, during her period of exile in the rural town of Barnesbury, that they discover the true depth of their love. Ironically, their maturation beyond jejune medievalism is signalled by a medievalist reference: when they are reunited after their trials, George is likened to the knight Geraint, who, in Tennyson's *Idylls of the King*, is reunited with his long-suffering bride Enid after he has driven her into exile in the land of Doorm.

In Chapter 4 of Martin's *An Australian Girl*, we find another gargantuan shrine to material medievalism, and especially to medievalism as associated with the Aesthetic movement. The sympathy extended to Uncle Piper is absent here: domestic medievalism is unambiguously associated with tasteless modishness and the worst kind of *nouveau riche* ostentation. Godolphin House, the luxurious town residence of self-made magnate Sir Edward Ritchie, nestled at the foot of the Adelaide Hills, has been riotously made over in the Aesthetic style:

[21] Montana, *The Art Movement*, p. xv.

> in an evil hour, the emissary of a great 'decorative' firm had prevailed upon Sir Edward to have the 'mansion' 'done up' from top to toe. This took the form of a carnival of unlimited expenditure, and that unhappy outburst of British Philistinism known as the aesthetic craze. (p. 43)

The Ritchies' parvenu slavishness is underlined in Sir Edward's desire to be '*en rapport* with a rampant art-decorator' (p. 44) and his ready acquiescence to the judgement of the firm, which his daughter Laurette declares 'just the thing' (although she later redecorates when it is no longer as fashionable). Decorated with such medievalist touches as 'sage green portières' (fabric doorway hangings), the house's most vulgar Aesthetic interior is 'one apartment known as the peacock-room', which is depicted humorously as driving people away with what one guest calls its 'damned staring eyes' (pp. 43–44).

It may well be that Martin, as an Adelaide-based writer, was aiming her satire close to home. It is difficult to read the description of Godolphin House without thinking of the famed patronage of Morris and Co. by Adelaide's hugely wealthy Barr Smith family, who decorated their many homes extensively using the firm's furnishings, wallpapers, carpets, and curtains. Christopher Menz says of the family:

> [b]ecause of the number and vast size of the Barr Smith houses, their orders for Morris & Co. were some of the most extravagant of the period. During the 1880s and 1890s this family was one of the firm's most significant international clients.[22]

Just as Godolphin House is decorated 'top to toe' by the unnamed decorative firm, so too the Barr Smiths' Torrens House was, according to Menz, 'furnished from 1884 largely under the direction of the firm'.[23] The Barr Smiths were, it is true, far from the only prominent colonial family to engage an Arts and Crafts firm to decorate their home; indeed, it was a mark of distinction among the mercantile classes to have one's grand residence made over to the last detail, and at great expense, by one of the increasing number of local firms specializing in both imported and bespoke Aesthetic furniture and décor. Perhaps Martin is even making fun of those lesser families who did not decorate with the taste and authenticity of the Barr Smiths. Nevertheless, it is strongly tempting to read this as Martin's unflattering and recognizable portrait of a prominent local family's extravagant addiction to a décor that is ultimately un-British and hence decadent.

[22] Christopher Menz, *Morris & Co.* (Adelaide: Art Gallery of South Australia, 2002), pp. 136–37.

[23] Menz, *Morris & Co.*, p. 172.

Its possible local target notwithstanding, Martin is also arguably offering a generic satire of the interior design of the Aesthetic craze. Her readership in Australia and Britain could hardly have read Martin's reference to the 'great "decorative" firm' without calling to mind the 'Æsthetic High Art Company, Limited' lampooned in F. C. Burnand's 1881 smash-hit comedy *The Colonel*, which, along with *Patience*, was among the best-known satires of the Aesthetic movement. The generality of the critique is also especially likely given the ubiquity of the peacock-feather motif within Aesthetic interiors. Design historians often identify the Peacock Room produced in 1876–77 by James Abbott McNeill Whistler as the apogee of this phenomenon, while major London Aesthetic design houses such as Morris & Co. and Liberty & Co. had also developed their own peacock-derived designs in the 1870s and 1880s respectively. Indeed, Martin's account bears the hallmark of many satires of the Aesthetic craze from the 1870s on, including those that linked Aesthetic medievalism with decadence and orientalism. Despite her earlier description of the Aesthetic movement as a species of 'British Philistinism', the narrator goes on to describe Godolphin House's decorator as having 'forsworn the old honest British hideousness' in favour of 'a sickly unreality'. The style, furthermore, with its unsettling fusion of European medievalism and orientalism — the medieval portières are combined with oriental screens and fans — 'weigh[s] heavy on the spirits', leading to a state of decadence: 'It was a house in which above all others to taste the wormwood of ennui to its last dregs; in which to be overcome by [...] lassitude of body, and languor of mind' (p. 44).

Martin goes on to enumerate comically a symptomology of this ennui brought about specifically through contact with Aesthetic interiors. Chris Lee has argued for the closeness of these symptoms to the aetiology of neurasthenia, the nervous affliction commonly attributed to overeducated women in the nineteenth century, and has ingeniously suggested that the effect of the house on its inhabitants foreshadows Stella Courtland's breakdown when ill-fortune marries her into the Ritchie clan.[24] Martin's aetiology is, however, foremost that of decadence; it bears comparison with well-known descriptions of opium addiction in earlier texts such as Dickens's *The Mystery of Edwin Drood* (1870) and Gustave Doré and Blanchard Jerrold's *London: A Pilgrimage* (1872), as well as, more topically, in decadent texts such as Oscar Wilde's *The Picture of Dorian Gray*, which was published in serial form in the same year as *An Australian Girl*. The combination of medievalism and orientalism under the aegis of decadence was a particular satiric bête noir of the

[24] Christopher Lee, 'Strategies of Power and Catherine Martin's *An Australian Girl*', *Southerly*, 51 (1991), 189–206.

*London Punch*, which on 17 March 1894 published a cartoon by Edward Tennyson Reed in the style of an orientalist woodcut, punningly entitled 'Japanese Fan de Siècle Illustration by Mortarturio Whiskersly'. The yoking together here of 'Mortarturio' and 'Whiskersly' creates an absurd amalgam in which Pre-Raphaelite Arthurianism is linked (via pretentious continentalism) to an infantalized version of the name of Aubrey Beardsley, the artist synonymous with Art Nouveau and Decadent art, whose style is unmistakably imitated in the cartoon. *An Australian Girl*'s satiric triangulation of medievalism, orientalism, and decadence is more subtly configured than that of other satirists such as Reed, but is very clear nevertheless: just as opium and *Japonisme* encapsulate the insalubrious seductions of the Orient, so too the decadent medieval-orientalism of Godolphin House threatens to leech away the vitality of the robust colonials who enter its doors.

Lest Martin's description seem purely comic, we discover that as the novel proceeds, the narrator's architectural prediction comes tragically true: the young colonials reared within the house have indeed been infected with decadence. The daughter Laurette is a brittle socialite whose malicious nature is exposed when she sabotages Stella Courtland's engagement to her true love, Anselm Langdale; her brother Ted, although devoted to Stella and disarmingly forthright, is revealed after his marriage to Stella to be an alcoholic, a fact his relatives have colluded in concealing. Martin's mistrust of oriental-medievalism as being on a continuum with moral and racial degeneration aligns her with those women authors and activists who were keen to dissociate the cause of the New Woman from those socially destabilizing movements with which it had been identified by its critics, including Aestheticism and Wildean decadence. Although Stella does marry into the decadent Ritchie family, this is a tragic rebound marriage resulting from her being tricked by Laurette into believing Anselm is a would-be bigamist. It is true that Martin does not travel down the eugenic path carved out by some British novelists such as Sarah Grand, who promoted the New Woman's vital maternal role in racial regeneration; but the clearly stated preference in *An Australian Girl* for 'old honest British hideousness' over the 'sickly unreality' of Aestheticism is an Australianized version of British nationalist rejections of the movement, including *Punch*'s 1895 call for 'plain sturdy Britons' to throw off the racially endangering 'cant' of the decadents.[25]

Medievalism is not universally condemned in the novel, however. The decadent orientalist-inflected medievalism of Godolphin House is contrasted with Stella

[25] *Punch*, quoted in Sally Ledger, 'The New Woman and the Crisis of Victorianism', in *Cultural Politics at the Fin de Siècle*, ed. by Sally Ledger and Scott McCracken (Cambridge, London, and Melbourne: Cambridge University Press, 1995), pp. 22–44 (p. 31).

Courtland's more cultured interest in Teutonic romantic medievalism, which takes the form of translating not only Goethe's *Faust* but also an unnamed 'old ballad in early German' (p. 80), the latter suggesting she is also familiar with medieval linguistic forms. Stella's pastime closely parallels Martin's own interest in German literature, a legacy of her earlier years among the German communities of the Mount Gambier district of South Australia. Martin, like Stella, translated the work of Goethe along with medievalist and folkloric verses by German Romantic poets and thinkers Heinriche Heine, Ludwig Uhland, and Johann Gottfried von Herder.[26] Germany is twinned with England in Stella's pan-Germanic historical consciousness as 'two old civilizations firmly rooted in the past' (p. 189), and the two are combined ideally in her beloved, Anselm. As Tanya Dalziell has discussed,[27] it is a part of Stella's characterization as Australian Girl that her notion of 'old civilizations' extends beyond the European premodern past to the deep past of Aboriginal mythology, which for her occupies as profound a role for its culture as Greek myth does for the West, 'giv[ing] an account of the origin of things' (p. 68). Furthermore, when repeating a conversation she had with a German archaeologist, Professor Kellwitz, Stella heartily applauds his condemnation of the European past as mired in social inequality, and tacitly agrees with him that a nation's grand history of 'great kings and nobles' (p. 73) is of little account to its hungry and oppressed masses. The Professor's realist perspective on the (in)significance of the medieval past for the modern working poor reminds Stella, and us, of the centuries of inequity that marked the period she is otherwise apt to romanticize as a result of her Germanophilic reading habits.

Stella also leans towards, and finally adopts, a personal spirituality that is affiliated with a well-known medievalist impulse of nineteenth-century High Anglicanism. This religious orientation, known variously as the Oxford movement or Tractarianism, sought to restore to the modern Anglican Church the ancient apostolic inheritance of the Old (that is, Catholic) English Church. The figures most prominently associated with this movement were Edward Bouverie Pusey and John Henry Newman, who in 1845 converted from Anglicanism to Catholicism, famously rising to the rank of Cardinal; but it also attracted a number of writers and artists with medievalist leanings such as Gerard Manley Hopkins, Charlotte

[26] See the 'Translations' in Martin's *The Explorers and Other Poems* (Melbourne: Robertson, 1874), especially pp. 228–46. For a discussion of Martin's early exposure to Germanic influences, see Margaret Allen, 'What Katie Might Have Learnt in Mount Gambier, or Some Early Influences on C. E. M. Martin', *Barcelona University Australian Studies Papers*, 1 (1996), 1–19 (p. 9).

[27] Tanya Dalziell, *Settler Romances and the Australian Girl* (Crawley: University of Western Australia Press, 2004), pp. 74–105.

Yonge, Christina Rossetti, and William Morris. Stella's leaning toward Tractarianism is presented early in the novel as a kind of immature provocation, as those around her are bemused by her interest in such 'papist' things as worship of the Virgin Mary and joining a convent (although this could just as easily refer to the orders of Anglican nuns founded in the mid-nineteenth century as a by-product of Tractarianism). Her quasi-Catholicism continues on a persistent but essentially playful note for most of the novel, with snatches of liturgical Latin and her beloved Anselm calling her 'St Charity', although we later learn that she has indeed read Newman's Tracts and been 'deeply stirred' by them — a detail that suggests her leanings toward convent life reflected her genuine scepticism about matrimony. At the end of the novel, this devotion is confirmed and strengthened. In London, barely recovered from a breakdown and struggling desperately to reconcile herself to the fate that has separated her from Anselm and married her to Ted, Stella stumbles upon the end of a church service conducted by none other than Cardinal Newman. Gazing upon his 'austere, ascetic countenance' (p. 453) she experiences an extreme state of contrition and self-abnegation. After this she forms a new spiritual resolve to accept her unfair fate, saying '[t]hough I may never be an orthodox Catholic, yet the old faith had so far revived as to be an inspiring rule of life' (p. 462). Her adoption of the penitential economy of this Anglo-Catholicism eventually softens into Protestant good works, but her Tractarian epiphany has changed Stella forever. The novel's sure-footed course from Aesthetic materialism to Tractarian spirituality offers testament to Martin's familiarity with the wide significance of medievalism in the nineteenth century.

A particularly intricate exploration of medievalist Aestheticism, femininity, commodity culture and colonial desire can be found in Ada Cambridge's novelette *The Perversity of Human Nature*, which first appeared in the 1887 Christmas Supplement of the *Illustrated Australian News*. Described somewhat surprisingly by Audrey Tate as 'a light-hearted piece, written to entertain Christmas readers',[28] this is in fact an unsettling little tale whose rather sordid narrative traces an arc through marital desertion, bigamy, subterfuge, and death, to a morally unredemptive conclusion. In this tale, English-born and -educated Alexandra (Lexie) has married the young Australian stock agent Robert Brown, whom she met at that mecca for Aesthetes, the Grosvenor Gallery, during his art-collecting visit to London.[29] As a

[28] Audrey Tate, *Ada Cambridge: Her Life and Work: 1844–1926* (Carlton: University of Melbourne Press, 1991), p. 149.

[29] Alison Inglis has written an excellent article on the fact that there was a temporary Grosvenor Gallery in Melbourne. See 'Aestheticism and Empire: The Grosvenor Gallery

'nervous' melancholic, another of the 'neurasthenic' New Women identified by Chris Lee in Australian fiction, Lexie is unfit both for marriage and for life in colonial Melbourne. After a bitter and protracted marital dispute, Lexie deserts Robert for England, returning many months later to discover that he, thinking her dead, has remarried. Her reappearance causes such distress to his new wife Mabel that she goes into premature labour and dies, after which Lexie and Robert reunite and raise the baby 'while Mabel [...] mouldered to dust in the St Kilda Cemetery, abandoned and forgotten'.[30]

This tale is of significance because Cambridge presents us with another colonial domestic interior in which the emotional disorder of the inhabitants, as well as the suburban circumscription of the heroine, is augured by a medievalist aesthetic. The tale opens with a detailed description of 'The Nest', the bungalow in St Kilda, Melbourne, owned by the young couple. At first it would appear that the cultural signification of this interior could not be more different from that of Godolphin House:

> Persian carpets on the dark floors; Liberty stuffs at the window; Morris chintzes on the chairs and sofas; good, though not rare, pictures on the walls, which are tinted on purpose to suit them; low book cases running like dados around the room [...] bearing dainty *bric-à-brac*, of which each piece has been selected for its merits, and not at the command of vulgar fashion. A thoroughly refined and harmonious house, in short; such a house as could only belong to cultivated and enlightened people. (p. 2)

In sharp contradistinction from the overwrought interiors of Martin's Adelaide mansion, The Nest's medievalist-orientalist flair is presented as the pinnacle of domestic good taste. But once we are introduced to Lexie, it quickly becomes clear that the room's apparently harmonious Arts and Crafts interior is in fact infected by the enervation and restlessness that characterizes the devotee of Aestheticism, especially if that devotee happens to be female. Unlike Sir Edward's ignorant embracing of the Aestheticist trend, Lexie's devotion is genuine and abiding, if clichéd: even before her marriage, when she had spent her days dispensing Fabian-

Intercolonial Exhibition in Melbourne, 1887', in *Seize the Day: Exhibitions, Australia and the World*, ed. by Kate Darian-Smith and others (Melbourne: Monash University ePress, 2008), pp. 16.1–16.17. DOI: 10.2104/sd080016. Interestingly, Cambridge wrote *Perversity* in the last month of the Melbourne Grosvenor's tenure.

[30] Ada Cambridge, *The Perversity of Human Nature*, from *The Illustrated Australian News Christmas Supplement* (Melbourne: Syme, 1887), p. 16. All future references are to this edition.

style charity in London's East End, the one pleasure she had allowed herself was her 'aesthetically furnished lodgings', with their 'rush-bottomed chairs and high art cups and saucers' (p. 2). But her Aestheticism has estranged her from conventional middle-class femininity, an estrangement which is further confirmed by the fact that she is an alumna of Girton College, Cambridge University's relatively recently opened college for women. Sally Ledger describes 'The Girton Girl' as 'much maligned and ridiculed'[31] as an exemplar of unsexed womanhood throughout the *fin-de-siècle* period, and Cambridge's portrait of Lexie certainly relies on this apprehension, especially as before her marriage she shared her 'aesthetic' lodgings with another Girtonian, Emily Price, in a relationship whose jealous volatility and virulent anti-marital stance hints at an 'unnatural' bond between the women. Highly educated, financially independent, and ensconced in graceful surrounds, Lexie is also deeply unhappy, a malcontent whose medievalist affectations are an index of her unspecified sense of superiority over the 'intellectually benighted people' around her in her new colonial domicile.

Despite proudly identifying as a Girtonian, Lexie does not dress in the mannish 'rational' attire frequently attributed to such 'over-educated' women in the British popular press. She chooses instead to express her anti-conventionalism by donning Arts and Crafts costumes that harmonize meticulously with her domestic surrounds, modelling herself on any number of famous Pre-Raphaelite paintings featuring interiors with women. She dines with her husband 'picturesquely dressed in sage-tinted Liberty silk' (p. 2) draped in loosely girdled antique folds, an unequivocal declaration of herself as an Aesthetic woman. This style of dress was not antithetical to New Womanhood; rather, as Elizabeth Wilson and others have pointed out, the simple antique shift allowed women to move more freely, and shed their pinching stays to embrace the more natural 'antique waist' of ancient Greece and pre-Elizabethan England as advocated by Aesthete, feminist, and Chaucer popularizer Mary Eliza Haweis in her widely praised 1878 treatise on women's dress, *The Art of Beauty*.[32] On the rare occasions when Lexie ventures unwillingly into the prosaic backdrop of metropolitan Melbourne, her incongruous clothes attract ridicule from the conventionally fashionable women around her, whom she in turn thinks of as 'the Philistines of the tight waists' (p. 2), preening herself on her

[31] Sally Ledger, 'The New Woman and the Crisis of Victorianism', p. 27.

[32] Mary Eliza Haweis, *The Art of Beauty* (New York: Harper, 1878), pp. 45–48, 62–66. Haweis's book received positive reviews in Australian newspapers. See also Elizabeth Wilson, *Adorned in Dreams: Fashion and Modernity*, rev. edn (New Brunswick, NJ: Rutgers University Press, 2003), pp. 209–10.

New Woman credentials. These women apply to her the moniker 'Mrs Cimabue Brown', after George du Maurier's satiric portrait of the narcissistic 'Aesthetic woman' made famous in the *London Punch*. This character, whose name fuses that of the duecento Florentine painter Cimabue with a thoroughly commonplace surname, was promptly popularized and Australianized in the colonial press, where she also featured as an embodiment of the risible female Aesthete: 'Shades of Murray and Flinders defend us! Mrs Cimabue Brown has arrived', mocked the *Melbourne Bulletin* on 12 November 1880, in its satire of Aesthetic elements at the 1880 Melbourne International Exhibition. Bearing the surname Brown herself, surely not accidentally, Lexie becomes an Australian counterpart of this much derided caricature.[33]

This satirical characterization, which renders Cambridge complicit with Lexie's detractors, is especially noticeable when we consider that the author appears to look favourably on free-waisted Aesthetic dress when worn by the gracious King sisters in *The Three Miss Kings* (1891); but she is careful to detach the sisters' dress sense from other Aesthetic tastes, attributing it instead to good sense and natural gentility, while Lexie's couture, by contrast, is placed within the full gamut of Aesthetic clichés. Her love of 'high art cups and saucers', for instance, a predilection lampooned mercilessly in the popular press and in George Grossmith's 1876 anti-Aesthetic play *Cups and Saucers*, contrasts strongly with Elizabeth King's emphatically professed ignorance of historical and oriental ceramics.[34] A similar distinction is made in Cambridge's 1889 serialized novel *A Woman's Friendship*, where the Aesthetic interior created by urbane would-be New Woman Margaret Clive is portrayed as mercifully free from all signs of the medieval-orientalism we see in Lexie's interior.

Yet Tate's description of Lexie as 'a spoiled and petulant child'[35] does not do full justice to the narrator's disposition toward her as Aesthetic New Woman, which is not simply satirical but, rather, shot through with ambivalence and moments of sympathy. Furthermore, it diminishes the complex portrait of New femininity embodied in this character, who appears to retain her progressive views on female independence even as she abandons her hostility to marriage and finds redemption through caring and planning for baby Mab, whom she declares 'should never wear

[33] *Melbourne Bulletin*, 12 November 1880, p. 9. Mrs Brown is also mentioned in the fashion column of the *Australasian Sketcher*, 13 August 1881, as part of its discussion of Aesthetic fashions.

[34] Ada Cambridge, *The Three Miss Kings*, with a new introduction by Audrey Tate (1891; London: Virago, 1987), p. 107.

[35] Tate, *Ada Cambridge*, p. 150.

stays, and should go to Girton, and become the woman of the future generally' (p. 16). Most notably for our purposes here, Lexie does not abandon her predilection for medievalist aestheticism despite her eventual acquiescence to matrimonial custom. Rather, the most unequivocal sign of her renewed tenure at The Nest is her prompt replacement of Mabel's gaudy furnishings with her own harmonious Arts and Crafts arrangements of yore. Far from treating interior decoration as incidental, Cambridge makes a point in this story of tethering the main female characters' domestic tastes to their ideological dispositions as women, and telescopes their later conflict through their separate disapproval of one another's interior decoration. Just as the highly conformist Mabel 'thought the colors [sic] of the Liberty stuffs rather dingy, and the patterns of the Morris chintzes [...] *old fashioned*' (p. 7) and soon rids herself of them, Lexie, with her horror of conventionality, becomes enraged at the sight of the commonplace tapestry chairs with which Mabel has usurped her Morris chintzes. With a Ruskinesque posture of disdain for the fruits of mass production, she notes witheringly that Mabel's furniture was 'exactly like all of the chairs and sofas in the windows of all the furniture shops' (p. 13). Her own fastidious partiality for bespoke items does not go uncriticized, however. Once her remorse over Mabel's death passes, her reinstatement of her Aesthetic décor, which she enacts with ruthless efficiency, clearly declares her victory over her rival. As the novel ends with a cosy vignette in which Lexie sits down with to Christmas dinner with her little family, swathed in gold-tinted Liberty silk, it appears that the spirit of Aesthetic medievalism, and the New Woman aspirations that accompany it, of which little Mab is to be beneficiary, reign triumphant. But the cost, we are reminded in a narrative aside, has been another woman's life. Even as Lexie enthusiastically embraces her new nurturing role, the narrator's pointed characterization of her as 'the pseudo-mother' (p. 16) bestows on her conditional honours only, leaving intact the equation of Aesthetic medievalism with aberrant femininity.

Cambridge uses interior decorative medievalism, furthermore, to point with great subtlety and insight to an unresolved contradiction, even hypocrisy, at the heart of Aesthetic New Womanhood. For all its rejection of contemporary mass culture philistinism, Aesthetic taste is, the story suggests, arguably just a form of niche consumption, through which professedly 'artistic' but essentially bourgeois women in Australia could mark both their distinction from their less discriminating peers and their affiliation with British cosmopolitanism. In this respect, Cambridge's work corresponds with that of women writers in Britain, which Regenia Gagnier describes as 'consistently sensitive to the manifold politics of aesthetic production and consumption'.[36] Montana's insightful reading of Australian women's involvement in what he inclusively names the 'Art Movement' deftly draws out the contradictory possibilities held out to women by Aestheticism, particularly due to its complex intersection with the emerging women's movement:

> At its popular levels the Art movement was framed as feminine and women's ambitions for social autonomy were channelled back into artistic home decoration [...] Women's broader social concerns were thus diverted into the making, buying, and arranging of artistic decorations for the domestic interior. But there was a side-effect: art and women's independence were confused [...] Many interiors in which the prescribed 'artistic' reforms were applied became symbolic enclaves of women's frustrated ideals.[37]

On the one hand women could use the domestic space as a canvas for expressing their tastes and ambitions; on the other hand this relegated them to the role of consumers. In their capacity as arbiters of domestic taste, and hence potential clients, middle-class women with a taste for oriental-medievalism were courted avidly from the 1870s on by the proprietors of the numerous Aesthetic emporia springing up in the colonial metropolises, as well as by the organizers of the numerous Great Exhibitions that were mounted throughout the colonies as part of the international craze for such events, and which regularly included courts featuring medievalist and orientalist Aesthetic objects.[38] Although Montana's account is wide ranging, he could have been talking specifically about Lexie, so close is her situation to the one he identifies. Indeed, he singles out Cambridge's fictions for their shrewd diagnosis of the sham autonomy offered to women by Aestheticism and of the movement's deep implication within aspirational consumerism in the Australian metropolis. Despite Lexie's conviction that she is 'Aesthetic', educated, and therefore emancipated, she is, on closer scrutiny, caught utterly within an international circuit of Aesthetic commodity fetishism. Far from adhering to the Ruskinian ethos of preindustrial unalienated production, she imbibes the niche-consumerist fantasy of a premodern 'beautiful life'. Indeed, her

[36] See Gagnier, 'Women in British Aestheticism and the Decadence', p. 240.

[37] Montana, *The Art Movement*, p. 18. This ambivalence is also taken up in a number of the essays in *Women and British Aestheticism*, ed. by Talia Schaffer and Kathy Alexis Psomaidis (Charlottesville: University Press of Virginia, 1999).

[38] Susan K. Martin discusses the central importance of the Melbourne Great Exhibitions for Cambridge and notes that, within the Exhibition setting, her female characters are both objects of consumption (and exportation through marriage) and consumers of display objects. See Martin's excellent '"Surmounted by Stuffed Sheep": Exhibitions and Empire in Nineteenth-Century Australian Women's Fiction', in *Seize the Day*, ed. by Darian-Smith and others, pp. 13.1–13.11. DOI: 10.2104/sd080013.

'personal' taste corresponds closely to the medievalist aesthetic promoted to bourgeois Melbourne in such commercial documents as the 1874 catalogue *Remarks on Furniture and the Interior Decoration of Houses* by William Henry Rocke, proprietor of the Collins St Aesthetic emporium W. H. Rocke and Co., and Cullis Hill and Co.'s advertorial 'Artistic Houses for the People', which was reprinted repeatedly in the *Argus* throughout 1882.[39] Indeed, Cambridge's readers would very likely have recognized that the opening description of 'the Nest' draws heavily on the seductive language of the catalogue genre, and would ideally have registered the critical end to which this advertorial discourse was being used.

Cambridge again critiques this same fantasy in *A Woman's Friendship*. When describing the domestic interior assembled by Margaret Clive, she makes sceptical use of the word 'kalizoic', an Aesthetic *mot du jour* meaning 'beautiful life' which was also the name of a Melbourne Aesthetic warehouse.[40] In *Perversity*, possibly because of its more compressed form, the critique is more intense and more searching. While a single woman in London, Lexie's medievalist rejection of the ills of industrial modernity had led her into Fabian charitable works, but now, married in Melbourne, her sphere of agency has become so circumscribed that once her interior decoration projects are completed, she is without occupation or means of self-expression. Montana argues that this as a particular symptom of colonial Aestheticism, which experienced, he says, 'the effect without the cause'; untethered from the forms of social activism which had accompanied its inception in Britain, including women's advocacy of work reform and female industry, it became merely a bourgeois Anglophilic fashion statement.[41] Lexie's disconnection from her former ideals of useful beauty is so extreme that does not engage even in the limited form of Aesthetic production offered by the traditional domestic arts of needlework, an occupation which was pursued by many Australian women specifically under the aegis of the Aesthetic movement. So Cambridge's references to Lexie's coveted Liberty and Morris fabrics do not just signify her medievalist tastes, but are allusions to what today would be called her brand loyalty as well as her Anglophilic social aspirationalism.

This condemnation of fatuous consumption needs to be read in the context of Cambridge's social conservatism, which includes, as we have seen, recourse to

[39] See Montana, *The Art Movement*, p. 111.

[40] Ada Cambridge, *A Woman's Friendship*, ed. by Elizabeth Morrison (Kensington: New South Wales University Press, 1988), p. 38. Montana also discusses this passage, *The Art Movement*, p. 54.

[41] Montana, *The Art Movement*, p. 19.

medievalist racial typologies. Her account of entrapped consumerist Aesthetic women, whilst accidentally serviceable to Marxist-feminist inflected analyses of women under Victorian capitalism, is framed within what Jill Roe has described as Cambridge's indictment of a world where arriviste money counts more than ancient 'blood',[42] a point overlooked in Montana's reading of her work. While Tasma's *Uncle Piper* celebrates this disdain for genealogy in the name of colonial egalitarianism, for Cambridge it is more troubling. The social hubris of Melbourne's post-gold-rush boom period is famously condemned in her memoir *Thirty Years in Australia*, while the Depression that followed in the 1890s is presented as a providential moral correction.[43] Within this larger conservative commentary, medievalist Aestheticism functions for Cambridge as a potent meeting point for cultural imperialism, caste confusion, conspicuous consumption, and feminine entrapment. Her works offer us a singularly nuanced, female-orientated but also socially conservative insight into the modern commercial interests and colonial aspirations served by the apparent antimodern nostalgia of Aestheticism.

Rosa Praed's 1889 novel *The Romance of a Station* offers another fascinating critique of the deleterious effects of medievalist aesthetics on the colonial New Woman. This seemingly conventional settler romance surprises us with a highly sophisticated linking of the objectification of women within aestheticism/pre-Raphaelitism with the commodification of female beauty within the contemporary marriage market.

In Chapter 16 of this rather meandering tale, we meet Weeta Wilson, 'The Veiled Princess', daughter of a Queensland speculator-landowner and his ferociously ambitious wife. When we first come across Weeta, the description of her is highly painterly in a way that bears unmistakable reference to the visual idiom of the Pre-Raphaelites:

> At one end of the house grew a poinciana-tree, now a canopy of gorgeous flame-coloured blossom. Young Thurston was gathering sprays of the flowers and giving them to a most curious and attractive-looking woman, who stood in a statuesque attitude against a background of orange and green. She herself was a harmony of green and orange [...] she must have found it a difficult matter to achieve the soft, clinging, 'Liberty-looking' dress which was draped from her shoulders and seemed to be caught at her waist by a girdle of poinciana flowers. She had a wreath of the same flowers on her head, and they were just two tones more vivid than her hair. I never beheld such hair. It hung to her waist in

[42] Jill Roe, '"The Scope of Women's is Necessarily Less": The Case of Ada Cambridge', *Australian Literary Studies*, 5 (1972), 388–403 (p. 393).

[43] Ada Cambridge, *Thirty Years in Australia*, intro. by Louise Wakeling and Margaret Bradstock (Kensington: New South Wales University Press, 1989), p. 157.

> a natural ripple, and each strand seemed to fall by itself. In colour it was simply magnificent. She wore it parted in the middle and standing out from her forehead as it does in some Venetian portraits.[44]

Complementing her burnished hair, Weeta's face has a natural Pre-Raphaelite quality, with an equine length, a 'too high' brow, a 'full mouth' and 'heavy lidded' eyes (p. 209) — features reminiscent of the strong-featured beauty of Jane Burden Morris, whose queenly visage dominates the paintings of Dante Gabriel Rossetti and her husband William Morris. Indeed, Weeta's wreath of flame-red poinciana flowers reads like an antipodean translation of the crimson wreath worn by Jane Morris in William Morris's iconic 1858 painting *La Belle Iseut.* But as Praed's opening description of Weeta avers, her persona as Pre-Raphaelite beauty is highly self-conscious and obviously costs her considerable effort to maintain. The 'blunt' remark to Weeta's father by the narrator Rachel Ansdell's husband, 'What a pity it is that Rossetti couldn't have painted your daughter' (p. 210), exposes the studied nature of the pictorial effect Weeta is straining to create. This is not the only occasion in the story, either, where the narrator notes the girl's habit of striking Pre-Raphaelite poses in settings calculated to harmonize with her autumnal tones and Titian hair: 'The girl put herself into one of her attitudes. The sitting-room wall was of cedar, and its rich brown made an effective background for her red-gold and green, and her odd mediaeval style of beauty' (p. 221).

The narrator Rachel is fascinated but unsettled by this beautiful but remote girl, whose inner turmoil is hinted at in her eloquent violin playing. Later Rachel learns the circumstances that led to Weeta's current status as 'mediaeval angel' (p. 253): formerly a gormless girl, teased mercilessly for her carroty hair and for 'ha[ving] a shingle loose' (p. 218), she has now been rebadged as an ethereal Pre-Raphaelite beauty as a result of the passing admiration of a visiting Prince (this presumably refers to Prince Alfred's visit to the Eastern colonies in 1867–68). Although Weeta privately confesses to Rachel her doubt at the Prince's sincerity, her mother seizes the opportunity to niche-market her previously unmarriageable daughter, and devotes herself to forming Weeta into a living Rossetti muse. Weeta's father builds a room onto the house with high windows that let in a minimum of the strong Queensland light, and her mother confines her to this room through the hot midday hours. When she does venture out, she is made to wear an impenetrable veil to protect against the dreaded return of a freckle that had once marred her now-flawless complexion.

[44] Praed, *The Romance of a Station: An Australian Story* (London: Chatto and Windus, 1893), p. 209. All future references are to this edition.

Praed's portrayal is striking in its anticipation of much later feminist-influenced critiques of the Pre-Raphaelites' fetishistic objectification of women, such as Deborah Cherry and Griselda Pollock's pioneering discussion of how Rossetti saluted his own genius by way of his obsessive portrayal of wife and favoured model Elizabeth Siddall.[45] In the initial portrayal of Weeta, the narrator wonders whether her aristocratic English admirer Archie Thurston, who is a 'dilettante in art', had been instructing the girl on her appearance, a thought that positions the Pre-Raphaelite woman as a passive product of the masculine imagination. The fact that we discover that it is her parents rather than Archie who fashion her, and that Weeta submits herself to their medievalizing regimen, does not make her any less of a masculine object, as her highest purpose is to attract male regard. Her complete object status is especially evident when we compare her with Praed's earlier Queensland Pre-Raphaelite, Angela Ferris in the 1881 novel *Policy and Passion*. Angela's appearance corresponds with another Pre-Raphaelite type, the pale and abstracted waif:

> Angela was slender and fair, with the appearance of frail health which is denoted by great delicacy of limb, waxen complexion, and violet stains beneath the eyes [...] [h]er features were of the purity of a cameo, her forehead low, and her eyebrows full and extremely arched. Her mouth, pale rather than red, was of almost infantine softness [...] [h]er grey eyes, lovely in colour and shape, had a blank abstracted gaze, and were at once dreamy and shallow.[46]

Physically she is a wan blonde Elizabeth Siddall to Weeta's regal Jane Morris. Like Weeta, Angela attires herself in Pre-Raphaelite ensembles, such as a 'white dress with a fantastic wreath of flowers adorning her yellow hair' (p. 118). But there are two crucial differences between the girls. The first is that in Angela's case her Aesthetic persona is entirely uncalculated. She has, it is true, been immersed in romantic poetry, music, and art by her fanatically aesthetic father, as well as in folklore, that favourite pastime of amateur Victorian medievalists; but Praed is also at pains to emphasize the almost chthonic naturalness of her medieval persona. In

[45] Griselda Pollock, revised version of Deborah Cherry and Griselda Pollock, 'Woman as Sign in Pre-Raphaelite Literature: The Representation of Elizabeth Siddall', in Griselda Pollock, *Vision and Difference: Feminity, Feminism and the Histories of Art* (London: Routledge, 1988), pp. 91–115; the original essay was written in 1984. A similar argument about Elizabeth Siddall's image as a reflection of Rossetti's genius is made in David G. Riede, *Dante Gabriel Rossetti Revisited* (New York: Twayne, 1992).

[46] Praed, *Policy and Passion: A Novel of Australian Life* (London: Richard Bentley and Son, 1881), p. 90. All future references are to this edition.

a medievalizing gesture that likens Angela to the Rhine dryad Lorelei from the medieval German legends she loves to read, Praed repeatedly describes her as a mystical sprite, 'a true incarnation of the spirit of these Australian wilds' (p. 124). Her surface Aestheticism might gesture to contemporary medievalist trends, but beneath this she is an authentic fay, not neo-medieval but truly folkloric. The other crucial distinction between Angela and Weeta is that Angela is an artist to Weeta's model. The analogy to Elizabeth Siddall again seems apt, as Siddall was an accomplished artist as well as Rossetti's muse. Although Angela is, like Weeta, also the focus of obsessive parental ambition, her father's determination that she become an artist means that he keeps her away from those 'petty interests of womanhood', including courtship, which he believes will stunt her creative development. While he is misguided in his cosseting of her and in his denial of her capacity for womanly passion, his ambition for her art (and she is an excellent, though still unformed, artist) emancipates her from the narrow path of marital objectification on which other girls her age have anxiously set out. She is utterly naïve, but also, compared to Weeta, free. And, vitally, although she is the object of a painting in the novel, it is a self-portrait. She does not complete it before dying from unrequited love — in the novel's flurry of medievalist references, she is also a Lady of Shallot figure, lured from art to passion by the 'highbred' Hardress Barrington — but by painting this self-portrait Angela is able to assert her artistic subjectivity in a way that defies the Pre-Raphaelite object status her appearance might otherwise invite. By contrast, Weeta's stylized posturing suggests that despite her donning of loose Aesthetic shifts, she is no uncorseted New Woman, breathing easy in her Greco-medieval folds; rather, she is a one-woman *tableau vivant*. Profoundly disempowered, she aspires neither to be an artist like Angela nor even to be like one of Cambridge's consuming Aesthetic women; rather, she contents herself with being turned into an Aesthetic-medieval commodity to be consumed by others. As we discover, she perceives this visual consumption to be part of an objectifying continuum in which she will also be consumed materially as a wife.

*Romance of a Station* also draws a clear link, as later scholars have, between artistic representation and female commodification. Numerous feminists have related how the Pre-Raphaelite 'stunners', including Jane Burden and Elizabeth Siddall, were, famously, lower class English women whose antique beauty had vaulted them into illustrious company;[47] in Weeta's case, Praed has her mother boast of her daughter being painted by the artist accompanying the Prince, but then rue that the family's financial situation does not permit them to travel to

[47] See Pollock, *Vision and Difference*, pp. 102–05.

England to capitalize on the portrait by snaring a highborn English husband for her daughter. Weeta's entrapment within representation is figured literally in the glass-encased volume containing a description of her, which takes pride of place in the Wilsons's drawing room. This lovingly bound volume, the published diary of one of the Prince's entourage, has become a domestic reliquary, carefully preserving the remnants of the exulted admiration Weeta once excited.

Praed's criticism of this economy of objectification is most powerfully registered in a blistering outburst she puts into Weeta's mouth on the subject of finding a husband. Before this tirade we have been led to believe that the girl is, on the whole, compliant with her parents' marketing of her, although we have an inkling from her confession to Rachel that she is equally amused and anguished by the terms on which she has become 'a person of consideration' (p. 218). But when she overhears her mother's wish to hitch her to the already-engaged Archie, she makes her view of her situation appallingly clear. Accusing her parents of seeing her as 'only a doll [...] with no brains and no pride, except pride in my complexion' (p. 228), she goes on to disclose an unexpected mercenary sensibility that shocks even her mother, vowing to 'make the best bargain' for herself by pursuing Archie, fiancée notwithstanding, because he is an aristocrat and thus 'quite our best opportunity' (p. 230). From this point on it is clear that beneath the wistful Rossetti-esque persona lurks a bitter and despairing resignation that she has no value for others beyond her medieval beauty. Although Weeta does not possess the New Woman's considered determination to either avoid marriage or enter it on her own terms, she not only shares with such women a keen and unromantic insight into the commerce of the marital marketplace but also clearly understands, and cynically exploits, the ironic role played by her medievalization as a tactic to distinguish her within that market.

Praed's exposé of the sexual politics of Aesthetic medievalism is, moreover, given a particularly colonial inflection. Montana argues that '[h]ow to look "ancestral" in a new colony became a burgeoning preoccupation amongst many of [the] nouveau riche'.[48] While, as discussed in the last chapter, Paul de Serville focuses on colonials' hot pursuit of medieval pedigrees, Montana's concern is with the accumulation of aspirational domestic goods of a medievalist cast. Weeta clearly recognizes that her meticulously crafted appearance is of a piece with, say, decorating the house with gothic prie-dieux or leadlight windows; that is, she has been drafted into the service of 'looking ancestral', thereby giving her family the aristocratic appearance that they believe will secure their upward social mobility via the marriage market. Weeta, despite her furious resentment, is determined to fulfil

[48] Montana, *The Art Movement*, p. 61.

her 'duty' to 'raise' her family from their shameful origins, outlining her motive in the bluntest of revelations: 'mother and I think a great deal of family because we haven't got it. My grandfather was a shepherd who died knocking down his cheque in a bush public-house' (p. 229). This stinging attack on her parents' instrumentalization of her, which freely uses the language of the marketplace, slices through to the heart of the colonial desire for ancient breeding, and exposes it for the aspirational opportunism it is.

When Archie describes Weeta's studiedly offhanded manners as those of a duchess, it appears the ruse is working. Eventually she wins him, and the impending title of Lady Colworth, after a typical Romance set-piece in which she stakes her claim in a three-way confrontation with him and his fiancée Isabel, who turns out to be her (lightly freckled) doppelganger. Yet in the last paragraphs the plot takes a sharp turn. We learn via a two-line note from Weeta to Rachel that she has not gone through with her socially ambitious engagement but has, instead, eloped with Mr Humphries, the dim but affable son of a local landowner, who has recently made his own large fortune. Her reasons for reneging on her engagement are withheld, pronounced an 'enigma' by Rachel. We are left to contemplate a range of possibilities. Was Weeta finally unable to live with her stated knowledge that Archie does not truly 'in his heart of hearts' love her? Did she feel compunction about luring him away from his long-term betrothed Isabel, whose appearance so closely mirrors her own? Such explanations, while morally gratifying, fail to persuade because they reduce the conclusion to a matter of personal conscience, ignoring the undertow of colonial and *nouveau riche* anxiety that churned incessantly beneath the tense surface of the union. Even in the climactic scene where Archie must make his choice of a future wife, Weeta cannot conceal her unease over their difference in social rank, fearing that one day he may come to despise her for it: '[i]t would kill me if you were sorry afterwards [...] if you were ashamed of me, or of my people'. A more convincing alternative, then, is that with her contempt for the charade of man-catching and her deep sensitivity to caste distinctions, Weeta has finally rejected a union that had been forged on a sustained and intolerable illusion of her ancient nobility and has opted, instead, to marry within her own rank of colonials.

Since this is the most encompassing explanation, it is intriguing that it is not tendered by Rachel. And the effect of this refusal is subtly powerful, because rather than granting Weeta full rational or moral agency in her decision, it implies that she has succumbed to the ineffable but incontestable rightness of class endogamy. Weeta's medieval 'passing' had a paradoxical, 'backwards-and-forwards' valency: by securing her an entrée into the feudal remnant of modern English society, it could not help but disturb that caste's claim to ancient patrimony and purity of blood. But this threatened social disturbance is ultimately dispatched and the characters neatly squared away in a world where caste apartheid is both natural and desirable. Despite the novel's progressive approach to sexual politics, its class ideology is distinctly conservative. At the novel's conclusion, the line between the English aristocracy and newly wealthy Australian is elegantly but firmly drawn.[49]

But what exactly is being criticized in these novels? Aesthetic medievalism itself, or its distorted vulgarization at the hands of the ignorant and misguided? As Montana points out, attacks on popular Aestheticism did not necessarily reflect a wholesale rejection of it, but rather a rejection of its fate at the hands of popularizers. As an 1881 article by 'Lancelot' in the *Argus* indicates, mocking Aestheticism's ersatz manifestations marked out the truly discerning from the docile masses, the 'would be aesthetes — camp-followers and pretenders to taste and culture', who could not grasp the true Aesthetic spirit and so turned to the consumer objects that were its crude simulacra.[50] On this point Australian women writers seem to be far from unanimous. Tasma, as we have seen, seems more tolerant of its vulgarization as part of her rejection of medievalist snobbery; *Uncle Piper* is thoroughly meritocratic in its assertion of earned over inherited nobility. He has his crenellated tower because he deserves it: he has paid for it with the sweat of his hands. But Martin, Praed, and Cambridge most of all, arguably retain an ideal of 'real' medieval Aestheticism and offer examples of women (Stella Courtland, Angela Ferris, Elizabeth King) who embody this ideal. In addition to her fiction, the fact that around 1889 Praed engaged fellow Australian expatriate artist Mortimer Menpes to decorate her house partly in Aesthetic style (dados, blue-and-white china) suggests that she favoured this style in its 'authentic' form,[51] while, as we have seen, Cambridge's critique was aimed more at the objectionable combination of old-world beauty and new colonial money.

In stark contrast to this, medievalism has a more redemptive quality when associated with the freedom of Australian girlhood rather than the constraints and pressures of womanhood. Praed's *Australian Life: Black and White* was written

[49] This is one of what Len Platt incisively calls Praed's 'all-Australian resolution[s]'; Platt notes that this was a preferred dénouement in a number of Praed's novels in the 1880s and 1890s. See '"Altogether Better-bred Looking"', p. 36.

[50] 'Lancelot', 'Modern Aestheticism', *Argus*, 16 July 1881, p. 4.

[51] See Patricia Clarke, 'Two Colonials in London's Bohemia: Rosa Praed and Mortimer Menpes', *National Library of Australia News*, 13.12 (2003): <http://www.nla.gov.au/pub/nlanews/2003/ sep03/article4.html>.

four years before *Romance of a Station*, and thus right in the thick of the Aesthetic-medievalist craze to which Weeta has fallen victim; and yet here Praed looks back with affection and indulgence at the medievalist reading habits of her youth, as well her and her young friends' love of history and staging of fun medievalist *tableaux vivants* based on the twelfth-century story in Walter Scott's *The Bridal of Triermain* (p. 190). Arguably the fullest account, however, in which medievalism functions as an index of the freedom of girlhood and, conversely, of society's curtailment of that freedom, appears in Richardson's *The Getting of Wisdom*. Here medievalism has been firmly detached from the domain of domestic consumerism and returned to the site of innocence. The novel is, of course, principally about Laura Rowbotham's development as a musician and her associated transition from rural girlhood to metropolitan (and, finally, cosmopolitan) young womanhood. But cleverly woven into its *Kunstlerroman* fabric is a tandem narrative that traces the gradual stripping away of Laura's romantic and imaginative approach to the past. The changing form of her medievalism is presented as a kind of snapshot of her shift from imagination to empirical knowledge, dilettantism to mastery, and from freedom to discipline.

When we first meet Laura in the novel's opening chapter, she is narrating, in the persona of 'Wondrous Fair', a medievalist romance to her younger siblings. Her tale, about a Prince and 'a beautiful lady in a long white dress', adheres closely to the standard idiom of Tennyson and Scott, both of whom she has read, and as she continues she glosses such stock terms as 'glade' and 'sward' for the benefit of her young listeners (p. 1). Its conventionality notwithstanding, the romantic medievalism of Laura's tale reveals to us the rich imaginative landscape of her bucolic (though impoverished) childhood — which, like her tale, is about to come to an abrupt and unwelcome end as she prepares for a new life at a boarding school. Once at school, Laura begins to view the 'Wondrous Fair' approach to history with the regretful eye of her newly institutional self, realizing that her imaginative and histrionic impulses had left her with a piecemeal understanding of the past, made up chiefly of medieval vignettes:

> History she knew in a vague pictorial way: she and [her sister] Pin had enacted many a striking scene in the garden — such as 'Not angles but angels' or did the pump-drain overflow, Canute and his silly courtiers — and she also had out-of-the-way scraps of information about the characters of some of the monarchs, or, as the governess had complained, about the state of London at a certain period; but she had never troubled her head with dates. Now they rose before her, a hard, dry, black line from 1066 on, accompanied, not only by the kings who were the cause of them, but by dull laws, and their duller repeals. (p. 70)

At this point, Laura, still not absorbed fully into the school's educational culture, is wistful, and resentful about the conversion of her beautiful mind-pictures of 'spreading trees [and] hoary old cathedrals' (p. 73) into military and legal facts. But later, when she has come to submit herself to the school's values, she acknowledges without complaint that '[i]t was facts that were wanted of her; facts that were the real test of learning; facts she was expected to know' (p. 91). Accepting her teacher's explanation that her bower-bird medievalism is a result of her having 'a woman's brain' (p. 57), she castigates herself and vows to overcome her dilettantism:

> until now, she, Laura, had been satisfied to know things in a slipslop, razzle-dazzle way [...] [s]he had never set to work to master a subject, to make it her own in every way. Bits of it, picturesque scraps, striking features [...] were all that attracted her. (p. 89)

This anti-romantic endeavour meets with success, as Laura, by dint of rigorous obedience, comes to 'cut a dash in history' (p. 260). It would appear that the key to her intellectual and artistic development has been the exile of Wondrous Fair. But this is not the end of the story. After neglecting her studies due to her infatuation with another student at the school, she cheats, significantly, in her final history exam. She is not caught, but has lost faith in the institution and the emptiness of its empirical teaching. On her graduation day, she declares that she 'never want[s] to hear a date [...] again' (p. 270). In the novel's famously open conclusion, we are left with the image of Laura sprinting through the streets of Melbourne and out of sight, forwards into a future that, we are told, will restore her to the realm of 'men's best thoughts [...] hopes [...] fancies [...] the dream' (p. 272).

Turning her back on the institution that has imposed its rational demands on her medievalist imagination, Laura resembles many of her sisters in Australian women's fiction. For even as she runs toward an unknown freedom, she is also fleeing back into a past blissfully of her own (re)making. This premodern past, with all the perilous fantasies it engenders — racial fantasies, consumer fantasies, romantic fantasies — not only feeds into the present for these women, but plays a unique role in the shaping of a feminine vision of the Australia to come.

Chapter 3

# BUSH IDYLLS AND GALLOPING ROMANCES: MEDIEVALISM IN THE POETRY OF ADAM LINDSAY GORDON

Lamenting the widespread indifference to poetry in the colony of New South Wales, the Reverend John Woolley attempted to alarm the audience of his 1861 speech 'Schools of Art and Colonial Nationality' with the prospect of a cultural tragedy. Among them, he warned, might lurk an unsung 'provincial Tennyson', his gift withering on the vine through neglect and lack of opportunity.[1] The warning was calculated to hit home: Tennyson's popularity was, at the time of Woolley's speech, cresting new heights after the publication in 1859 of the first four portraits in his Arthurian epic *Idylls of the King*, a poem which was, for colonial readers as for British readers, the acme of poetic achievement. Reaching in another speech for a favourite medievalist commonplace, Woolley rallied to the idea that the colony's harsh cultural climate might produce a hardy and self-willed laureate, opining that 'severe discipline is good for the literary postulant, as for the knightly champions of old'. Yet he ultimately conceded that Sydney, with its fetish for commerce and its notorious philistinism, was a 'weary place' for the aspiring local Tennyson, who would likely die in obscurity and despair, his Arthurian epic probably unwritten, and certainly unread.[2]

[1] John Woolley, 'Schools of Art and Colonial Nationality: A Lecture Delivered at the Inauguration of the Wollongong School of Arts, May 28th 1861' (Sydney: Reading & Wellbank, 1861), p. 12.

[2] Woolley, Lecture IX, 'The Idylls of the King', in *Lectures Delivered in Australia* (Cambridge: Macmillan, 1862), p. 286.

Eulogized by the poet Henry Halloran as 'the poet's comforter',[3] Woolley, who was also the inaugural Professor of Classics at the University of Sydney, did not stop at verbal promotion of local poetry but also attempted to offer patronage to Australian poets, among them the then-rising talent Henry Kendall, who would later be lauded as the greatest poet to emerge out of nineteenth-century Australia. Kendall's rejection of Woolley's offer, which was based in part on the grounds that the professor was 'a crammed man who admires Tennyson by rote',[4] suggests the wrong-headedness of Woolley's positing of Tennyson, and in particular the Tennyson of the sprawling Arthurian epic *Idylls of the King*, as the model for an Australian laureate. In mocking Woolley thus, Kendall was not, as will become clear later, spurning Tennyson *in toto*; but the notion of an Australian local slavishly reiterating Tennysonian verse was clearly anathema to the young poet, who made it his quest to identify, and eventually cultivate in his own work, a distinctive voice in Australian verse.

Looking at the medievalist output of colonial poets, it would seem that Woolley's prediction may have come to pass. There is no 'provincial Tennyson' to whom we can definitively point, unless we count Tennyson's statesman son Hallam, whose career in antipodean colonial administration included a brief period as Governor of South Australia (1899–1902) and then an even briefer stint as Governor-General of Australia (1903–04). Colonial Australian poetry boasted no major medieval epic like Tennyson's *Idylls*, Swinburne's *Tristram of Lyonesse* (1869–82), or William Morris's more eclectic *The Earthly Paradise* (1868–70), and it fostered no feverish production of shorter works by a dedicated medievalist collective in the mode of the Pre-Raphaelite Brotherhood. Tennyson had legions of admirers in the Australian colonies, but no serious imitators or rivals.

Woolley's pathetic image of the impossible colonial Tennyson would, furthermore, appear to be corroborated by a number of his fellow Englishmen in Australia. The best known of these is Marcus Clarke, who firmly dismissed the possibility of local medievalist verse in his famous meditation on the essence of Australian scenery and its impact on poetry. While, says Clarke, even the mediocre poet is provided with mythic inspiration in 'historic Europe, where every rood of ground is hallowed in legend and in song', Australia offers no such inspiration to its aspiring bards. In Europe, the poet 'lounging at sunset by some ruined chapel'

[3] From a memorial poem by Henry Halloran, published in the *Sydney Morning Herald* on 27 March 1866. Quoted in Ann-Mari Jordens, *The Stenhouse Circle: Literary Life in Mid-Nineteenth Century Sydney* (Carlton: Melbourne University Press, 1979), p. 82.

[4] Quoted from Jordens, *The Stenhouse Circle*, p. 87.

experiences a human sympathy with the past that makes Tennysonian historical epic possible: 'we partake of the varied moods which belong not so much to ourselves as to the dead men who, in old days, sung, suffered, or conquered in the scenes which we survey'. Australia, by contrast, Clarke claims in a statement notable today for its breathtaking (though conventional) Eurocentricity, 'has no past, no story' with which the poet can engage, and hence the poet is drawn away from history and thrown back upon 'Nature's teachings', or his own soul, for inspiration. Even more explicitly, he goes on in one of his best-known statements to deny the possibility that the Australian environment could generate medievalist verse:

> Europe is the home of knightly song, of bright deeds and clear morning thought [...] in Australia alone is to be found the Grotesque, the Weird, the strange scribblings of Nature learning how to write. Some see no beauty in our trees without shade, our flowers without perfume, our birds who cannot fly, and our beasts who have not yet learned to walk on all fours. But the dweller in the wilderness acknowledges the subtle charm of this land of monstrosities [...] the Poet of our desolation begins to comprehend why free Esau loved his heritage of desert sand better than all the bountiful riches of Egypt.[5]

The Australian poet's covenant is with haunting barrenness rather than the 'bright deeds' of heroic tradition. Interestingly, when this passage has been quoted by critics, which it has been frequently, the first sentence has generally been left out. This omission is significant, for it has had the effect of suppressing the important fact that Clarke explicitly defines Australian poetry against medieval forms such as chivalric romance or *chansons de geste*, which he takes to be the quintessence of the European verse tradition.

There is an irony here, though. For all Clarke's claim that the monstrous strangeness of Australia impedes the emergence of 'knightly song', his much-quoted passage in fact, as indicated in the Introduction to this book, accomplishes a complex medievalizing of the antipodean landscape by virtue of his appeal to a number of recognizably Gothic tropes when describing it. Many have discussed the ongoing instability of the relationship between notions of the Gothic and the medieval throughout the eighteenth and nineteenth centuries. In some cases of what Stephanie Trigg has called the 'historical Gothic' (neo-Gothic architecture is an obvious example), the Gothic was taken to be synonymous with the medieval;[6] in other cases it represented the barbarous obverse of the civilized world of

[5] Marcus Clarke, 'Preface' in Gordon, *Poems*, p. ix. Unless indicated, all references to Gordon's poems are from this edition.

[6] Trigg, 'Introduction', *Medievalism and the Gothic in Australian Culture*, ed. by Trigg, pp. xiii–xvi, xv.

medieval chivalry and romance. Elsewhere still, as in colonial Australian nature writing, it came to mean, in Peter Otto's words, 'a primitive (natural) world able to renovate a lifeless modernity'.[7] In Clarke's text, the invocation of the Gothic creates an unstable medievalism. On the surface it seems that the highly charged Gothic scene encountered by the hypothetical Australian poet is presented as the primitive antithesis of the refined world that inspires 'knightly song', thus corresponding with what Andrew McCann has brilliantly described as the colonial sensationalist use of the '*frisson nouveau* of the Gothic' to evoke the 'spectral alterity' of the Australian landscape.[8] Yet, at the same time, Clarke's memorable use of pathetic fallacy (the mountains are 'funereal, secret, stern', the gums are 'melancholy', the hills are 'frowning') obliquely medievalizes the Australian 'natural' scene by imputing to it those characteristics of otherworldly horror, dereliction, and engulfing gloom that in the Gothic genre were commonly associated with medieval castles and baronial halls. This has the secondary effect of domesticating this apparently alien landscape by rendering it intelligible to readers familiar with the medievalist architectural tropes of the Gothic.

A more immediate irony in Clarke's disavowal of the possibility of Australian 'knightly song' is that it originally appeared in his preface to the 1880 collected works of the horseman-cum-versifier Adam Lindsay Gordon, who was arguably colonial Australia's closest contender for the Tennysonian mantle. While Gordon, who arrived in Australia as a young man in 1853, was at least as well known in his own lifetime for his skill (and his recklessness) as a steeple-chaser, it is his verse that has made him posthumously famous. Considering his work in relation to Clarke's assessment of Australian verse, it is certainly true that the poems by Gordon which have outback and bush settings are filled with haunting images of a distinctly Gothic cast. To take just one of many available examples, 'Gone', Gordon's *memento mori* meditation on the tragic death of the explorer Robert O'Hara Burke (who has 'gone where we all must go') places before us images of the ill-fated explorer perishing in 'the sand waste lone' amid 'the blighted herbage', brooded over by eagle-hawk and dingo (pp. 7–9). Similarly, his portrayal of a South Australian seascape in 'The Swimmer', in spite of its later recollection of the coast's sun-drenched brilliance, places before us a tempestuous scene in which 'the swirl of the

[7] Peter Otto, 'Romantic Medievalism and Gothic Horror', in *Medievalism and the Gothic in Australian Culture*, ed. by Trigg, pp. 19–40 (p. 19). See also Smith and Hughes, *Empire and the Gothic*, pp. 1–3.

[8] Andrew McCann, 'Colonial Nature-Inscription: On Haunted Landscapes', in *Five Emus to the King of Siam*, ed. by Tiffin, pp. 71–84 (pp. 80, 82).

surges livid' dashes against 'the crag and the cliff', and engulfs the 'grim, grey coast and a seaboard ghastly, / And shores trod seldom by feet of men' (pp. 129–32).

Alongside these Gothicized images of Australia, Gordon also produced at least eight examples of 'knightly song', some of which were of considerable length. Although Gordon's reputation to this day is that of a bush balladeer, albeit of a strikingly melancholy cast, his literary engagement with the Middle Ages was not only abiding throughout his brief poetic career but also far from incidental. As will be explored in this chapter, Gordon's depictions of the medieval period as beset by agonizing contradictions — faith and doubt, honour and shame, loyalty and treachery, hope and despair, atonement and perdition — were central to his sense of its unique, if unexpected, correspondence with modern Australia. Gordon's Middle Ages were dominated by sombre religiosity and romantic intensity, with a decorous surface that strove, yet failed, to contain the dark passions that simmered beneath. As such, this period held particular significance within his historicized vision of humanity's failing struggle against futility, and offered poignant settings for the expression of Gordon's own rather conflicted version of stoicism, in which nihilistic resignation contended against hope for redemption. We see his early fascination for this conflicted world and its tortured souls carried over into his portrayals of Australian bush life, while his idea of the Middle Ages was, conversely, also strongly inflected by the modern, nihilistic sensibility that dominates his verse set in Australia. Before any discussion of the thematic and, more importantly, the moral significance of these poems within Gordon's oeuvre, some introduction of the poems themselves is needed.

The earliest of Gordon's medievalist poems was 'The Feud', published under the somewhat transparent pseudonym 'A. Lindsay' in 1864 by the proprietors of *The Border Watch*, a newspaper produced at Mount Gambier in South Australia.[9] A six-part poem written in Scottish border ballad style, this poem, as its title indicates, recounts the tale of a blood feud between a knight and an ancient noble clan over the terms of a dowry. Gordon's poem enters the story late, at the point where the feud culminates in a duel that in fact turns out to be a deadly ambush, during which the knight and all eight of the brothers who set upon him are killed. The poem participated squarely in the fashionable Romantic enthusiasm for folk story, having been inspired by a set of six engravings taken from Sir Joseph Noel Paton's paintings depicting the old Border ballad 'The Dowie Dens o' Yarrow'. Although Scott's influential collection *The Minstrelsy of the Scottish Border* contained

[9] The edition being referred to here is in Frank Maldon Robb's *The Poems of Adam Lindsay Gordon* (London: Oxford University Press, 1912), pp. 342–52.

a ballad based on the same tale, Frank Maldon Robb states that 'the district could not furnish a copy of [Scott's *Minstrelsy*], but Gordon, who knew well the story but not its words, undertook to weave it afresh into ballad form'[10] (p. xliv). The poem sets its medieval scene not by specifying dates, but through recognizably medievalist allusions — castles, escutcheons, feudal foes, recumbent staghounds, trusty steeds, broadswords, bloody frays, and, finally, requiem masses. This is a Scottian Middle Ages to the point of cliché: noble yet bellicose, studded with cavernous stone castles and wooded glens, and populated by sturdy chieftains, Rhenish-quaffing hot-heads, and spirited Border maidens. As the original print-run was only thirty copies, the poem did not enjoy a wide readership until it was re-published after Gordon's death, in the journal *Literary Opinion* in 1891 and again in *The Bulletin* in 1902, where it was nevertheless proclaimed (probably by Gordon's great critic A. G. Stephens) 'colourless doggerel verse, which has merely the interest of anything attaching to Gordon's name'.[11]

The next medievalist poem, which was Gordon's lengthiest (and indeed the longest of all his poems), was *Ashtaroth*, a ponderous dramatic lyric in thirty-one scenes, set in medieval Normandy and Rhineland (*Poems*, 219–325). Unlike the allusive setting of 'The Feud', *Ashtaroth*'s setting is made explicit in its *Dramatis Personae* page and in its scene descriptions. It features Hugo, a Norman knight whose initial crisis of faith, tortured devotion to astronomy, and generalized existential angst (driven apparently by a Faustian thirst for knowledge, and possibly the result of an unexplained compact made with his shadowy Mephistophelian companion, Orion) are compounded by a rekindled infatuation with his friend's daughter Agatha, who once jilted him by eloping with his rival, and whom he is now escorting to a Rhenish nunnery where she will join the congregation. While the central section of the poem is devoted to the married Hugo agonizing over his forbidden desire for his charge, the later stages take an unexpected turn as, having reached the convent, Hugo and his men find themselves defending it against a band of brigands led by the outlaw Count Rudolph of Rothenstein. The convent is saved, but Hugo, we learn later, is killed in the battle, and the poem ends with a monastic dirge punctuated by a *Miserere Domine* chorus in medieval Latin.

Portentous in both language and setting, with a narrative that is chaotic yet also elliptical at times to the point of obfuscation, *Ashtaroth*, according to Robb, did not

[10] Robb, *The Poems of Adam Lindsay Gordon*, p. xliv.

[11] *The Bulletin*, 15 February 1902.

find a readership in Gordon's lifetime.[12] Furthermore, from the time of its publication to the present, those critics who have read it have united in condemning it, and indeed it is difficult not to join in the chorus of derision. Apart from its muddled plot, its clutch of red-herring characters, and its Faustian pretensions, all of which have been roundly criticized by others, it must be admitted that the medievalism of *Ashtaroth* furnishes the weapons for some of Gordon's worst crimes against poetry. Among these is the use of some wincingly redundant cod-archaic dialogue, included so as to sustain the poem's dogged adherence to metre and rhyme scheme. Consider the following:

> *Osric:*
> I am a Norseman, frank and plain;
> Ye must read the parchment over again.
> *Eric:*
> Jarl Osric, twice we have read this scroll;
> *Osric:*
> Thou hast read a part.
> *Eric:* I have read the whole. (p. 294)

Its medieval setting provides Gordon, moreover, with the vocabulary for some of the most egregious rhymes of his poetic career, as we see from the unintended hilarity of the following:

> What ho! Art thou drunk, Sir Norman?
> Has the wine made thy pale cheek red?
> Now, I swear by Odin and Thor, man,
> Already I count thee dead. (pp. 310–11)

and

> Beneath us they throng, the fierce Norsemen,
> The pikemen of Rudolph behind
> Are mustered, and Dagobert's horsemen
> With faces to rearward inclined. (p. 317)

Perhaps predictably, given Gordon's dual equestrian and medievalist predilections, the 'Norsemen / horsemen' rhyme is given an outing several times, and reappears later, in 'The Rhyme of Joyous Garde', in its more abbreviated form: Norse/horse.

At the same time as *Ashtaroth* was released, Gordon also published his first collection of twenty-three poems, *Sea Spray and Smoke Drift*, of which five are medievalist poems. Taken together, the medievalist poems in this volume read like

[12] Robb, *The Poems of Adam Lindsay Gordon*, p. liv.

a primer of experiments in genre, style, and subject. They do not adhere to a consistent medieval mythology (Arthurian, Norse, or Celtic, for instance), or maintain a national focus, or achieve a consistent poetic register in relation to the Middle Ages. 'Unshriven', a short and somewhat cryptic ballad of nine stanzas, tells the tale of a knight who, having been involved in what the reader guesses is a deadly swordfight, returns to the scene of conflict to face retribution despite the pleas of his new bride, who points out the danger of courting death with a soul 'unassoiled and, aye, unshriven' (*Poems*, 10–11). The knight is killed before he can confess and atone for his previous murder, and the poem ends with his horse returning riderless to his horrified bride as nearby monastery bells toll. As with 'The Feud', the medieval setting is evoked through a series of commonplaces: architectural (hall, tower, bower, monastery), martial (trusty blade, swift courser, cloak, spurs and belt), and social (binding oath, revenge pact, ritual of confession). Gordon also uses archaic spelling ('merrilie' 'drearilie') to strengthen the poem's link to old ballad tradition. In 'Rippling Water', also a ballad, a beautiful peasant girl contemplates her forthcoming marriage to the bloodless aristocrat Lord Marmaduke, whom she has chosen for his wealth over the reckless, dashing Brian of Hawksmede and her former love, the virile but low-born Stephen (*Poems*, 51–53). The medieval setting is only sketched in here as backdrop to the ambitious maiden's musings, mainly for the purpose, it seems, of heightening her dilemma by placing it in a world where the hierarchy of status and wealth is deeply entrenched. At the same time, however, the vanity of her social ambition is implied by the ballad's refrain: each stanza ends with 'the rippling water murmurs on', an image of nature's indifference to human wishes.

In the same volume we find the more vividly drawn chivalric world of 'Fauconshawe', an inconclusive murder-mystery ballad in thirty-one stanzas. In this poem a Norman knight, Sir Hugh de Vere, is forced to determine whether his betrothed, the Saxon Lady Mabel, has been involved in the murder of a rival knight, who was also possibly her lover and whose corpse has been discovered outside her castle, Fauconshawe (*Poems*, 44–50). The poem offers neither moral nor narrative closure, but ends with Sir Hugh's permanent departure after the possibly innocent Lady Mabel has scorned to confirm or deny her fiancé's accusations of infidelity and murder. The poem is replete with the same medievalist commonplaces as 'The Feud' and 'Unshriven', but is more detailed, adding such touches as turrets, a funeral bier, a parchment billet-doux, faithful retainers, and a possibly treacherous maidservant. 'Confiteor', briefer at fourteen stanzas, is a shipboard dialogue between a sinning priest and a knight who is about to depart with his men for the Crusades. The knight's Eastern destination is only vaguely alluded to, by a reference to the 'West-wind' that fills the ship's sails, so Gordon relies here on assumed knowledge in his readers, who were probably most familiar with the character of the jaded Crusader in the form of the knight Brian de Bois-Guibert from Scott's *Ivanhoe.* The knight encourages the priest to shrive his men but refuses absolution for himself, despite the fact that he is a sinner and that imminent death is a real prospect for him as a soldier. As with the other poems, the narrative is somewhat cryptic, but it seems that the knight's moral jaundice has emerged in response to the death of his virtuous beloved, and his belief that if her prayers could not induce him to feel compunction, then neither could the exhortations of this priest, whom he calls a 'wither'd branch'. The poem's highly ambivalent final stanza, in which the priest admits that he too feels he is damned but must continue to plead for absolution, strikes the note of agnostic irresolution that is the hallmark of all Gordon's medievalist poems.

A more controversial inclusion in *Sea Spray and Salt Drift*'s group of medievalist poems is 'Ye Wearie Wayfarer: Hys Ballad in Eight Fyttes', which was published in instalments in the sporting journal *Bell's Life* between October 1865 and November 1866 (*Poems*, 12–35). Despite the promising archaic spelling of its title and the use of the Middle English term 'fytte' for its eight discrete sections, we soon discover that the title is almost the beginning and end of its engagement with medievalism. Gordon makes us wade through seven meandering 'Fyttes' on hunting, fishing, and riding before finally reaching his rousing but decidedly brief allusion (also discussed in Chapter 1) to the idea that Australians' equestrian fanaticism has a post-conquest racial origin:

> if we efface the joys of the chase
> From the land, and outroot the Stud,
> GOOD-BYE TO THE ANGLO-SAXON RACE!
> FAREWELL TO THE NORMAN BLOOD! (p. 28)[13]

Taken out of context, this much-quoted passage can give a false impression of committed Anglo-Saxonism — an impression, we recall from Chapter 1, encouraged by Francis Adams's interpretation of these lines in 'Melbourne and Her Civilization' — but in fact it stands virtually alone in this poem as an overt engagement with a recognizable medievalist discourse. Brian Elliott argues that the

[13] W. H. Wilde notes that these lines 'were included in Wyndham Lewis's anthology of bad poetry, *The Stuffed Owl*, and drew from Lewis the comment that Gordon evidently believed the future of the Empire depended on Tattersalls, where the largest horse sales in England were conducted'. Wilde, *Adam Lindsay Gordon* (Melbourne: Oxford University Press, 1972), p. 29.

poem's 'conscious antiquarianism', which chiefly involved the spelling of the title and 'the playful use of a little gothic 'black letter' in the typography', was all in the name of fun.[14] And yet, not quite. Gordon's inclusion, at the opening of each 'fytte', of epigrams from Scott, Robert Browning, Charles Kingsley, Tennyson, and William Makepeace Thackeray (from *Rebecca and Rowena*, his burlesque on *Ivanhoe*), as well as a number of old ballads, places his poem into dialogue with a number of well-known medievalist texts, thereby performatively reinforcing the notion of an old English heritage for the contemporary Australian sporting life.

Gordon's second and final verse collection, *Bush Ballads and Galloping Rhymes*, contains two medievalist poems. The first of these is the forty-stanza Arthurian dramatic monologue 'The Rhyme of Joyous Garde', considered by many to be among the best of Gordon's poems. In this poem the ageing Lancelot looks back with regret over his ill-fated affair with Guinevere and the destruction wrought to his relationship with Arthur and the entire kingdom of Camelot (*Poems*, 170–79). Nostalgic and stoic by turns, the poem adopts the tone of a personal *ubi sunt*, recalling the splendours of Camelot yet ultimately laying them to rest as fleeting and emerging out of 'earthly ill-doing'. Although the poem revels in the images of medieval warfare (caparisoned steeds, mail-clad knights, fights in the lists) when recounting the principal events of the *Morte D'Arthur*, its centre of gravity lies elsewhere, in its anatomizing of Lancelot's burdened heart and his rueful realization of the vanity of worldly pursuits. His stoic resignation is, again, incomplete; for while his fervent prayers for the salvation of Guinevere's soul suggest a belief in redemption, he is unable to seek the same for himself.

*Bush Ballads* also contains 'The Three Friends (From the French)', adapted from an Alfred de Musset poem, which tells the tale of three inseparable Christian knights who fell in love with the same maiden, and so entered into a mutual pact of death by sword and poison, in which the last one standing wins the maiden (*Poems*, 180–83). As arranged, the knight who survived his friends did engage in passionate embraces with the maiden, but she fled soon after, and the poem hints at the possibility that she may have been the architect of the friends' deadly pact. Narrated retrospectively, the poem is the dying confession of the surviving knight, who lies expiring from self-inflicted wounds after his beloved's unexplained departure. Like 'Joyous Garde', 'The Three Friends' presents us with a brooding and tragic Middle Ages, in which the noble bond of chivalric fraternity is destroyed by the primal and violent passions that it ultimately cannot hope to master.

[14] Brian Elliott, *Adam Lindsay Gordon* (Melbourne: Sun Books, 1973), p. 23.

One of the many ironies attaching to Gordon is that while he was the closest thing colonial Australia had to a budding medievalist laureate, he also finally, and tragically, became John Woolley's nightmare made flesh. Racked with debt, ill-health, and despair, he took his own life in June 1870 at the age of 36, nine years after Woolley's prophesy and one day after the publication of *Bush Ballads and Galloping Rhymes.* He was not the only colonial poet to sink into ignominy and suicidal despair. Not many years later, Barcroft Boake, whose best-known work is the Gordon-esque 'Where the Dead Men Lie', would hang himself with his own stockwhip at the age of 26, while Gordon's friend (and Woolley's would-be protégé) Henry Kendall would struggle with alcoholism and melancholy, spending time in the Gladesville asylum in Sydney. But given that one of Gordon's mature poems was 'The Rhyme of Joyous Garde', one can only wonder whether this was the beginning of a dazzling local Arthuriad that was not to be. The crowning irony, accomplished many years after his desperate, destitute end, was that Gordon was to become, in 1934, the first, and so far the only, Australian poet to be given a memorial bust in Poets' Corner in Westminster Abbey. It is curiously fitting that at the same time as he was hailed as 'Poet of Australia' and 'the voice of the national life of one of the young nations of the British race',[15] he took his place among the English poets he revered, including his immediate neighbour Tennyson, in the surrounds of a thirteenth-century cloister.

No analysis of Gordon can properly consider his work without bringing it into the orbit of passionate opinion that has long circulated around him. This is even more pointedly the case with Gordon's medievalist poems, for we are compelled to assess them in relation to the impact they have had on his literary reputation. Unlike the writers considered in the previous two chapters, whose medievalism has gone largely unrecognized, Gordon's medievalism is central to his reputation. Given that his medievalist output was modest relative not only to the giants of British medievalist verse but also to his own oeuvre, it has had a disproportionate role in determining how his work has been received. His affiliation with nineteenth-century medievalism has loomed large in the rather varied, even contentious, critical tradition that has evolved since his death, figuring significantly for not only a number of his earliest readers but also, though often in a barely acknowledged way, for his more recent critics, whether detractors or defenders. His admiration for, and at times flagrant imitation of, a number of the major British

[15] These two descriptions are taken, respectively, from Gordon's memorial in Westminster Abbey and from the Archbishop of Canterbury's address at the unveiling of Gordon's memorial there, as reported in *The Herald*, 21 June 1934.

medievalists has been the subject of prolonged discussion by critics such as Robb, whose detailed analysis of 'Gordon's Debt to English Literature' not only explored the influence of Tennyson, Swinburne, and Byron on the poet, but made a particular case for his deep affinity with Browning.[16] Exploring Gordon's relationship to his sources is a valuable approach to his work, and has occupied many fine scholars, but it will not be central to this chapter. For, it is in the local reception of Gordon's poetry, rather than in his adaptation of British models, that a unique story of Australian medievalism unfolds. Across the various posthumous fortunes of Gordon's medievalist poems we can trace his readers' quest to define, and thereby discover, a local laureate — a desire that, while constant, has been shaped by a set of criteria that was unstable and shifting. Put simply, the significance of Gordon's medievalism lies primarily in the ways in which his Australian readers have assimilated it into, or separated it from, his Australianness.

Clarke, with his express denial of a medievalist impulse in Australian verse, was an early example of a critical strain that has suppressed, or at the very least downplayed, the medievalism of Gordon's verse. Clarke's preface, as one of the most influential commentaries on Gordon, spawned a long-standing tradition of commentary that has emphasized the poet's intimate engagement with the Australian bush and outback over any European affiliations his work might display. Reading Clarke's preface, which expressly mentions *Ashtaroth*, one wonders how conscious he was that his claim about the absence of 'knightly song' in Australia did not in fact apply to the poet whose work he was introducing. It appears that the incongruity might not have been lost on him, for before embarking on his rhapsody to Australian Gothic, he briskly declines to analyse the details of Gordon's work. What Clarke seemed unwilling to entertain was any notion that medievalism, except in the displaced form of its menacing sibling, the Gothic, could furnish an idiom expressive of a modern Australian sensibility. So for him, Gordon's preoccupation with the passions and intrigues of medieval knights and nobles became a Europhilic embarrassment to be side-stepped.

Another influential early criticism that suppressed Gordon's medievalism rather than trying to reconcile it with his 'Australianness' was Francis Adams's essay 'Melbourne and Her Civilization as they Strike an Englishman', also mentioned in Chapter 1. Openly surprised that the poorly educated middle classes of Melbourne could be reading the work of their local poet, Adams rather speciously conflated Gordon with his readers, proclaiming him to be the voice of wealthy post-gold-rush Melbourne, with its 'sense of movement, of progress, of conscious power', and its

[16] Robb, *The Poems of Adam Lindsay Gordon*, pp. lxxxiii–cxx.

'contempt for the pedantry of the Old World'.[17] The fact that this same Melbourne was, at the very moment Adams was writing, in the process of expressing its status as a modern metropolis through the undeniably medievalist idiom of Gothic revival architecture, suggests that Adams's sharp distinction between medievalism and the modern involved something of a sleight-of-hand. When Adams's essay was published, a number of conspicuous medievalist buildings were casting their increasingly ample shadows across Melbourne's landscape and public consciousness. To mention two of the most unavoidable edifices Adams would have encountered: the splendid Gothic Revival St Patrick's Catholic cathedral, designed by William Wardell, had been under halting construction for close to three decades in East Melbourne, while central Melbourne witnessed the much more rapid rise (between 1883 and 1887) of the massive Venetian Gothic ES&A Bank, also designed by Wardell. It would seem that Adams's commitment to presenting late nineteenth-century Melbourne as a quintessential New World metropolis, and Gordon as its prophet, prevented him from considering that in the city's built environment, as in Gordon's colonial poetry, medievalism did not just survive as a fossil of, or retreat to, a former age, but flourished as an unexpected but powerful expression of colonial modernity. He even cited, more than once, Melbourne's banks as the embodiment of her 'movement, progress, [and] conscious power', without alluding to the fact that one of these banks unmistakably evoked the great mercantile and banking culture of medieval Venice as an intrinsic part of its lavish statement about the prosperity of 1880s Melbourne. This critical tradition, which was committed to the idea of Gordon's verse as quintessentially Australian, continued into the twentieth century, reaching its pitch in the promotion of Gordon by Douglas Sladen, the devoted lobbyist chiefly responsible for the installation of Gordon's memorial bust in Westminster Abbey.[18]

Although these readers have chosen to overlook Gordon's medievalism, it has proven highly significant for generations of others also attempting to evaluate Gordon's legacy to Australian poetry, and especially for those who have debated whether, or how, he could properly be called an Australian poet. This latter debate, which was a *leitmotif* of Gordon scholarship up until the 1970s, has been examined

[17] Adams, 'Melbourne and Her Civilization as they Strike an Englishman', p. 5.

[18] For Sladen's (ands others') efforts in promoting Gordon's reputation, see Richard D. Jordan, 'Adam Lindsay Gordon: The Australian Poet', *Westerly*, 2 (1985), 45–56 (esp. pp. 48–49); and Leonie Kramer, 'The Literary Reputation of Adam Lindsay Gordon', *Australian Literary Studies*, 1 (1963), 42–56.

exhaustively elsewhere,[19] so only its barest contours will be sketched here. Essentially, this debate revolved around whether Gordon was too Eurocentric, both in his representation of the Australian bush and in his devotion to European legend, to be deemed a truly Australian poet. Although this debate is well-trodden ground, a new look at it through the lens of Australian medievalism discloses the centrality of Gordon's devotion to the Middle Ages — or, more accurately, the centrality of perceptions of this devotion — to his posthumous reputation. Looking at what has been said about Gordon's status as an Australian, we find the question of his position as 'Australia's first national poet' repeatedly tethered to the question of his relationship to the European Middle Ages. Indeed, for a number of Gordon's commentators, the Middle Ages came to stand in for, and be synonymous with, the 'Europe' that proved to be such a thorny obstacle to his status as an Australian poet. Michael Ackland notes that until quite recently, Gordon's critics, most of them Australian, condemned all that they disliked about his writing under the rubric of 'medieval escapism'.[20]

This is perhaps best exemplified by Geoffrey Hutton's 1978 commentary. Having reminded those overenthusiastic claimants who saw Gordon as Australian that he was in fact a 'Scottish laird' by heritage and hence genetically linked to the Middle Ages, Hutton went on to say:

> While he picked his way on horseback through the stony potholes of the Mount Gambier district of South Australia, his mind was far away, living in a mediaeval world of fantasy, or fighting battles long ago.[21]

This fanciful medievalism is proffered by Hutton as literary evidence that Gordon 'felt himself *déclassé* among the pushing *nouveaux riches* of the Colonies' and, more comprehensively, that he 'was never more than an honorary Australian'. Furthermore, Hutton's later comparison of Gordon to Don Quixote cannot help but cast Gordon, to anyone familiar with Cervantes's deluded self-appointed knight errant, as a hapless victim of the dangerous spell cast by medieval romance, with its implausible heroic excess. Gordon's love of medieval story and old ballad, then,

[19] To Jordan's and Kramer's discussions can be added C. F. MacRae, *Adam Lindsay Gordon* (New York: Twayne, 1968).

[20] Michael Ackland, 'Martial Code: Meditation and Action in the Verse of Adam Lindsay Gordon', *Westerly*, 2 (1993), 53–65 (p. 53). Much of this article reappears in Ackland's *That Shining Band: A Study of Australian Colonial Verse Tradition* (St Lucia: University of Queensland Press, 1994).

[21] Geoffrey Hutton, *Adam Lindsay Gordon: The Man and the Myth* (London: Faber, 1978), p. 18.

rendered him not only un-Australian but also a worrying fantasist. Even worse, in the eyes of some assessing his national value, was the fact that Gordon's medievalism was derivative, emerging out of his admiration for the nineteenth-century English medievalist poets mentioned earlier. For those using the equation that 'Australian' equals 'original' (for which read 'inspired by the local scenery, society, and vernacular') this was an insurmountable obstacle on which Gordon's status as 'Australian poet' foundered. Among his most vehement and influential critics on this score were Joseph Furphy, A. G. Stephens in his *Poems of Adam Lindsay Gordon* (1918), and, later, H. M. Green in his *History of Australian Literature* (1961), Judith Wright in her chapter in *The Literature of Australia* (1964), and Vivian Smith in *The Oxford History of Australian Literature* (1981), who, much like Hutton, pronounced Gordon an exiled Englishman.[22]

The literary nationalists of the twentieth century might have been bluntest in their dismissal of Gordon as an Australian poet, but his readers began almost immediately after his death to ponder the difficulty of assimilating his medievalism into the image of him as Australian laureate. The apparently irreconcilable tension between his medievalism and his portrayal of Australian life and landscape is obliquely but definitely suggested in the raw elegy 'The Late Mr A. L. Gordon: In Memoriam', written by Gordon's Melbourne comrade Henry Kendall only days after the poet's death. Early on, the poem appears to reconcile medieval and Australian by locating Gordon, as the singer of 'the first great songs these lands can claim / To be their own', within an ancient bardic tradition, describing him as:

> The bard, the scholar, and the man who lived
> That frank, that open-hearted life which keeps
> The splendid fire of English chivalry
> From dying out.[23]

The bardic image is repeated toward the poem's end, where it is reinforced by Kendall's description of his own poetic commemoration as a 'poor wreath', a metaphor that doubles as a funereal tribute to Gordon and as a laurel for his head. This homage is complicated, however, by the deceptively dense Arthurian allusion found in the poem's famous final lines:

[22] This critical reception of Gordon as 'un-Australian' is discussed in Jordan, 'Adam Lindsay Gordon: The Australian Poet', pp. 46, 50–51.

[23] Kendall's elegy is regularly incorporated into editions of Gordon's work. See Gordon, *Poems*, pp. iii–iv.

I stand to-day as lone as he who saw
At nightfall through the glimmering moony mists,
The last of Arthur on the wailing mere,
And strained in vain to hear the going voice. (p. iv)

Readers familiar with 'The Rhyme of Joyous Garde', which had been positively reviewed by Kendall only a week earlier, can appreciate the poignancy of the Arthurian reference in these lines. Here, in farewelling the departed Gordon, Kendall cast himself as Sir Bedivere, the knight who in Sir Thomas Malory's *Morte Darthur*, and more recently in Tennyson's 'The Passing of Arthur', witnessed the dying king's journey to Avilion. These lines' mythic evocation of lost leadership seems to imply by analogy that Gordon's death has left the formerly 'shining band' of Australian poesy bereft and rudderless, like Camelot before it. The Arthurian conceit and the ventriloquizing of Tennysonian vocabulary in phrases like 'the wailing mere' also clearly align Gordon, as author of 'Joyous Garde', with the Tennyson of the toweringly influential Arthurian *Idylls*. But, as Peter Otto's nuanced reading of Kendall's final lines has suggested, the Arthurian allusion warrants careful attention, because in it we can see Kendall using this myth to channel his ambivalence about Gordon's poetic legacy. For a start, in ventriloquizing the Tennysonian idiom, Kendall could just as easily be aligning himself, rather than Gordon, with the laureate. Furthermore, in what Otto describes as 'Kendall's curious misrepresentation' of Bedivere's final moments with Arthur, we see a subtle but significant alteration of the myth as presented by Tennyson. In Tennyson's 'The Passing of Arthur', Bedivere hears not only Arthur's rather fulsome parting speech but also, though more faintly, the king's welcome in Avilion 'as if some fair city were one voice / Around a king returning from his wars'.[24] Kendall as Sir Bedivere, conversely, strains 'in vain' to hear any final words from Gordon who, unlike Tennyson's Arthur, does not issue parting instructions or a promise to return, but is simply a 'going voice'. In Kendall's compressed antipodean Death of Arthur, the reassuring communicative link between king and knight — that is between poet and poet — is broken. The motif of Gordon as an indistinct 'going voice', for all its elegiac power, in fact marks subtly but powerfully Kendall's final revocation of Gordon's rank as 'once and future' laureate of Australia.[25]

[24] Alfred, Lord Tennyson, *Idylls of the King*, ed. by J. M. Gray (Harmondsworth: Penguin, 1983), p. 300.

[25] See Otto, 'Romantic Medievalism and Gothic Horror', pp. 37–40.

Kendall's qualified tribute was the first of many critical responses that not only acknowledged the significance of the medieval to Gordon's work but also developed a poetic persona for Gordon that located him within an imagined medieval past. Interestingly, it is Kendall's description of Gordon as a bard that arguably 'medievalizes' him more than the Arthurian image, insofar as it portrays him as a primitive ancestral figure in an Australian poetic tradition to come: just as the creators of the medieval ballads, epics, and lyrics were believed to have spawned the illustrious national traditions of the Old World, so too Gordon sings Australia's 'first great songs'.

We can detect a comparable medievalizing impulse among a number of others who have aimed far less ambiguously than Kendall to defend Gordon's right to the title of Australia's first poet. A fascinating and complex case in point can be found in the commentary of Robb. In the closing paragraph of the introduction to his edition of *The Poems of Adam Lindsay Gordon* (first edition 1912) entitled 'Australia's Debt to Gordon', Robb enacts a quite idiosyncratic medievalization of Gordon, not by simply associating him, as others had, with the events and legends of the medieval past, but rather by an arresting act of historical projection in which he looks ahead several hundred years to a time when the poet's tomb will be one of the nation's august ruins:

> Centuries hence, when men go up beside the banks of the noble stream of great poetry, which we believe will one day gladden the city and humanize and fertilize and deepen our Australian national life, as they climb reverently to its source, they will find on a broken memorial column, in letters that cannot fade, the name of ADAM LINDSAY GORDON.[26]

Robb's imaginary projection of Gordon as future ancestral poet here echoes verbally the visual message Gordon's early followers aimed to convey when they commissioned the monument above his grave in Brighton cemetery. Apparently not content to leave Gordon's ancestral status to evolve over the coming centuries, these devotees organized for his grave to be marked by a broken stone column. While the broken column clearly symbolized Gordon's early death, its unmistakable evocation of the ruins of former civilizations also had the effect of endowing the poet, less than twenty years after his death, with instant ancestral gravitas. Of course, there is no denying the classical, rather than medieval, flavour of a laurel-wreathed broken Doric column. But the desire to memorialize Gordon in this way can nevertheless be described as 'medievalist' in that it echoed, in Australian terms,

[26] Robb, *Poems of Adam Lindsay Gordon*, p. cxxvii.

the frenzied pursuit among the medievalists of nineteenth-century England and Europe to locate founding figures whose work could give credence to their nations' competing claims to ancient national poetic traditions. In recent years, a lot of excellent work has examined the ideological potency of medieval literature for nineteenth-century scholars and antiquarians, who regarded it as the fountainhead and authentic expression of national culture. Poetry in particular was singled out as an expression of national *geist*, with August-Wilhelm von Schlegel saying of it in 1818, 'it is always null and artificial, when it is not national'.[27] In colonial Australia, the most common response to the embarrassing absence of a local Middle Ages was to insist on a continuous racial, cultural, and literary link to medieval England and Europe. But with others, including Gordon's promoters, we see something quite different. Rather than invoking a bond with the historical Middle Ages, they instead endowed Gordon with the primal authenticity attributed to the medieval poets.

This desire to characterize the present day as the 'medieval past of the future' is detectible in a number of nineteenth-century discussions of local poetry. In Rosa Praed's *Policy and Passion*, the aesthetically inclined character Mr Ferris, obviously a devotee of the widespread Romantic fetish for Celtic bard Ossian, cries out,

> will there never be an Australian Ossian, to strike a wild note in tune to the cry of the curlews, the moan of swamp oaks, the rushing of streams, the hum of butterflies, and sighing of leaves! Is Nature to be always eloquent here, and Art mute?[28]

Nor did this motif die with the nineteenth century, as David Matthews has demonstrated in his insightful discussion of Australian literary debates in the 1930s. A most striking return of this motif can be detected is a comment made in 1935 by literary critic P. R. Stephensen, who asserted of Australian poetry '[w]e are on the threshold of Australian self-consciousness, at the point of developing Australian nationality, and with it Australian culture[;] we are in our Chaucerian

[27] A. W. von Schlegel, *Observations sur la langue et la littérature provençales* (Paris: Librarie Grecque-latine-allemande, 1818), p. 73. Of the numerous discussions of nineteenth-century nationalistic medieval philology, see R. Howard Bloch, 'Naturalism, Nationalism, Medievalism', *Romantic Review*, 76 (1985), 341–60; John Graham, 'National Identity and the Politics of Publishing the Troubadours', in *Medievalism and the Modernist Temper*, ed. by R. Howard Bloch and Stephen G. Nichols (Baltimore: Johns Hopkins University Press, 1996), pp. 57–94; and Hans Ulrich Gumbrecht, '"Un Souffle d'Allemagne ayant passé": Friedrich Diez, Gaston Paris, and the Genesis of National Philologies', *Romance Philology*, 40 (1986), 1–37.

[28] Praed, *Policy and Passion*, p. 274.

phrase'.[29] For Stephensen, Chaucer's quest to elevate the national vernacular into a legitimately literary tongue was, in Matthews's words, 'an authentic medieval moment' that was being repeated in the early twentieth century in the new national environment of Australia.[30] What this suggests is that the gesture of portraying the Australian present as a 'medieval' moment in the nation's literary evolution has had an undeniable rhetorical appeal. The Australian literature of the present becomes, by analogy, a foundational literature — crude and primitive, perhaps, but a vigorous tradition in the making.

And yet the self-interest and naïve idealism underlying such a medievalizing gesture had been satirized wickedly decades before Stephensen's statement, in the 1897 poem 'An Australian Mummy' by Victor Daley.[31] This very odd but quite remarkable poem demands our attention for the way its description of contemporary Australian society relies on, yet simultaneously lampoons, the nostalgic impulse of nineteenth-century antiquarianism. Its premise is a novel one: apparently produced three thousand years in the future (according to its prose prologue, which is in the form of an extract from a newspaper article written in the year 4897), the poem purports to be verses written by a leading Australian poet of the fifth millennium, Alexander W. Mudlarque, in response to the recent excavation of a mummy that had been buried in 'the ancient city of Melbourne' in 1897. Contemplating the 'dumb, shrouded shape' of the nineteenth-century mummy, Mudlarque is drawn into an idealistic retrospective fantasy in which late nineteenth-century Melbourne is conjured up before him as a feudal paradise in which squatters, as 'Monarchs of the Land' — extend benevolence toward their contented and well cared-for workers. Mudlarque's rosy misapprehension of labour relations in the economically depressed 1890s offers a clear parody of the Victorian fantasizing of medieval Europe as a pre-industrial paradise in which feudal lords and serfs live in goodwill and mutual obligation. Its description, for instance, of 1890s Melbourne as a 'fair and goodly Guild of Work and Wealth' is modelled on the widely held notion of medieval guilds as brotherhoods where workers stood shoulder to shoulder in bonhomie and un-alienated labour. The effect for the

29 P. R. Stephensen, 'The Foundations of Culture in Australia' (1935), in *The Writer in Australia: A Collection of Literary Documents, 1856 to 1964*, ed. by John Barnes (Melbourne: Oxford University Press, 1969), pp. 204–44 (p. 211).

30 Matthews, 'Marcus Clarke, Gothic, Romance', pp. 4–6.

31 This poem first appeared in *The Bulletin*, 21 August 1897, p. 31. Reprinted in *Creeve Roe: Poetry by Victor Daley*, ed. by Muir Holburn and Marjorie Pizer, foreword by E. J. Brady, drawings by Roderick Shaw (Sydney: Pinchgut, 1947), pp. 128–32.

reader, however, is two-fold satire. Not only does Daley's Melbourne fall woefully short of this quasi-medievalist dream: the dream itself, it is hinted, is ridiculous, and perhaps even mendacious.

Of particular interest within this poem's futuristic antiquarianism is its assessment of Gordon's legacy to future Australian verse. In a humorous distinction from Robb's image of Gordon as future ancestral monument, Mudlarque presents Gordon's work, and indeed all late nineteenth-century Australian poetry, as an irretrievably lost corpus. Looking back at colonial Australia, he claims:

> Poets they have; long perished is their fame.
> Their Gordon Kendall is to us a name,
> And nothing more [...]
> Long ere the land to nationhood upsprang
> Its magic and its mystery they sang,
> And hoped for Fame Immortal. Well away!
> The tongue they sang in is as dead as they.

Recalling Kendall's respectful dismissal of Gordon as the Australian Laureate at the end of 'The Late Mr Adam Lindsay Gordon', we can appreciate the sly humour in Daley's reference to 'Gordon Kendall': on the one hand a joke on the inaccuracies committed by antiquarians in their misguided efforts to recover national ancestral bards, this bundling together of Gordon and Kendall into one long-vanished poet also consigns them equally to historical oblivion. Daley also condemns his own work to this oblivion: he is among the unnamed 'rest' who 'in silence sleep', their work lost forever to later generations of Australian readers. Far from presenting the poetry of his own era, and especially Gordon's work, as expressing a foundational Chaucerian moment in Australian literature, Daley envisages a future society in which this early verse has long passed into irrelevance.

Although one would expect that the poem's fifth millennium setting would lead Daley to make the present over in the image of the classical past, his double satire leads him more readily into a mirthful use of the idiom of nineteenth-century medievalism, and hence the poem's historical vision is recognizably medieval. The satiric intent of this last poem notwithstanding, Robb's, Stephensen's and Daley's attempts to historicize their present moment are alike in their depiction of present-day Australia as the antique past of future Australia, with a particular emphasis on the medieval complexion of that past.

It is possible to distinguish yet another, quite tenacious, critical approach to Gordon's medievalism, which has subscribed to what can be called the 'divided Gordon' thesis. One of the best-known early purveyors of this thesis was Robb, who, notwithstanding his promotion of Gordon as the font of Australian poesy, draws a strong distinction between 'His Debt to English Poetry' and 'His Debt to Australia'. According to Robb, what English verse imparted to Gordon was the art of poetry: with Byron he shared a morbid temperament, from Browning and Swinburne he learned technique and subject matter, and from Tennyson he took his 'sympathy with the old knightly times'. Australia, in contrast, inspired this unlikely wordsmith by striking a chord with his soul rather than his mind. C. F. MacRae's 1968 study followed the lead set by Robb and divided Gordon's narrative poems up into 'Stories from the Past' and 'Stories from the Present'.[32] But the reader who arguably takes the notion of a 'divided Gordon' furthest is Leonie Kramer in her 1963 essay 'The Literary Reputation of Adam Lindsay Gordon'. In this essay Kramer goes so far as to suggest that Gordon was riven by the two irreconcilable impulses that claimed him, to the point that we cannot treat his work as the product of a single poet:

> Indeed, it is arguable that he was two poets. On the one hand he was the nostalgic imitator of the poetic heroes and accents of his youth, of Swinburne, Browning and Tennyson in particular, and in this mood he was introspective and melancholy. On the other hand he was the sporting hero, naively appreciative of 'GOD'S GLORIOUS OXYGEN', writing for an audience which admired his galloping rhymes as much as his horsemanship.[33]

For Kramer, the medievalist and the bard of the turf were strangers. Kramer's firm grasp of the double cultural allegiance of colonial writers means that, unlike Hutton, she does not take this disjunction to be *prima facie* grounds for disqualifying Gordon from the ranks of Australian poets. Nevertheless, her statement that Gordon 'turned his back on the realities of the time in which he lived, and sought refuge in a self-controlled world of mediaeval idealism' equates medievalism with nostalgic escapism, denying its capacity to engage in commentary on affairs of the present. In subscribing to this notion of medievalism as flight from the modern, Kramer was clearly influenced by Francis Adams's long essay 'The Poetry of Adam Lindsay Gordon', written in 1885, five years after the publication of Gordon's collected works. Unlike Robb, Adams did not regard the dual influences of literary history and social modernity as complementary forces in Gordon's work: Rather, in this essay he not only proclaimed Gordon's life and work a failure but also, significantly, attributed this failure to the poet's unfortunate situation as a 'martyr [...] to our terrible period of transition from the Old World into the New, from Mediaevalism into Modernity'. Clustering him

[32] MacRae, *Adam Lindsay Gordon*, esp. pp. 35–52.

[33] Kramer, 'The Literary Reputation of Adam Lindsay Gordon', p. 43.

with other 'martyrs' such as Charles Baudelaire and James Thomson, Adams argued that Gordon and his verse were redolent of the unsettling and dispiriting nihilism characteristic of this historical transition: 'Gordon and his work are modern, but not wholly Modern [...] he has lost the Old and he has not won the New Faith'.

Yet, despite Adams's repeated avowals that Gordon's chief 'claim on our interest as a poet' is his tragic fall between the stools of nostalgic fantasy and progressive élan, his essay ultimately — although very possibly inadvertently — demonstrated that Gordon's nihilistic uncertainty was in fact one of the vital threads of continuity between his medievalist and modern work. The essay's extensive argument for the dominance in Gordon's 'modern' work of nihilism, which Adams calls 'the malady of our time', can clearly be seen to echo Adams's own earlier discussion of Gordon's portrayal of 'the once-loved knight' Lancelot in 'The Rhyme of Joyous Garde'. Old, broken, divested of all earthly ideals but uncertain of what death will bring, Lancelot's resigned musings as presented by Adams are of a piece with those of the world-weary personae of Gordon's bush ballads, who contemplate death with a mixture of trepidation and acceptance. However, while this parallel might strike the reader, Adams did not develop it, preferring to hive the medieval and the modern off from one another and to present them as opposing forces in Gordon's work.

A more recent critic who has issued a salutary corrective to this long-standing 'divided' model is Michael Ackland. In a 1993 article, Ackland argued that the poems of Gordon's oeuvre have 'an unsuspected degree of conceptual unity, irrespective of whether their subject matter is based on past or present, Old World or New World experience'.[34] Ackland's unifying gesture rests on his claim that Gordon's verse, far from jumping arbitrarily between the ninth and the nineteenth centuries, can be more productively understood as presenting us with 'exemplary' and 'representative scenarios' or 'parables' that assert a 'consistent (and consistently dark) view of life irrespective of setting or epoch'. Within this argument, characters from medieval knights to Australian jockeys are gathered together under the all-encompassing 'postlapsarian doom' that pervades Gordon's work; and whatever the poems' individual historical settings, they are united as 'timeless plaints against man's inescapable lot' in which 'both the past and the present afford the same crushing lesson'.[35]

[34] Ackland, 'Martial Code', p. 53.

[35] Ackland, 'Martial Code', p. 60.

Ackland's astute synthesizing, which teases out the thread that Adams picked up but did not unravel, provides a most welcome path out of the impasse of denial, condemnation, and segregation in which Gordon's medievalism has been trapped. But other problems emerge as a result of his suggestion that history is, for Gordon, an undifferentiated continuum of despair. Chief among them is that this account denies that the Middle Ages had any specific valency for Gordon as a poet, suggesting that their role was simply to furnish him with exemplars of human tragedy that were essentially interchangeable with those from other periods in human history. This is most apparent in Ackland's comment about 'The Rhyme of Joyous Garde', of which he says, '[d]espite the veil of Arthurian legend, the personal analogies are unmistakable with this writer who, in his youth, had light-heartedly commented: "I should make a good knight-errant at times, but I think a highwayman would suit me better"'.[36] To suggest that the Arthurian story was simply a 'veil' Gordon threw over what was effectively a personal meditation is to ignore the profound, complex, yet also quite specific constellation of meanings this story held for nineteenth-century British and colonial readers. As the epic of choice throughout the British Empire, it was regarded variously, and even simultaneously, as a celebration of the origins and the future of English greatness, an elegy to the vanished ideal of loyalty and social harmony, and a cautionary tale about governance and personal conduct. Others in the Australian colonies, including John Woolley, seized on Tennyson's version of the story as an allegory warning of the pitfalls of colonial life.[37] While it is true that Gordon's poem is more engaged with presenting a portrait of personal disaffection than with mining the ideological depths of the legend, much of its nostalgic reflection is directed at the loss of the noble society forged and ruled over by Arthur.

It is also true that Gordon does not draw exclusively from the medieval past but, rather, as Ackland rightly points out, roams more broadly for examples of human defeat and lost ideals. In 'Podas Okus', the first poem in *Sea Spray and Salt Drift*, and in 'Pastor Cum', a translation from Horace, he turns to the legends of Homeric Greece and Troy; 'The Romance of Britomarte', is inspired by the English Civil War, while 'The Roll of the Kettledrum' is set amid the fray of the Charge of the Light Brigade in the Crimean War. But we should not conclude from this that the Middle Ages has no special significance for Gordon. This having been said, though, it remains to uncover what this significance might be.

[36] Ackland, 'Martial Code', p. 62.

[37] See D'Arcens, 'Antipodean Idylls', pp. 237–56.

We might begin by taking up a conspicuous theme and argue that the disparate strands of Gordon's work are held together by a tribute to chivalry. Indeed, as much is suggested by his earliest posthumous commentator, Kendall, who describes him as the guardian of '[t]he splendid fire of English chivalry' in Australia (p. iii). This is not a generic evocation of chivalry by Kendall, but draws on a *leitmotif* in Gordon's work. In Fytte III of 'Ye Wearie Wayfarer' Gordon makes a clear case for the link between chivalric romances and contemporary tales of hunting, riding, and seafaring when he says that these modern tales '[s]eem legends of loyal knights' in which 'chivalry dawns' (p. 17). Given so many of his own poems focus on the chase, the turf, and the sea, they too by implication share in this chivalric legacy. This is overtly borne out in Fytte II of the same poem, where a doomed cavalryman of the light brigade is described, in unmissable upper case, as 'A TYPE OF OUR CHIVALRY' (p. 15), in that he perished in mounted combat upholding an ethic of self-sacrifice and protection that Gordon suggests was responsible for keeping alive the medieval code of chivalry.

Chivalry's elaborate social codes notwithstanding, Gordon's poems keep firmly before us this word's intimate etymological relationship to horsemanship, and the chivalric bond that is of most interest to him is not that between brothers-in-arms but that between horse and rider. The mystery and profundity of this bond is expressed best in 'The Roll of the Kettledrum', where the poem's persona says (channelling *Hamlet*, I. v) 'there may be more links 'twixt horse and his rider / Than all of your shallow philosophy guess'd'. This is most pointedly the case in *Ashtaroth*, where, in one of Gordon's most infamously bad rhymes, the knight Hugo's dying thoughts are concerned equally with the welfare of his own soul and the diet of his beloved mount, Rollo:

> How heavy the night hangs how wild the waves dash,
> Say a mass for my soul and give Rollo a mash. (p. 322)

Furthermore, as discussed in Chapter 1, he expressly attributes Australians' hippodromania (love of the race track) and love of the hunt to their Anglo-Norman heritage, in a gesture that presents these sports as characteristic of English chivalry. This motif of horsemanship, then, is the glue that binds the modern Australian bushman and jockey to the medieval knight.

Their shared equestrian devotion is, moreover, reinforced through a set of metrical patterns held common throughout Gordon's oeuvre. The metre used in both the medievalist poem 'Unshriven' and the bush ballad 'The Sick Stockrider' is a case in point. The opening exclamation of 'The Sick Stockrider' initially destabilizes this metre, but subsequently the poem's metre mirrors that of 'Unshriven', as demonstrated by the opening stanzas of both poems:

> Oh! the sun rose on the lea, and the birds sang merrilie,
> And the steed stood ready harness'd in the hall,
> And he left his lady's bower, and he sought the eastern tower,
> And he lifted cloak and weapon from the wall. ('Unshriven', p. 10)

> Hold hard, Ned! Lift me down once more, and lay me in the shade,
> Old man, you've had your work cut out to guide
> Both horses, and to hold me in the saddle when I sway'd,
> All through the hot, slow, sleepy, silent ride. ('The Sick Stock-Rider', p. 125)

What we discover here is a striking chiasmus. Just as Gordon had assimilated Australian equestrian sports and stockriding into the illustrious lineage of chivalry, so too he Australianized 'Unshriven''s tale of knightly honour-gone-wrong by casting the poem in one of the favoured 'galloping' anapaestic metres associated with the Australian horseback ballad and derived from George John Whyte-Melville, the dedicatee of *Bush Ballads and Galloping Rhymes*. This technical cross-pollination of the modern and medieval is also effected through Gordon's use of genre. As Richard D. Jordan has argued, his frequent recourse to the ballad form means that his bleak bush tales and sporting rhymes allude to literary traditions which include Old Scottish ballads and medieval romance.[38]

And yet chivalry seems more of a motif than a deep unifying theme in Gordon's work. It is part of the assumed backdrop of his medievalist poems, in particular those whose narratives involve the forging of loyal friendships ('Joyous Garde', 'The Three Friends') or the honouring of knightly pacts, including pacts of revenge ('The Feud', 'Unshriven'), but it does not feature centrally in his portrayal of the Middle Ages. Rather, when these poems are read together, we see that Gordon was far more fascinated by the moral, religious, and indeed existential complexion of medieval society. In particular, he seems to have been haunted by what he portrayed as a troubling gap between its seemingly reassuring Catholic rituals, most particularly its rituals of absolution, and the agnostic uncertainty that dogs his medieval protagonists as they contemplate the prospect, and in some cases the imminence, of death. It is true that Gordon's entire oeuvre discloses his preoccupation with the notion of being caught unready by death: to name but a few, we find it in such non-medievalist poems as 'Gone', 'The Sick Stockrider', 'De Te' (which ponders whether 'death absolves or cures / The sin of life /' or '[i]f the sin endures' (p. 147)), and the dramatic lyric 'The Road To Avernus', where a woman whose baby has just died questions the 'sad assurances of priests' by asking 'is it well

[38] Jordan, 'Adam Lindsay Gordon: The Australian Poet', p. 45.

for the sinner that the soul endure? / For the sinless soul is it well?' (p. 164). But the Catholic backdrop of his medievalist poems gives a historical poignancy to his characters' unconfessed sins. *Ashtaroth*, 'Unshriven', 'The Three Friends', 'Confiteor', and 'The Feud' all thematize repentance, or its absence, through the specific institutional forms of Catholic confession or through penitential and requiem masses; indeed, the very title of 'Confiteor' refers to the penitential prayer at the opening of the Catholic mass. Furthermore, these poems feature protagonists who are either troublingly unrepentant, or only incompletely penitent, about having succumbed to their erotic or violent passions. This state is most searchingly explored in 'The Rhyme of Joyous Garde', where the aged Lancelot, despite the daily counsel of a bishop, cannot bring himself to repent of his consuming, sinful love for Guinevere:

> When I well-nigh swoon'd in the deep-drawn bliss
> Of that first long, sweet, slow, stolen kiss,
> I would gladly have given for less than this
> Myself, with my soul's salvation. (p. 177)

Although 'Fauconshawe' is less explicit in its appeal to ritualized absolution, it still shares with the other poems a preoccupation with the peril of living with unabsolved sin and risking a spiritually unprepared death. As Sir Hugh examines the corpse of his rival for clues as to 'how the spirit had pass'd in the moments last', he finds that 'the hands were clench'd in a death-grip fast, / And the sods stamp'd down by the heel' (p. 45) — stark traces of the knight's struggle against death which gain an extra moral dimension when we learn that at the time of his death he was in the throes of a clandestine affair with Lady Mabel.

This is not to say that Gordon ultimately subscribed to Catholic dogma on confession. Indeed, it is the very insufficiency of confession, the whispering suspicion that its assurances are facile, that makes it most discomfiting to his medieval protagonists, who want to take comfort but cannot. This is registered most conspicuously in 'Confiteor', where the reprobate knight rejects the priest's offer of confession, saying 'I hold your comfort a broken reed; / [...] I've striven, though feebly, to grasp your creed,/ And I've grappled my own despair' (p. 65). The poem ends with a kind of Pascalian wager, in which the priest, admitting that he too struggles with doubt about his own salvation, finally resorts to confession not as a promise of redemption, but as an affirmation of hope:

> I too have sinn'd, even as thou,
> And I too have feebly striven,
> And with thee I must bow, crying 'Shrive us now!
> Our father which are in heaven!' (p. 66)

Similarly, in 'The Rhyme of Joyous Garde' Lancelot believes that his own transgressions have exceeded the ordinary 'sinfulness/ That through prayer and penance is pardon'd', implying that there is a level of sin for which ritual atonement is futile. Conversely, King Arthur's goodness was such that Catholic penitential rites are unnecessary.

> Now priests may patter, and bells may toll,
> He will need no masses to aid his soul;
> When the angels open the judgement scroll,
> His wrongs will be tenfold righted. (p. 175)

More ambiguously, but just as profoundly, the final line of 'Unshriven', in which the murdered knight's soul 'unshriven to its maker flies' (p. 11), appears to withhold judgement on the soul's eternal fate, thereby supplanting the power of institutional absolution by imagining, as Lancelot does with Arthur, a direct encounter between the individual soul and the divine. But despite the questioning of confession in some of the medievalist poems, their moral and metaphysical force depends upon Gordon setting them in a historical moment where their protagonists' salvation or damnation cannot be understood without recourse to the general medieval belief in the efficacy of ritual acts of penance. These medieval characters might share existential doubt with Gordon's modern characters, such as the famous sick stock-rider, who surmises agnostically that his soul will 'go where most men go'; but their end-of-life nihilism, or indeed regret, is thrown into relief as a lapse from Catholic institutional absolution and the hope it imparts.

The importance of recognizing the undeniably Catholic nature of Gordon's European Middle Ages is that we can see that he seizes on something that distinguishes this period from other civilizations and other moments in Western history, including his own. That Gordon was conscious of Christianity as an historical phenomenon is clear in 'The Road to Avernus'. Although the priestly character Melchior appears to subscribe to a universal dualism, saying 'God wills the inclination with the soul at war to be' (p. 157), he concedes that this war differs from age to age, contrasting the more bellicose saints of 'earlier Christian ages, while the heathen empire stood' with the passivity of 'so-called saints of latter days' (p. 156). Although his medieval characters' agnosticism engages in dialogue with the contemporary nihilism captured in his other poems, this should not lead us to say, with Ackland, that the Middle Ages simply furnished Gordon with 'timeless' exemplars of human frailty and misfortune. Rather, it is the particularity of the period, with its extremes of piety and barbarity, that makes it intriguing to Gordon. So even if we disagree with Francis Adams's statement that Gordon's work was a failure, the fact that Gordon reaches for medieval Catholicism to add moral weight to the experience of existential doubt confirms the perspicacity of Adams's diagnosis of Gordon's historical dilemma that 'he has lost the Old and he has not won the New Faith'.

The use of a medieval Catholic worldview also serves to heighten the emotional and spiritual drama experienced by his protagonists, and is thus crucial to Gordon's creation of an unmistakably Gothic Middle Ages. It is his exploitation of this idiom in all of its nuances that, more than anything, lends consistency to his oeuvre. Recalling Otto's taxonomy of the Gothic, we see that Gordon's use of the 'natural Gothic' to create bleak portrayals of the Australian landscape is supplemented by a Gothic portrayal of an overwrought, disordered medieval world that shadows the refined and highly codified world of chivalry and romance. The Gothic idiom is not just evident in the poems' wind-wracked landscapes, grim battlefields, or cavernous stone castles. The moral landscape of Gordon's medieval world is also Gothic, steeped in murder and treachery ('The Feud', 'Fauconshawe', 'The Three Friends', 'Unshriven') and populated by tormented souls (Hugo in *Ashtaroth*, Lancelot in 'Joyous Garde', the confessing knight in 'The Three Friends', the sinning priest and knight in 'Confiteor') who are locked in a battle between their primal erotic and violent drives and their desire to redeem themselves through obedience to social and religious codes. Lancelot is arguably the most famous example, but Hugo also wrestles with his passion for Agatha and his aspiration to live in the exalted realm of thought, while the dying knight in 'The Three Friends', despite being aware he is '[o]n the dread verge of endless gloom', is drawn back irresistibly to his memories of 'slow caresses that consume, / And kisses that devour' (p. 182). Even the female protagonist of the relatively anomalous ballad 'Rippling Water' embodies this struggle, as, on the eve of her wedding to the milk-livered but aristocratic Marmaduke, she meditates over the passionate kisses she once shared with her peasant lover Stephen, as well as her evident attraction to the gallant Brian of Hawkesmede.

We do not know the exact order in which Gordon composed his poems; but given that both his earliest published poems, 'The Feud' and *Ashtaroth*, have Gothicized medieval settings, it is arguable that Gordon's Gothic sensibility began with his medievalist verse and was then extended to the Gothic bush ballads for which he is most famous. Thus we can also query Ackland's 'one-way' model which suggests that Gordon's representation of the past is inflected by his peculiarly modern crisis of faith, but that the historical past does not influence his outlook as a modern. Rather, it is his poems with modern Australian settings that, in fact, owe much of their distinctive imagery, vocabulary, and stoic pathos to his fascination with the vivid Middle Ages of his imagination. In a way not dissimilar to the architects of Melbourne's banks and cathedrals, a Gothic vision of the Middle Ages provided him with a surprisingly apposite language for expressing his sense of life under colonial modernity. His use of the Gothic idiom functions as a kind of medievalist gesture of equivalence in which modern Australia assumes the sinister, irrational, and barbarous sensibility conventionally reserved for the Gothic Middle Ages.

Perhaps, then, Clarke was half-right in his assessment of Gordon's work. Although it clear that Gordon did, *contra* Clarke, produce 'knightly song', it is equally clear that he was not drawn to recount the 'bright morning deeds' of the romance or epic traditions. Instead, he preferred to dwell on dark deeds grieved over in the twilight of remorse. For his knights and their ladies, heroic feats and passionate love are but dim memories, blighted by calamity and contracting in the face of death's stalking approach. And just as his personae did not ultimately seek redemption through nostalgia, neither did Gordon. Rather, like them, and through them, he stood vigil between stoicism and nihilism, praying that the light would be shed on someone, though it was too late for him. This is, of course, not unique to his medievalist poems; but their singular place in his oeuvre, and more generally in nineteenth-century Australian verse, comes from their portrayal of a world whose painful contradictions, while starkly different from those of nineteenth-century Australia, resonated with the anguishing doubt that beset Gordon's age and, finally, claimed him as its own.

Chapter 4

# THE DRIVEL OF OUR FATHERS: MEDIEVALISM IN POPULAR AUSTRALIAN POETRY

In his satiric poem 'Correggio Jones', first published in *The Bulletin* on 11 June 1898, Victor Daley calls up the absurd figure of an Australian pre-Raphaelite painter, whose 'body dwells on Gander Flat' while '[h]is soul's in Italy'. The poem's opening stanza portrays the painter — whose name clearly evokes that of Mrs Cimabue Brown, the infamous aesthetic caricature discussed in Chapter 2 — as a pretentious dupe of Eurocentrism, saying:

> Correggio Jones an artist was
> Of pure Australian race,
> But native subjects scorned because
> They were too commonplace.[1]

Parodying conventional claims that the dullness of the Australian scene stymies creative genius, Daley has his artist blame his obscurity on the lack of historical inspiration in his surroundings:

> Now, look at those Old Masters — they
> Had all the chances fine,
> With churches dim, and ruins grey,
> And castles on the Rhine,
>
> And Lady Gay in miniver,
> And hairy-shirted saint,
> And Doges in apparel fair
> And things a man might paint!

[1] 'Correggio Jones', repr. in *Creeve Roe: Poetry by Victor Daley*, pp. 41–43.

> And barons bold and pilgrims pale,
> And battling Knights and King
> The blood-spots on their golden mail
> And all that sort of thing.

This cascade of medievalist commonplaces, from its opening Gothic clichés to the slapdash 'all that sort of thing', humorously exposes the banal, miscellaneous, and fundamentally *un*historical attitude underlying the colonial artist's fascination with the medieval past. The fact that Correggio (1489–1534) was a painter of the Italian high Renaissance, rather than the Middle Ages, only serves to underline the point that for Daley's artist the past is an undifferentiated mélange of romance. This slavish Europhilia is coupled, furthermore, with Jones's blindness to the possibility of an emerging heroic tradition in Australia. So removed is he from his Australian surroundings that he commits what for *Bulletin* readers would have been nothing short of sacrilege: he dismisses the doomed uprising of miners at the Eureka Stockade on the Ballarat goldfields in 1854 — a legendary event for the Australian Left, and iconic in the mythology of Australian anti-authoritarianism — as having 'no Romance'.[2] The fact that even Rolf Boldrewood, hardly a friend of the Left, recognized the romantic potential of the Eureka uprising and dramatized it in his novel *The Miner's Right* underlines the extent of Jones's Eurocentric refusal.

Despite its deflationary intent, Daley's poem, with its casual stream of medieval clichés, takes its place in a rich seam of Australian literary medievalism that has, as yet, received no critical attention: that is the large body of verse produced by Australian authors that makes reference to personages, events, and legends from the Middle Ages. Much of this verse has been forgotten partly because, unlike Gordon's 'Joyous Garde', it was not of the highest calibre. A good deal of it was unabashedly ephemeral, trite, superficial in its medievalism, and even at times unconcerned with medieval culture except as a repository of literary motifs and allusions. Indeed, many of these poems might be thought of as the literary counterpart to Correggio Jones's paintings — hackneyed, derivative, and knocked out in haste for the consuming public. In short, much of it was drivel, the 'drivel of our fathers', as James Edmond thunders in his 1888 poem of that name, which will be discussed later. Yet despite the undeniable mediocrity of much of this verse, this was also an indisputably pervasive and robust strain of medievalism, and we dismiss it to the detriment of understanding fully how the Middle Ages was represented

[2] Indeed, Daley went on to write his own Eureka poem, 'A Ballad of Eureka', three years later.

by colonial Australian poets and understood by their audiences. We need to register the significance of Australia's medievalist drivel, for although much of it does not bear up well under close literary analysis, it should be seen as a barometer of popular attitudes in colonial Australia to Europe and the pre-modern period.

So what exactly counts as medievalism in nineteenth-century Australian verse? Looking at many of the poems, we can discern what might be called an 'amnesiac' strain of medievalism in late nineteenth- and early twentieth-century Australia, in which medievalist allusions are frequent, but are often curiously dehistoricized. The oeuvres of poets great and small are festooned with an eclectic smattering of brief medievalist references as well as the occasional foray into medieval or more broadly antiquarian stylistics, such as that found in Gordon's 'Ye Wearie Wayfarer' and John Dunmore Lang's 1843 'Reliques of Auncient Poetrie', a poem which, despite its title's reference to Thomas Percy's 1765 *Reliques of Ancient Poetry* (indeed Lang's 'auncient poetrie' out-medievalizes Percy) is actually about the seventeenth-century hanging judge George Jeffreys, written in a confected 'olde' English consisting of medieval and loosely Shakespearean words. Dante and Petrarch are passingly evoked in Henry Kendall's verse ('Twelve Sonnets', 'Black Lizzie', 'Jim the Splitter'), while in one of Gordon's non-medievalist poems, 'Delilah', we find allusions to Lancelot and Galahad in verses about the biblical temptress. Generalized ideals and motifs associated with chivalry are evoked ubiquitously, yet often so briefly that they are almost emptied of association with the Middle Ages. In two of Gordon's horsiest poems, 'Hippodromania' and 'How We Beat the Favourite', for instance, we find passing mentions of figures from medieval history and literature, such as King Alfred and Iseut, but these allusions turn out to be to horses named after these legendary figures. In Henry Kendall's prize-winning poem celebrating The Sydney International Exhibition of 1879, displays of Viking culture jostle against an indiscriminate global mass of exotica such as island spices, while in the 1907 poem 'Avatar', Victor Daley — yes, he who had satirized Correggio Jones and his ilk — singles out the heroines of medieval legend (Bynhild, Ysolt, Gudrun, Guinevere) but then places them into a universal history of female allure ranging from Helen of Troy to the poet's beloved.

Nor, as will become clear later, is this Daley's only foray into Correggio Jones-style miscellaneous medievalism. He wrote at least a dozen poems with some kind of medievalist content — that is, at least four more than Gordon, despite the latter's posthumous reputation as colonial Australia's most committed medievalist. Like Gordon, Daley's poetic persona was also medievalist in flavour. This was partly cultivated by Daley himself, via his adoption of the pseudonym Creeve Roe (Red Branch) to align himself with the ancient Red Knights of Ulster, but was corroborated by his posthumous promoter E. J. Brady.[3] All of this would seem to fit Daley for the role of local Celtic bard singing ancient songs of romance — a kind of 'harp in the South'. But, as indicated in 'Correggio Jones', 'Avatar', and other poems, one possible reason he has not become Australia's iconic medievalist is that his poetic treatment of the Middle Ages, with its haphazard and often flippant allusions, reflects less complexity and less commitment than Gordon to medievalism as a paradigm for meditating on Australia and modernity. And yet it is arguable that Daley, as a bard of medievalist ephemera, is in fact the most representative poet of popular Australian medievalism. His work is typical of the many Australian-written poems in which the Middle Ages can be glimpsed among a miscellaneous assortment of historical references ranging from the classical to the Napoleonic, and beyond.

This kind of throwaway, dehistoricized allusion to the medieval period had a specific valency in the context of colonial Australia. It was simultaneously a reflection of that society's desire for continuity with the medieval past, and a sign of the cultural amnesia that was wrought by a vast distance that was both spatio-temporal and cultural. Furthermore, this verse is arguably, in its very lack of historical discrimination, distinctive of one major direction that Australian medievalism has continued to take up until the present. If we are to use the term 'medievalism' to refer only to usages such as Gordon's that convincingly demonstrate an awareness of the Middle Ages as a specific period, we would need to consign most nineteenth- and early twentieth-century Australian poetic usages to the limbo of pseudo-medievalism. To do so would limit considerably our understanding of the significatory richness of medieval events, personages, and cultural phenomena within an important and vibrant theatre of colonial creative expression.

In finding an image or model to describe the diffuse, promiscuous, amnesiac medievalism of colonial Australia, it is helpful to draw on the concept of 'the rhizome', as developed in the French poststructural philosophers Gilles Deleuze and Félix Guatarri's tome *A Thousand Plateaus: Capitalism and Schizophrenia*:

> Let us summarize the principal characteristics of a rhizome: unlike trees or their roots, the rhizome connects any point to any other point, and its traits are not necessarily

[3] Brady's pen-portrait of Daley, much like Daley's own verse, is a miscellany of medievalisms: the Irish-born Daley was, says Brady, descended from a family who were 'a bardic clan in classic Eire'; as a man, he 'trod the highway of life like a cavalier of old time — *sans peur et sans reproche*' (here he quotes the motto attached to the chevalier Bayard), while his pen was 'the sharp sword of the Crusader, flashing with unexpected fire'. See E. J. Brady, 'Personal Impressions of Victor Daley and His Work', in *Creeve Roe: Poetry by Victor Daley*, pp. 11–13.

> linked to traits of the same nature; it brings into play very different regimes of signs [...] [i]t has neither beginning nor end, but always a middle (milieu) from which it grows and which it overspills.[4]

The notion of the rhizome is useful not only because it captures the promiscuity and viral mutations of medievalist reference within the poetry examined in this chapter but also because it allows us to develop a paradigm that frees Australian medievalism from charges of being merely derivative. Applying this model, we see that Australian medievalism functions less according to what Deleuze and Guattari would describe as an arborescent model (that is, a tree-like model of inheritance in which the great fathers and canons of Victorian British medievalism beget children who continue their lineage in the colonial setting) and more like a rhizome (a decentred literary formation with multiple origins and entry points, pursuing multiple directions simultaneously and energetically, forming unexpected and mutually transformative conjunctions with local culture and indeed subcultures).

This decentred, rhizomatic appearance of the Middle Ages in colonial verse is reinforced, moreover, by the dominant pattern of its publication. Many of the verses discussed so far were eventually gathered into volumes, where they may appear to the modern reader to gather a critical mass. But in nineteenth-century Australia it was, in fact, the periodical press that was, as Elizabeth Webby's work has shown, the favoured site for original verse publication. Webby points out that in colonial Australia the costs of volume publication were prohibitive for many authors, who then chose to disseminate their work as individual poems in newspapers and magazines.[5] So, at the time of publication, these verses that we experience as collections were scattered nationwide across a range of mostly weekly and periodical publications, both metropolitan and regional. Gathering together the mass of medievalist verse published in these publications is a huge undertaking, and there is undoubtedly an enormous trove, both of precious gems and of tawdry trinkets, yet to be uncovered. But even a selective systematic search of the major broadsheets, journals, and pictorial monthlies between 1840 and 1910 yields a significant enough volume of poems to indicate a definite subgenre of popular verse. Given that some of these publications were read not only nationwide but also beyond Australia — *The Bulletin* was sold and read throughout the British Empire — we

[4] Deleuze and Guattari, *A Thousand Plateaus: Capitalism and Schizophrenia*, trans. and intro. by Brian Massumi (Minneapolis: University of Minnesota Press, 1987), p. 21.

[5] Elizabeth Webby, *Early Australian Poetry: An Annotated Bibliography of Original Poems Published in Australian Newspapers, Magazines & Almanacks Before 1850* (Sydney: Hale and Iremonger, 1982), p. ix.

have a medievalism that was ubiquitous yet, for that very ubiquity, imperceptible, scattered everywhere but concentrated nowhere. As early as 1840 we find a remarkably shrewd assessment of the subliminal power of the press, in the statement by Robert Montgomery, editor of the *Colonial Magazine*, who said that '[p]eriodical literature is an instrument of vast but almost unseen power'.[6] This is arguably another reason why popular Australian medievalist verse has exerted its stealthy influence and yet has passed beneath the radar of scholarly and cultural recognition. It could seem, then, that gathering a number of these poems into a single chapter skirts dangerously close to turning them into a coherent tradition, and thereby negates the very subliminal nature of their presence in the colonial cultural field. But it is strategically necessary to render them at least temporarily visible as the group that they never actually were, so we can begin to understand their numbers, their significance, and their uniquely diffuse force. Drivel many of them may have been, but they offer us vital insight into the everyday consumption of medievalism in the regularly and widely encountered medium of popular verse.

The fact that so many of these poems were published in popular newspapers is not only a reflection, as Webby has noted, of the status of poetry as a public form in colonial Australia,[7] and of their role in promoting literary cultivation amongst their readers,[8] but also is highly significant for diagnosing both the dissemination and the reception of the Middle Ages in colonial Australia. It suggests the presence of, and participates in constructing, a generalized 'knowingness' about the Middle Ages in Australian readers, built not on deep erudition but on what can be described as a 'general absorption' of medieval commonplaces which creates what Victorian popular culture scholar Peter Bailey has called a 'select conspiracy of meaning' about what the Middle Ages could mean.[9] Despite its apparent superficiality, the allusive portrayal of the Middle Ages made Australian periodical verse an effective vehicle for uniting a readership that Walter E. Houghton has

[6] Quoted in the Introduction of *Periodicals of Queen Victoria's Empire: An Exploration*, ed. by J. Don Vann and Rosemary T. VanArsdel (Toronto: University of Toronto Press, 1996), p. 5.

[7] Elizabeth Webby, *Early Australian Poetry*, p. ix.

[8] Elizabeth Webby, 'Australia', in *Periodicals of Queen Victoria's Empire*, pp. 19–58.

[9] Peter Bailey, *Popular Culture and Performance in the Victorian City* (Cambridge: Cambridge University Press, 1998), p. 137. The phrase 'general absorption' to describe the journalistic mode of reading appeared in 1866 in an English agricultural newspaper and is quoted by Joanne Shattock and Michael Wolff in their Introduction to *The Victorian Periodical Press: Samplings and Soundings*, ed. by Joanne Shattock and Michael Wolff (Toronto: University of Toronto Press/Leicester University Press, 1982), pp. xiii–xix (p. xv).

divided into 'the articulate classes' and 'the common reader'.[10] Those readers who were in possession of greater knowledge could engage with the medievalist allusions in these poems at a deeper level, and enjoy their own sense of distinction in doing so; but for the knowing, rather than erudite, public, the Middle Ages became, to use Bailey's incisive phrase, 'what everybody knows, but which some know better than others'.[11] This is perfectly demonstrated in 'To Molly — A Flirt', a poem written by 'Pagan', one of the pseudonyms of journalist and satirist Adam Cairns McCay (1874–1947) and published in *The Bulletin* on 24 August 1901. This poem takes as its reference point the popular legend surrounding Edward III's formation of the Order of the Garter in 1348, in which Edward defended the Countess of Salisbury's honour by donning her dislodged garter and proclaiming *Honi soit qui mal y pense* (shame be to the one who thinks evil of it). The comic tone with which the poem treats the legend implies an expectation that its audience knows it. And yet it is recounted fully enough that the uninitiated need not be too confused — or, indeed, embarrassed by their ignorance:

> Once, when our first King Edward sat
> An hour apart with some fair lady,
> And no one knew what they were at,
> Well hidden in an arbour shady,
> When they appeared, the courtiers skipped
> All ways at once to hide their laughter,
> For down her knees her hose had slipped
> And Ned himself had donned her garter.
> The gallant monarch saw at once
> The reason of their titillation,
> And '*Honi soit qui mal y pense!*'
> He cried, and saved the situation.

After this historical opening, the poem makes a rather abrupt shift in its later stanzas into a comic, slightly risqué *carpe diem* addressed to contemporary young women, embodied in the eponymous Mollie, urging them to pursue their youthful flirtations ('show your heels to Virtue') before their inevitable decline into maternal frumpiness. If anyone should question their moral lightness, Pagan supplies them, courtesy of Edward III, with the ultimate medievalist riposte: *Honi soit qui mal y pense.* The fact that the famous motto of the Order of the Garter goes untranslated

[10] Walter E. Houghton, 'Periodical Literature and the Articulate Classes', in *The Victorian Periodical Press*, pp. 3–27.

[11] Bailey, *Popular Culture*, p. 128.

again points to its general currency as part of the allusive, 'knowing' idiom of popular nineteenth-century medievalism.

An intriguing and complex visual example of this knowing medievalism can be found in a cartoon by John Henry Chinner published in the Adelaide satirical magazine *Quiz* on 23 March 1890 (Figure 5).

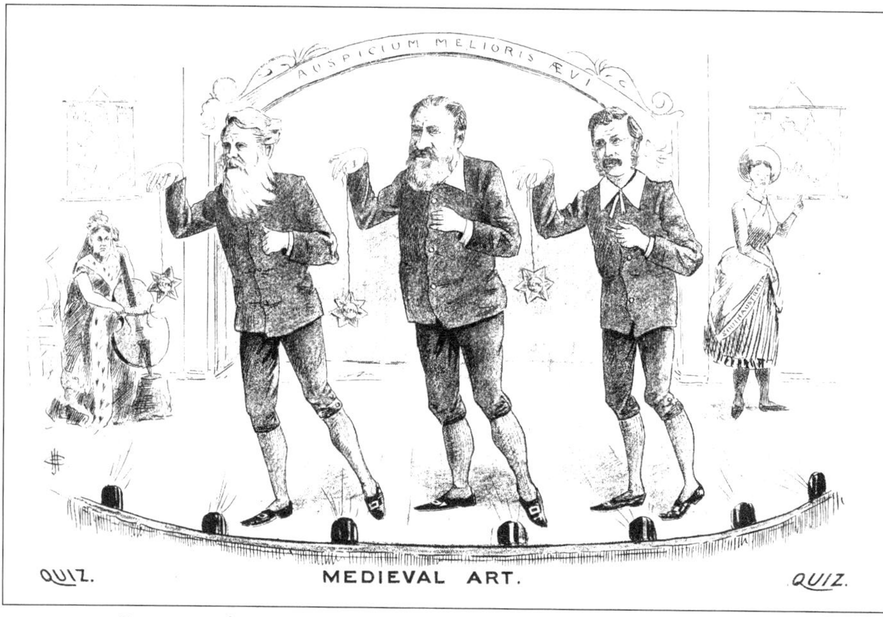


Figure 5. John Henry Chinner, 'Medieval Art', *Quiz*, 23 March 1890.

The Middle Ages is again evoked in relation to the colonial mania for recognition within the English honours system in this cartoon, which lampoons speculation over possible knighthoods for local politicians John Colton, Thomas Playford, and John Alexander Cockburn. Entitled 'Medieval Art', it takes its title from a song in *Patience*, Gilbert and Sullivan's enormously popular satire on Aesthetic medievalism, which had been performed at Adelaide's Theatre Royal by J. C. Williamson's Royal Comic Opera Company. The cartoon, which is modelled closely on a famous image from the operetta's original 1881 D'Oyly Carte production, depicts a stage on which the three politicians, dressed in the tight jackets and breeches associated with medievalist dandyism, stand in awkward 'aesthetic' poses, dangling before themselves badges engraved with 'K.C.M.G', the initials of the Order of St George and St Michael. Behind them on a proscenium arch we see the Order's motto, *auspicium melioris aevi* (token of a better time). On the left of the image is Queen Victoria standing before a map of England, while on the right a young maiden, South Australia, stands before a map of Australia. *Quiz*'s commentary on the image, despite a rather disingenuous denial, clearly associates these men's ornamentalist desire for honours with a ridiculous and effete medievalism, likening it to the 'devotion to a sunflower' that was iconically associated with the Aesthetes. This in turn is associated with colonial sycophancy, as they lean toward Queen Victoria, who 'anxiously await[s] the result of the bauble she has dangled before the trio', and away from South Australia 'in the character of Impatience', who 'angrily awaits the issue of the tomfoolery'.[12] Although Rob van den Hoorn has said of Chinner that 'many of his cartoons presupposed a degree of understanding of the classics, Shakespeare and English history',[13] this densely allusive image appeals rather to its audience's sense of knowingness: its reference to local current affairs demands little knowledge of the three figures' distinct political convictions, while its reference to 'medieval art' requires no direct knowledge at all either of medieval art or indeed of Aesthetic medievalism, only an awareness of how they are mediated through Gilbert and Sullivan's populist satire. Just as the *Sydney Morning Herald* review of the 1881 Australian premier of *Patience* tells us that audiences enjoyed the satire of medievalism, despite the fact that 'the aesthetic craze has not reached the colonies',[14] so too *Quiz*'s readers would not necessarily need anything beyond the generalized smattering of knowledge possessed by the newspaper-reading, 'informed' metropolitan colonial subject. Indeed, the only matter on which the readers are assumed to know any of the finer points is the Order of St George and St Michael, which would suggest that the obsession with knighthoods was not limited to the Melbourne described by Paul de Serville.

Alongside this incidental, 'amnesiac' medievalism, however, was a body of work in which medieval settings and themes were far more thoroughgoing, or at the very least more central to the concerns dealt with in the poems. These more thoroughly medievalist poems are found in collected verse volumes and scattered through the popular press. Among those poets other than Gordon who produced what could

[12] This unilateral satire was, in fact, unfair to Thomas Playford, the middle figure of the trio. Unlike Colton (on the left) and Cockburn (on the right), who were made K.C.M.G. in 1891 and 1900 respectively, Playford 'several times declined the offer of a knighthood'. See John Playford, 'Playford, Thomas (1837–1915)', *Australian Dictionary of Biography*, XI (1988), 245–47.

[13] Rob van den Hoorn, 'Chinner, John Henry (1865–1933)', *Australian Dictionary of Biography*, Supplementary Volume (2005), p. 67.

[14] *Sydney Morning Herald*, 28 November 1881.

be described as a modest medievalist corpus, Fidelia Hill (1790–1854) deserves an honourable mention. Her *Poems and Recollections of the Past* (1840), which is frequently cited as the first collection of poetry by a woman in Australia, contains no fewer than six serious medievalist efforts, which makes her possibly the earliest devoted medievalist, male or female, in Australian poetry. And yet, because of the general neglect of medievalism in Australian verse, this fact has gone unrecorded, even by those few who have written about Hill's work. As with so many other poets, the tendency amongst critics has been to focus on the Australian content in her work, especially her portrayals of the earliest years of white settlement in Adelaide.[15] But this oversight is also due to the neglect of female-authored medievalism that has been discussed in Chapter 2. Hill falls, then, under a double neglect, which it is now time to correct.

Three of Hill's medievalist poems, 'Knights [*sic*] Story', 'The Escape', and 'The Pleasaunce', do not appear in sequence in the volume, but appear to form a loose trilogy tracing the fortunes of a crusading knight and his lady, fair Estelle. Like the prose crusade tales discussed in Chapter 1, which were published in colonial Australian periodicals, these poems are typical specimens of Scott imitation, bearing the clear influence not only of *Ivanhoe* but also of *The Talisman* (1825) and *Count Robert of Paris* (1832). Familiar tropes include hardy Templars, throngs of wily 'paynims', a comely Saracen damsel with her siren-call to miscegenation (who also strongly recalls nineteenth-century depictions of Nicolette, the heroine of the thirteenth-century romance *Aucassin and Nicolette*) and, of course, the obligatory cameo appearance from Richard Coeur de Lion.[16] 'Knights Story' is narrated as a kind of epistle from the knight to lady Estelle, recounting the horrors of the battles in which the sabre-wielding Muslims are defeated by the Christian ranks. 'The Escape', again in the voice of the knight, narrates his escape, with help from the Saracen maiden Jumeli, from Damascus where he is being held prisoner, while 'The Pleasaunce', by far the least derivative of the three, offers a touching vignette in which the now-scarred knight, returned home, frolics with his countess Estelle and his small son in a field of wildflowers. The romantic, rather than antiquarian or

[15] See, for instance, Philip Butterss, 'Fidelia Hill: Finding a Public Voice', in *Southwords: Essays on South Australian Writing*, ed. by Philip Butterss (Kent Town: Wakefield, 1995), pp. 16–26; and Elizabeth Webby, '"Born to Blush Unseen": Some Nineteenth-Century Women Poets', in *A Bright and Fiery Troop: Australian Women Writers of the Nineteenth Century*, ed. by Debra Adelaide (Ringwood, Vic: Penguin, 1988), pp. 41–52.

[16] Fidelia Hill, *Poems and Recollections of the Past* (Sydney: Trood, 1840), pp. 7–10 ('The Knight'), pp. 28–31 ('The Pleasaunce'), and 44–47 ('The Escape').

ideological, impetus of these poems is evident in their unconcerned conflation of places, events, and characters from crusades that were decades apart into the one knight's story, coupled with their decisive foregrounding of the personal drama over concerns such as race, nation, or religion. Although 'Knights Story' and 'The Escape' make liberal use of the Islamophobic jargon typical of nineteenth-century Crusader tales, and 'The Plesaunce' engages in an idealization of Anglo-Scottish chivalry (the knight is called Ruthvyn, and so is presumably Scottish), these larger ideological concerns are mere window-dressing to Hill's central concern, which is the separation of the knight from his beloved.[17] She writes in the wake of Scott, but not with his breadth of canvas, being far more engaged by the sensational potential of separation, battle, imprisonment, escape, and reunion and their effect on the central heterosexual dynamic. While the final reunion of lovers named Ruthvyn and Estelle, and their fusion in the form of their 'beauteous boy', might arguably point to some kind of *Ivanhoe*-esque Scottish-Anglo-Norman accord, and their triangulated bliss evokes the Holy Family, Hill's touch is light, so that both national and Christian triumphalism are, at the very most, muted. Unlike *Ivanhoe,* the epic historical backdrop with which Hill's trilogy begins contracts until it is replaced by the vivid intimacy and artlessness of the field in which the young family romps.

The opening line of another of Hill's medievalist poems, 'Beatrice', in which the narrator tells us that s/he saw the eponymous heroine 'but once', strongly evokes Dante's *La Vita Nuova,* with its celebrated description of the brief encounter between the poet and his inamorata.[18] Given that Hill's poem was written by 1840, the portrait of Beatrice, with its description of 'auburn hair / In rich profusion', can be described as Pre-Raphaelite *avant la lettre,* and is uncannily prescient of Dante Gabriel Rossetti's image of Beatrice in his renowned painting *Beata Beatrix.* Although Hill's Beatrice, like Dante's, marries another and dies young, the poem ends (somewhat disappointingly) on a rather detached note, retreating from personal lamentation into stoic dictum: 'I heard a knell! — crowds with her bier passed by, / Sad type, methought, of man's felicity!'.

Hill's two final forays into medievalism are remarkable for their combination of familiar tropes from romance narrative with arresting expressions of female

[17] The persistent and widespread nineteenth-century interest in the crusades in North America and Britain is documented in Elizabeth Siberry's *The New Crusaders: Images of the Crusades in the Nineteenth and Early Twentieth Centuries* (Aldershot and Burlington, VT: Ashgate, 2000). A more extensive analysis of Hill's poems, in conjunction with the prose fiction discussed in Chapter 1, would offer a valuable supplement to Siberry's trans-Atlantic account.

[18] Hill, *Poems and Recollections,* pp. 49–50.

erotic longing. 'Ellinor's Lament' is a ballad narrated by a forlorn young woman who, in good romance (rather than medieval) fashion, has just learned that Oswald, the peerless knight with whom she has fallen in love, is in fact her half-brother.[19] As Ellinor unfolds her tale, we learn that she is preparing to go on pilgrimage, in pursuit of a cloister; indeed, as she sings she dons her pilgrim's sandals, cloak, and cockle hat. Hill's medievalism here services her instinct for gender and sexual melodrama, as the pilgrimage affords her heroine a means for setting out into the world unchaperoned and essentially cross-dressed. This historical melodrama is intensified by the drama of the heroine's unrepentant love for her half-brother, whom she continues to call her 'mate' despite knowing their love is forbidden. 'The Tournay' is a lengthy verse narrative which recounts, as its title suggests, a fatal stoush between two rival knights, Sir Aylmer and an unnamed rival who, having been dispossessed by Aylmer, foils him doubly by not only unhorsing and slaying him but, further, by stealing the regard of his beloved, the Lady Amoret.[20] For the most part, the poem is a chivalric set-piece, stocked with the predictable cast of peerless damsels and richly accoutred champions, whose battles take place against the received backdrop of pennants and waving kerchiefs. It is, moreover, dotted with Anglo-Normanesque phrases (attendants are 'poursuivants', a bleeding horse is 'lav'd in blood', a daisy is a 'marguerite'), and sprinkled with archaic interjections of a Chaucerian cast ('I ween', 'I trow', 'I wot', 'I wis', 'certes'). What makes the poem most noteworthy is the startlingly erotic female gaze couched within this conventional chivalric tale. Although the poem is narrated in the third person, we are made privy to Lady Amoret's unconcealed desire for the anonymous rival knight, whom she prefers to her suitor Aylmer. We follow as her eyes (and indeed Hill's by proxy) roam all over the 'perfect symmetry' of his virile 'dauntless form', resting finally on his 'blood-red plume [that] does graceful swell', an image whose priapic connotations are difficult to ignore.

A concern with the female perspective within medieval story can also be detected in Ada Cambridge's 1870 verse collection *The Manor House and Other Poems.* Michael Ackland has offered a sensitive reading of the place of Cambridge's early medievalist poems within her larger oeuvre. Ackland traces a persuasive link between Cambridge's scepticism about the entrapment of women in romance narrative and the more general scepticism that emerges in her later work, such as

[19] Hill, *Poems and Recollections*, pp. 24–28 ('Ellinor's Lament').

[20] Hill, *Poems and Recollections*, pp. 51–60 ('The Tournay').

the novels discussed in Chapter 2.[21] Taking up his argument, we can point to a generalized questioning of the Middle Ages in Cambridge's work, which was not limited to gender dynamics but extended to religion, militarism, and the rigidity of the feudal caste system. Given the highly critical stance she would later take in her novels against the delusions of Aesthetic medievalism, this explosion of medievalist gender mythologies does not seem surprising. But what is most striking about Cambridge's seven separate critical depictions of the medieval world is that they are still infected by a nostalgic fascination with the period. In 'The Legend of Lady Gertrude', for instance, it is true that Cambridge condemns the 'fettering' of her Alpine heroine by her possessive brother, the robber-baron Freiherr, and laments the deadly outcome of Gertrude's ill-fated love for a rival knight, who is killed by her brother's forces on the same day he and Gertrude have wed. As Ackland says,

> the medievalism of this tale, far from being escapist, serves to highlight the central attributes of a timeless predicament which enshrines female beauty as an inestimable treasure, yet confers power not on its embodiment but on its male possessor.[22]

Ackland is perceptive in noting how Cambridge's form of medievalism links to her critique of contemporary gender relations. Yet there is no denying, in her portrayal of the poem's dark Teutonic setting, Cambridge's deep aesthetic fascination with the world she is condemning. From its 'castle on the crag' and steep mountain passes to its dragon-crested lover-knight and velvet muzzled hounds, Cambridge's tale is intended to seduce us with its compelling Gothic glamour.[23]

A different kind of tension can be seen in the poems 'The Old Manor House', 'A Story at Dusk', and 'Dead'. Dwelling on the tragedies of characters compelled to marry without love in order to uphold caste, all three poems present this fate as a cruel legacy from the hidebound medieval past. And yet the scenery and characters in both 'The Old Manor House' and 'A Story at Dusk' carry vestiges of the medieval past as a purer, more beauteous age.[24] In 'The Old Manor House' Lady Margaret, as the last surviving descendant of a now-impoverished great Saxon house, is compelled to marry her rich cousin Sir Hildebrand to save her family's crumbling manor, in the process sacrificing the love between herself and the poem's

[21] Ackland, *That Shining Band*, pp. 155–74.

[22] Ackland, *That Shining Band*, p. 165.

[23] Ada Cambridge, *The Manor House and Other Poems* (London: Daldy, Isbister, 1875), pp. 171–97.

[24] Cambridge, *The Manor House*, pp. 1–36 ('The Old Manor House'), 81–101 ('A Story at Dusk'), and 141–46 ('Dead').

narrator, Guy. This sad legacy, however, has also bequeathed her the proud beauty and noble bearing so admired by her lover, as well as the affinity for medieval story; she and Guy read Chaucer and Tennyson's *Idylls* together, the second of these surely also intended to provoke a comparison between them and Lancelot and Guinevere. In 'A Song at Dusk', the unnamed high-born protagonist is induced by the blandishments of the worldly Lady Alice to abandon his peasant beloved Jeanie. Again, though, the poem's indictment of this inherited feudal rigidity is offset by a number of details that point to the Middle Ages as a nobler, purer time. The comforting backdrop of an old Norman church is a symbol of cultural and moral continuity; Jeanie, despite her low station, possesses, rather like Thomas Hardy's Tess, a dignified *je ne sais quoi* that is 'the noble trace of long-forgotten knights'. Conversely, when the lover abandons her for London society, he describes himself as having 'lost the tender chivalry of my love'. 'Dead' is more straightforwardly critical. A kind of feminine partner to 'A Song at Dusk', in it a countess laments the death of Dick, the sailor beloved of her youth whom she left to marry a great Earl. Although this is a modern tale, the medieval legacy of the heroine's loveless marriage is expressed in the costume her husband is wearing to a costumed ball: he is dressed as a knight, with 'plume and crest and linked mediaeval steel'.

In all of these poems the medieval past is woven into the present as a haunting presence. This is explored most conspicuously in 'A Dream of Venice', a dream-vision poem in which the heroine, caught up in the romance of holidaying in Venice, falls asleep and has a lengthy (and meticulously researched) dream in which a pageant of the city's medieval past passes before her.[25] The scenes before the dreamer are opulent, populated by hosts of crusading knights, grand emperors and dukes; but as the dream unfolds, this grand past descends into chaos and violence. When she awakes to the warm domesticity of her young family, both she and we are relieved. Cambridge's later work continues to pursue this course into the modern and the personal (though its path is more agonized than in 'A Dream of Venice'), and the fascination with the medieval retreats.

For sheer volume of output, another later nineteenth-century poet who earns mention as a serious Australian medievalist is the pseudonymous 'Gerontius', the poet featured at the outset of this study. Unlike Hill and Cambridge, who published their poetry as volumes, Gerontius's medium of publication was more typical of Australian medievalist verse, as it is found in two regular columns he wrote for *The Fremantle Herald:* 'Legends of the Kings', and 'Sonnets on Tennyson

[25] Cambridge, *The Manor House*, pp. 37–59 ('A Dream of Venice').

— Ideals'. Ranging less expansively across the spectrum of popular medievalist discourses, Gerontius's repeated excursions into Teutonic and Arthurian mythology in the 'Legends of the Kings' column disclose tastes and ideological preoccupations that were, as we saw in Chapter 1, typical of the imperialist, Christian triumphalism that dominated Anglocentric nineteenth-century medievalism. His 'The Saga of Frithiof', for example, is a wishful pan-Teutonic amalgam in which the eponymous hero of the Icelandic Friðþjof's saga becomes an attendant of the Saxon king Alfred, who also manages to Christianize him. Other Anglo-Saxonist efforts include 'Blynhilda of the Golden Hair', 'Sir Alban of Caerleon', 'Sir Galahad of Ivor', 'The Lady of Camelot', 'Elvira and Edgar'; and 'Walburga of Merlin'. The feature shared by all of these poems is their singular fusion of Arthurian legend and Anglo-Saxon history. In Gerontius's synthetic Old English mythscape, documented historical figures such as the seventh- and eighth-century abbesses Ermengild and Walburga and the seventh-century abbot Alnoth have been blithely imported into the firmly de-Celticized legendary world of Camelot, to the point, in some cases, of being transformed into the offspring of Arthurian characters. This fusion seems to bespeak a desire on the part of this self-identified Australian writer to forge a seamlessly integrated medieval past in which his favourite characters, events, and locales come together in a unified tribute to English greatness and cultural continuity. Compared to these, the 'Sonnets on Tennyson — Ideals', which include such poems as 'Eleanore, Serene, Imperial Eleanore', 'Adeline', and 'Margaret', do not engage our interests to the same degree. Despite the promising title, with its punning reference to the *Idylls of the King*, these sonnets are only diffusely medievalist. The wellspring of their Tennysonian influence seems to be less the Laureate's medievalism than his preoccupation with women in the first four *Idylls*, for the sonnets are, as their titles aver, all woman-worship poems.

More interesting, arguably, than Gerontius's strange but conformist Anglo-Saxon fantasies are the commentaries he offers on them. These give the reader insight into the sources of inspiration for the poet's medievalism, and offer sketchy but revealing glimpses into the local response to his verse, and indeed to medievalist verse more generally. The commentaries attached to 'Sir Alban of Caerleon', 'Blynhilda', and 'Sir Galahad of Ivor', which make liberal reference to Ruskin, Tennyson, Disraeli, and the Arthurian verse of Aubrey de Vere, leave us in no doubt that Gerontius was well versed in the major nineteenth-century medievalist trends, a fact also suggested by his use of Friðþjófs saga, which, according to Andrew Wawn, had been widely popularized in the nineteenth century in the wake of Esaias

Tegnér's 1825 Swedish 'poetic paraphrase' of the saga.[26] Gerontius's commentaries also reveal, however, that this same medievalist erudition led him to a recognition of the interpretive plasticity of medieval stories, which in turn freed him to mould them according to his interests. In his notes to 'Sir Galahad of Ivor', a poem in which he turns the famous virgin of Arthurian tradition into an amorous husband, he admits with rueful humour that even though Tennyson himself had preserved the knight's purity, 'as the poem grew under my hands [...] I felt bound to *fix* Sir Galahad'. This 'fixing' proved so compelling that it spilled over into another poem, 'Elvira and Edgar', which narrates the courting of Sir Galahad's peerlessly beautiful daughter. While it could be that Gerontius's heedless experimentation is attributable, at least in part, to a liberating sense of distance from Old World narrative tradition, it is equally arguable that his sense of license with medieval legend and history emerges precisely out of his assured sense of participating in the long and varying dissemination of these infinitely adaptable tales.

Gerontius's dark insinuations about certain readers' 'complaints', as mentioned in this book's Introduction, suggest that notwithstanding the currency of his poems, they were not unanimously embraced by the *Fremantle Herald*'s readership. The prefatory remarks to 'Sir Alban of Caerleon' are especially telling:

> [The author] is well aware that there are tastes not aesthetic to please, and that there are many who cannot see why our latest poets [...] should 'speculate so largely' (to be practical) in medieval romance and 'old world notions'.

He goes on to refute these critics by arguing that medievalism does offer a 'fresh' and practical view of contemporary affairs, and asserting, in the sentence with which this book's Introduction opened, that it is entirely possible to unite peaceably a rational Australian outlook and a proclivity for ancient song. (Perhaps it was this combination that led him to give the virginal martyr Galahad a happy marriage and prosperous old age). But the cat is out of the bag: Gerontius's defence makes it clear that the voluminous output of 'serious' medievalist verse in colonial Australia should not lead us to make easy assumptions about its popularity with

[26] For discussions of the popularity of Tegnér's Frithiof in Victorian British culture, see Geraldine Barnes, *Viking America: The First Millenium* (Cambridge: Brewer, 2001), p. 177; and Andrew Wawn, *The Vikings and the Victorians: Inventing the Old North in 19th-Century Britain* (Cambridge: Brewer, 2000), pp. 117–41. Wawn mentions that Tegnér's highly praised poem was translated into English no fewer than fifteen times between 1833 and 1914 (p. 121), and he says, '[i]n nineteenth-century Britain Tegnér's Frithiof outshone the Icelandic Friðþjófr, though the two figures were cheerfully confused and conflated by Victorian readers' (p. 122), a point which can arguably also be applied to Gerontius.

readers. Although it is fair to assume that this verse's ubiquity suggests its intelligibility to later nineteenth-century and early twentieth-century readers, it is in many cases easier to know what people were reading, and even how they interpreted it, than to know whether they liked it.

Alongside the more solid oeuvres of Hill, Cambridge, and Gerontius, we find a mass of single poems scattered throughout separate verse collections and the popular press. Picking just a few of the many discovered so far (with many more still to be found), we find, first of all, E. J. Brady's 'On Tapestry', published in *The Bulletin* on 14 July 1910, yet another earnest tale of Crusading glory in which Sir Maurice of Arcady, beloved of Lady Alice and, the 'crow-haired maid' in the castle keep, loses his life in the service of humbling 'Paynim pride'. 'A Roundelay', by 'Leo' in *The Fremantle Herald* (4 January 1868), is a brief trifle about the knight Sir Guy de Vare, who, presumed dead, is returning home from war to claim Lady Clare as his bride. The poem by 'Burke', 'Sir Hope and the Black Horsemen', in *The Queenslander* (6 March 1880), is an eight-stanza chivalric allegory that gallops through a series of tried and tested chivalric motifs (harness bright, dusky charger, lowered visor), only to surrender its hero Sir Hope to death at the hands of Despair (and his two attendants, both named Doubt). The unattributed poem 'The Toast', also in that rich resource *The Fremantle Herald*, is pattern-book chivalric banquet scene with knights pledging toasts to their 'ladyes' until its last line, where the woman whose face is graven on the heart of Sir Leon 'the flower of chivalry' turns out to be his mother.

Despite their individual variations, what is most noteworthy about these 'serious' medievalist poems as a group is that as stand-alone pieces there is very little, or in most cases nothing, in them that indicates their Australian provenance. It is true that their immediate contexts are highly localized. Hill's chivalric verses, for instance, are flanked by antipodean-themed poems such as 'Adelaide' and 'Recollections', which opens with the lines 'Yes, South Australia! Three years have elapsed / Of dreary banishment, since I became / in thee a sojourner' (p. 64), while Gerontius's work is surrounded by local news items and advertisements for local businesses. But far from 'localizing' the poems, these contexts only serve to highlight the extent to which these poets appear to subscribe to the notion of medievalism as a poetic *lingua franca* that offers access to a universal imaginative heritage.

In a tradition quite different from these non-specific poems, other medievalist verse produced in nineteenth-century Australia captures our attention for its reflective awareness of what medieval scholars over the past thirty years have come to call 'the alterity of the Middle Ages' — that is, its status as an era irreducibly different from the Australian present.[27] These 'alterist' poems appear to fall into two categories: those that nostalgically lament the passing of a more beauteous and courteous age, and those whose celebrations of modernity form a kind of collective obituary to the Old World and its feudal order. But these categories are far from discrete, for in the midst of seemingly nostalgic poems we repeatedly find surprising breakaway moments of modernity, while poems apparently devoted to ridiculing the Middle Ages in fact disclose a keen respect for this era and the nobility of its lost traditions.

Of the poems written in the register of nostalgia, we find that chivalry, as a code of moral values and, especially, as a model for heterosexual relations, is again a dominant motif. Of course, as Mark Girouard and others have shown, this is hardly remarkable, for the revival of chivalry as a model for nineteenth-century masculinity was ubiquitous throughout Europe and the British Empire.[28] Many of these poems appear to have been written in response to more general cultural debates around the impact of modernity on society, with the two main emphases 'the death of romance', that is, the loss of social cohesion and heroic ideals in the wake of industrialization and urbanization, and 'the death of chivalry', that is, the changing dynamics between men and women, a debate conducted under the star of the modern 'death of chivalry'. Few poems are as straightforwardly nostalgic as 'Netley Abbey', by G. F. A., in *The Adelaide Observer* 24 February 1844. Contemplating the 'crumbling pile' and 'ruined aisle' of the ancient English abbey, the reader is left in no doubt that the 'echoing minstrelsy' and 'tinted pane' that once adorned the abbey have gone forever, leaving only a void where 'thought may brood, and drink its pensive fill'. While moonlit nostalgic contemplation is

[27] Although the concept of 'medieval alterity' been analysed critically since the early 1970s in the work of Paul Zumthor and Peter Haidu, the landmark moment in the scholarly debate around the 'alterity' or 'modernity' of the Middle Ages was the 1979 'Medieval Literature and Contemporary Theory' issue of the journal *New Literary History* (vol. 10.2) and the 1997 revisitation of this topic in the same journal. The most famous defender of medieval alterity in this debate was Hans Robert Jauss, in 'The Alterity and Modernity of Medieval Literature' (pp. 181–229), while the most prominent critic was Zumthor, in 'Comments on H. R. Jauss's Article' (pp. 367–76). This issue continues to re-emerge regularly within medieval studies.

[28] Mark Girouard's *The Return to Camelot: Chivalry and the English Gentleman* (New Haven: Yale University Press, 1981) is the classic study on this, and is handsomely illustrated with nineteenth-century examples. In recent years there have also been more searching and critical studies of medievalism's role in developing modern military masculinities. See, for instance, Allen J. Frantzen, *Bloody Good: Chivalry, Sacrifice, and the Great War* (Chicago: University of Chicago Press, 2004).

presented as a genuine pleasure, it is conditional upon acknowledging that the past is irretrievable. Another unambiguously nostalgic poem, awash with chivalric cliché — plumèd knight, trusty sword, armour bright — is 'Romance' by 'L. D.' (possibly Alice Werner) in *The Bulletin*, 15 August 1885. Having evoked in its first stanza a world of 'castles and maidens forlorn' and 'chivalry and courtly ways', the poem goes on to lament the irredeemable loss of this world, which 'Ages ago [...] faded out and died'. The impossibility of romance's survival is underlined by the erosion of the lively opening tournament scene into a Gothic ruin by the poem's end:

> Gates of a spectral hall open wide;
> Deserted is the court, empty the stall;
> Mould'ring in silence in the ghostly hall
> Banner and lance and shield rest side by side.

The nostalgia in this melancholy poem is not coupled with any attempt to reanimate the spirit of nostalgia in the present. In this respect it is atypical of the nostalgic impulse that is characteristic of much colonial verse, which sought either to recreate the values of the medieval past in some way or to discover their unexpected continuation into the present. A response to L. D.'s poem, while not necessarily directed at it specifically, can be found in a later poem of the same name by Victor Daley. 'Romance', published in *The Bulletin* on 13 December 1902, takes up the cudgels against those 'fools supreme' who have pronounced Romance dead, by offering a series of touching scenes that reveal Romance's survival in a modern, urban Australia dominated by industry, progress, and 'iron-handed circumstance'. Significantly, however, in Daley's poem it is the world of medieval legend that is ultimately presented as the quintessential domain of Romance; but it is an accessible domain, a 'green and pleasant' sanctuary where refugees fleeing the pressures of modernity can rub shoulders with a motley cast of characters drawn from Celtic, English, and European legend:

> There you will see brave company, all making gay and gallant cheer,
> Blanaid the Fair, and Deirdri rare, and gold Gudrun, and Guinevere;
> And Merlin wise, with dreaming eyes, and Tristam of the Harp and Bow,
> While from the wood of Broceliande the horns of Elfland bravely blow.

Although here, as in L. D.'s poem, romance is firmly located in the world of chivalric legend, a crucial difference is that it is nevertheless retrievable in the Australian present, if only in the imagination of the nostalgic modern subject.

Daley (this time writing as Creeve Roe) also figures in the poetic debate on the apparent death of chivalry. In a brief editorial written above his poem 'Chivalry' in *The Bulletin* on 15 September 1904, he states:

> Many letters have appeared in the papers lately mourning over the alleged decease of Chivalry. The writers (women mostly) complain that men are losing their old-time reverence for the sex. They also say that the males of these degenerate days might as well be made of galvanized iron for all the romance in them.

Daley's poem, addressed to 'Woman', argues in defence of chivalric spirit nestled deep within the apparently taciturn Australian male, who is embodied in the uncouth but well-meaning figure of 'Plugger Bill':

> What if he could not rhyme his sighs?
> What if he could not sing a note?
> The sonnet shining in his eyes
> Is worth all Petrarch ever wrote.

Again we recognize in this poem a double move, both toward, and away from nostalgic reclamation. On the one hand it asserts that the essence of romance and chivalric woman-worship, epitomized in the sonnets of Petrarch, survives intact in the apparently romance-free soul of the Australian male. On the other hand, the mute, gruff devotion celebrated in this poem supersedes the devalued wordiness of the Petrarchan tradition as the new antipodean model for chivalry. Conversely, while Daley admits that mature men understand that women are not the 'angel-avatar' of chivalric tradition, the poem nonetheless exhorts them to go along with the fantasy: 'try to be, some day, / What younger men believe you are' — a plea that ultimately brings the poem into conformity with the dominant nostalgic celebration of the Old World gender dynamics of chivalry in which the pure, helpless damsel relies on superior masculine strength.

Daley's attempt to reinstate romantic and chivalric values in the present is more characteristic of the treatment of this theme in early Australian popular verse. In a similar gesture, E. J. Brady's 'Knights of Chance', published on 26 May 1900 as part of *The Bulletin*'s 'Bards of the Back Blocks' series, models the figure of the contemporary bushman, roaming the countryside and working at will, on the figure of the knight-errant. In looking forward to a future time of workers' emancipation, the poem is firmly rooted in the nineteenth-century Socialist-oriented nostalgic medievalism associated with William Morris and his followers, which is renowned for its criticism of the loss of community and the alienation of workers under modern industrial capitalism.[29] Opening on a romantic anti-urban, anti-industrial

[29] This is epitomized in the futuristic medievalism of Morris's 1890 utopian novel *News from Nowhere*. Morris's ideas, in *The Commonweal* and particularly in *News from Nowhere*, were well known and influential for the Australian labour movement. See B. Mansfield, 'The Socialism of William Morris: England and Australia', *Historical Studies*, 7 (1956), 271–90. Brady read *News*

note, Brady's poem goes on to advocate an adventuring life in which the worker, having turned his back on the alienation of capitalist enslavement, can reclaim the lost liberality of spirit enjoyed by the rural elite of the Middle Ages:

We shall be lords and masters, we shall be Knights of Chance,
Barons of Bold Adventure, Kings of the stout free lance,
Ours are the unwalled waters, ours are the Westlands wide,
Rovers and rovers ever, sons of the Outer-Side.

This stanza's conspicuous inversions of rank — the swagman is likened to a lord, a knight, a baron, a king — nostalgically evokes the spiritual sovereignty of the medieval noble castes, but, importantly, divests them of their manors. So here it is the landless swagman, not Boldrewood's squatter with his broad acres, who is the true inheritor of medieval nobility, embodied in the freelance knight rather than the landed aristocrat.

'On Keira', also by Brady (in *The Bulletin* 16 June 1910), offers another complex example of the operation of nostalgia. A kind of inversion of Keats's *La belle Dame Sans Merci*, it is a semi-allegorical ballad in which Youth, 'a callow knight untried, / With golden spurs to win', rejects the siren call of Love in order to pursue Gold and Praise. It is hard not to be amused by the risible image of the youth riding 'bright in armor' along the crest of the Illawarra escarpment south of Sydney; but this detail seems tame compared to the bizarre figure of Love, who is part-medieval 'maiden of old fairyland' and part-indigenous Spirit of Place calling her beloved back to the 'bush infinities' of Mount Keira near Wollongong. Brady's medievalist nostalgia lies primarily in his use of linguistic and poetic convention of a Tennysonian cast: when the youth rejects the maiden, he has 'scorned the guerdon he had won'; when the sun comes out, it is 'like an earl [...] flaunt[ing] his banner brave'. Yet the poem is most distinctive for its unapologetic insertion of the chivalric into the local and the local into the chivalric, although it is also true that this is also the source of much of poem's unintended humour. The image of the knight galloping through the Illawarra asserts this region's claim to old-style romance, as does the poem's localization of the medieval blazon, which boldly replaces the similes of the English/European romance tradition with images taken from the local environment:

Oh, whiter than the surf was she
That breaks those coasts along,
And redder by the coral tree
That grows by Gerringong;

*from Nowhere* as early as 1890: see Bruce Scates, *A New Australia: Citizenship, Radicalism and the First Republic* (Cambridge: Cambridge University Press, 1997).

> And graceful as the springing palm
> On Illawarra hills;
> And sweeter than the meadow balm
> By cool Shoalhaven rills.

Its borderline absurdity notwithstanding, the poem's peculiar ingenuity lies in the fine balance it strikes between nostalgic preservation and local innovation. With its lost-love tale likened to those 'by primal poets sung', and its setting on the ancient peak of Mount Keira, the poem inserts itself into deep natural and poetic time, and yet the very incongruity of this combination marks its departure from poetic tradition.

In a related but distinct strain of Australian popular verse, we find many other poems that were scathingly critical of the Middle Ages. Much of this poetry adopted a speaking position that is not just overtly, but indeed defiantly, Australian, in that it articulated a definitive severance from those values regarded as Old World. Central to James Edmond's verse polemic 'The Drivel of our Fathers', published in *The Bulletin* on 15 September 1888, is the charge that British imperial force is buttressed by the dissemination of medieval heroic legend. In his caustic evocation of such figures as 'warriors who skedaddled', 'the saints who liquored for their faith', and 'Vikings who were sick upon the waves', Edmond appeals to his readership to condemn this absurd mythology and the corrupt ideology it serves. And he was not alone in this. 'The Sagamen', by 'Prospect Good' (a.k.a. Francis William Ophel), while less vituperative in tone and less overtly anti-imperialist in stance, also questions the fabrications at the heart of the Viking mythology so beloved of imperialists, and suggests that the sagas were essentially 'songs of swords' buried beneath an avalanche of fantastical and distracting details: witches, trolls, Valkyries, runes, haunted cairns, flaxen-haired maidens, fjords, and so on. This poem's purpose differs subtly from Edmond's in that it does not so much set out to ridicule Teutonic mythology (indeed Ophel's recitation of what he identifies as the sagas' standard tropes suggests a long history of enjoying them), as to suggest that the impulse to turn violent history into heroic myth continues into the present:

> The skalds of ancient Iceland
> With many words made play
> Peopled with witch and warrior,
> Fjord and scarp and bay,
> And faith, our modern sagas
> Vie with these songs of swords,
> The naked truth is hidden
> Beneath a web of words.

Without saying it directly, the poem implies, in quiet agreement with Edmond, that this mythologizing impulse is strongest in those who have the greatest stake in creating 'modern sagas' out of the bloody *Realpolitik* of imperial conquest. As we have seen in Chapter 1, it was these same people who also happened to be the most enthusiastic devotees of the myth of Anglo-Teutonic destiny.

It is not surprising, given its anti-imperialist temper, that *The Bulletin* published so many of the poems in which the Middle Ages were represented as despotic and barbaric. Feudalism in these poems was a byword for the inequality and oppression of the Old World that Australia must leave behind. W. E. Carew's thunderous 'Federation — 'Under the Crown: (A Battle Hymn)', published on 14 July 1894, is a strong case in point. The poem's immediate target is the unwelcome prospect of Imperial Federation, the political model in which the united Australian colonies would be federated with other former colonies under English rule. The poem, with its clearly nationalist position, rejects this model as an imperialist threat to Australian political autonomy, attempting to incense its readers with the feudal image of an Imperial Federated leadership made up of 'mimic Court and king', 'knighted leaders', and a 'titled host'. This is presented not just as political interference but as an assault on the democratic spirit of Australia, an attempt to impose the 'outworn lie' of the English caste system in a new land where it is widely known that 'that a man is king and noble by the accident of birth'. Rousing its readers to take 'axe in hand', an image which calls up the ghost of pre-modern warfare, the poem calls upon them to be martyrs to independent Australian nationhood. Another prime example of workingman's anti-feudalism can be found in 'The Rule of the Many' by 'A. X. C.', which appeared on 20 December 1890. After its robust proclamation that 'the rule of the feudal despot's dead in the world's new onward swing' it goes on to call for a new, democratic regime: '[a]way with the past, with its king and its caste! / The people must be supreme'. Turning then to address 'lords', the poet again celebrates the decay of feudalism, which is presented as a dead tree, from which the withering depots hang like 'rotten limbs [...] swung on the gale with the fungus of feudal years'.

Surprisingly, Henry Lawson, much better known for his work's realist Australian settings, also wrote a number of poems set in the Middle Ages. But the strongly anti-medieval sentiment in these poems, which expose the hollowness of courtly love and chivalric *noblesse oblige*, means that they are at home in his larger realist oeuvre. 'As it is in the Days of Now' published in *The Bulletin* on 12 March 1908, is an anti-nostalgic demystification of chivalric heroism, recounting the cuckolding of the naïve crusading knight Sir William by his mistress and his best friend, with the guilty complicity of all around him, including the narrator, a knight who was Sir William's former page. The poem's reference to the crusades as unholy and brutal is matched by its depiction of courtly love and chivalric bonds as treacherous, loveless, and cowardly. Lawson's refusal of medievalist nostalgia is summed up in the poem's chorus, which presents the chivalric age as a counterpart of the self-interested present: 'For love or honor or faith or gold / For good or for evil, I trow — / It was in men's hearts in the days of old / As it is in the days of now'. A number of the same characters from this poem reappear in 'The Old Squire', which was published in *The Bulletin* the same year on 28 May. In this poem, Swithin, the aged squire of Sir William, who has long been overlooked for a knighthood, accompanies his master into a town gripped by the black death, where he dies rescuing a plague-ridden child. While he finally receives his long-overdue knighthood (not from his ungrateful Lord, but from the king), it comes too late: he has just perished from his heroic efforts. This poem is distinct insofar as it does not offer overt anti-medieval commentary; but its tale of faithful service unrewarded implicitly condemns aristocratic arrogance and the entrenched inequity of the feudal system.

A more affectionate adieu to the medieval past can be found in Mary Hannay Foott's 'The Future of Australia'. She admits that '[w]e love the legends of olden days', a category which includes not only 'border tales and minstrel lays', but also

> The fireside carols and battle rhymes,
> And romaunt of the knightly ring;
> And chant with hint of cathedral chimes,
> Of him 'made blind to sing'.[30]

Yet she goes on soon after to make an explicit appeal to Australians to supplant these Old World heroic mythologies with others that have greater local meaning:

> The Past is past — with all its pride–
> And its ways are not our ways,
> We watch the flow of a fresher tide
> And the dawn of newer days.

Exhorting 'Sing us the Isle of the Southern Seas', she spends the rest of her poem doing just that, extolling the bounty, equality, and prosperity enjoyed by the 'Old World's outcast starvelings' in the new land. Foott would again take up her own call for the writing of Australian epic. 'The Australiad', written in 1884, is an ambitious attempt to place its celebration of white Australian pioneering history (the only

[30] Mary Hannay Foott, *Where the Pelican Builds and Other Poems* (Brisbane: Gordon and Gotch, 1885), pp. 13–15.

mention of indigenous Australians is a single metonymic reference to 'savage spears') within a paean to the universal quest for liberty in recent world history. But the poem's celebration of liberty as an attribute of modernity leads it into some rather muddled ideological commitments and historical representations. Its allusion to the 1872 uprising in Paris, for instance, celebrates the Communards' smashing of 'the fetters of the Feudal Age' and 'the vile Bastille' yet represents contemporary France as 'ill-fortuned'. Similarly, its commentary on Ireland's place in the British Empire acknowledges a history of cruelty reaching back to the twelfth-century Anglo-Norman invasions of Ireland ('Strongbow's arrow rankled long within her wounded heart') and yet seems obliquely to applaud British-Irish union. The poem is consistent, however, in making the Middle Ages synonymous with the oppression and cruelty found in 'each distressful page' of history, a history that can be surpassed by the utopian future being built in Australia.[31]

The tone of these anti-medieval poems was, as we have seen, either deeply aggrieved at the injustices of the past or rousingly optimistic about the antipodean future. But there was another, more satirical, strand of popular anti-medievalism whose dominant note was far less earnest. Of these only a few representative samples can be mentioned here. In *The Bulletin* on 16 May 1885 we find 'Lays of Contemporary Chivalry', in which two knights Sir Peblar de Bart and Sir Jago Phipp, vie, along with the gallants Lord Golfo McGuff, Sir Perryman Pym, and the Marquise of Manganese, for the hand of Lady Podophylline Musa Miggs, the daughter of 'The Baron of Potts Point'. It is difficult to grasp the point of the poem's nebulous and rather silly narrative (the suitors plot to kidnap the father; he finds out and dispatches them to Antarctica; the daughter marries a coachman); but certain separate details point to a two-pronged satire. Its portrayal of competing suitors and a single remote lady clearly lampoons courtly convention, while its wildly incongruous names, combining ancient peerage with colonial new money (the Marquise of Manganese being the most extreme), pokes fun at the dubious pedigrees and social pretensions of wealthy colonial parvenus. Daley's 'Alfred and Adalgisa' (19 March 1887), a sort of predecessor to 'Correggio Jones', takes its satirical knife to the current taste for romance narrative conventions, with its central drama revolving around the staple romance feature of two babies switched at birth. It is set in present-day Australia, but the mock-medieval names of its lovers clearly point to the popular borrowing of medieval motifs in post-Scottian romance fiction, as well as to the mythic settings of popular opera (Daley's audience would have recognized Adalgisa's name as that of the druidical priestess in Bellini's *Norma*).

[31] Foott, *Where the Pelican Builds*, pp. 38–43.

On a related theme, Gerontius's 'The pathetic story of Heloise and Abelard. After "Beranger"' satirizes the popular sentimental attachment to medieval history, epitomized in the fetishization of the legendary twelfth-century lovers Abelard and Heloise. This poem is not simply a surprising departure from Gerontius's usual ponderous fare but in fact is a flaying (though, it must be said, not very funny) satire of the historical impulse that informs his own verse, a fact he himself appears to acknowledge in his self-satirizing column title: 'Some More Legends (not of the Kings, but very respectably connected)'. Set in Paris's Père Lachaise cemetery, the poem's narrative frame presents vulgar scenes of what we would today call heritage tourism, in which flocks of hysterical female visitors weep over the medieval lovers' memorial. Its middle stanzas offer a rather lame satire of the lovers' relationship that is remarkable only for its intense discomfort on the subject of Abelard's castration at the hands of Heloise's uncle Fulbert; this is represented in the deeply baffling line '*Cher oncle*'s grief; ring scandal, dong dell!'. After this the poem returns to its main target, the 'weeping damsels screw[ing] a tear' over 'that strangely hallowed tomb'. The scattergun quality of the poem's satire is continued into its commentary, which aligns this medievalist vanity with local instances of misplaced charity: 'One has as little patience with the fashionable craze for *historical sympathies* as one has with 'Top Boot and Blanket Associations for the South Sea Islanders'. Opining that '*sympathy* like charity begins at home', Gerontius seems momentarily to have sided with his critics, suggesting that Australians should not have any truck with this dusty and irrelevant past. Equally curious is the fact that after so roundly exposing the folly of sentimental medievalism, he went on unperturbed in his production of sentimental medievalist verse. Perhaps by equating medievalist 'historical sympathies' with femininity and hysteria he was able to distance himself from the implications of his own satire.

A perusal of colonial dailies and periodicals from the late nineteenth century also discloses the frequent use of medievalist verse as a vehicle for political satire. Of the available medievalist discourses, the one we find most commonly brought into the service of political satire is chivalry. Throughout the colonial press we find local politicians and other prominent (almost always male) citizens presented as knightly aspirants engaged in battle. 'Ye Civic Fytte', in the Adelaide journal *The Lantern*, 17 January 1885, in which 'fytte' is used punningly to denote both the poem's form and the aggressive and unseemly style of parliamentary and public debate that it is satirizing. Ironic recommendations that the Adelaide councillors should wear 'tights' and deliver 'flowery speeches' marks their decline from the courteous exchanges of their more chivalric predecessors, a point reinforced in the lines

> The shades of former Councillors
> Shall rush to see the fun;
> For that table was their field of fame,
> Where many a fight was won.

The reference to the Council chamber as a 'field of fame' evokes a former era when civic politics were conducted according to the genteel rules of the knightly tournament, with clear victors and losers, unlike the indecorous, interminable, and inconclusive 'squabbles' of contemporary Council meetings. The poem's haphazard ransacking of Middle English is evident in the inconsistent usage of the word 'ye'. In the title, it is a Middle English-esque definite article in which the 'th' is represented as a 'y' ('Ye Civic Fytte'), but elsewhere it appears as the second-person plural, as in 'Ye rowdy Councillors'. Although clearly motivated by current local politics, this poem's object is reasonably non-specific. For the most part, however, these poems were highly topical in their allusions, referring to events such as court cases, political debates, and public events. Thus the point of their satire has generally been blunted by time and can only, in many cases, be recovered through a dogged chasing-down and contextualization of the names and events to which they obliquely allude. For instance, in *The Bulletin* on 13 March 1880 we find the anonymous poem 'Light Verses'. This satire takes as its subject the recent inauguration of the construction work for the new Macquarie lighthouse, on the South Head of Port Jackson (Sydney Harbour):

> Two knights one day last week assistance lent
> To lay the stone, on which to found the lights
> To lighten Gentiles o'er the vast extent
> Of Jackson's waters through the dusky nights.
> [...]
> Once they were foes, their sharp lances lifted,
> They tilted — each strove to draw his foe's blood.
> Front is now changed, position is shifted,
> They bleed the poor public, for public good.
> [...]
> 'Let there be light', and prompt was the reply
> Sir 'Enery said it, all on him rely,
> He would his promise sacredly fulfill–
> All should be *light*, except the *heavy* bill.

The figure it lampoons with the faux-knightly moniker 'Sir 'Enery' is Sir Henry Parkes, elder statesman of New South Wales politics and, as discussed in Chapter 1, emerging figurehead of the Australian Federation movement. The evocation of the tournament in this poem is less flattering than in 'Ye Civic Fytte' as an analogy for politicians' conduct, for the emphasis here is on the tournament (and hence the parliament) as merely a spectacle of chivalric combat, a kind of theatre sport, rather than an expression of genuine antagonism between opponents. The poem not only represents as opportunistic and self-serving the alliance Parkes has struck with his unnamed former 'foe' (presumably Sir John Robertson, dubbed 'the Knight of Clovelly' by the Sydney press, with whom Parkes had recently formed a coalition cabinet), but also implies, via its tilting metaphor, that perhaps their longstanding rivalry had been little more than theatre.[32] Another *Sydney Punch* poem from twenty-four years earlier (25 August 1866) demonstrates the tenacity and serviceability of this metaphor for satirizing public affairs. 'Sir Pot and Sir Kettle', as a humorous commentary printed above it explains, satirizes one of the many libel court cases involving Sydney politician and barrister David Buchanan. The courtroom is described, with chivalric cliché, as 'the open lists', and Buchanan as 'the Fenian knight', the presiding Judge Sir Alfred Stephens is 'fair lady Alfreda', the tournament's Queen of Beauty, and the prosecution and defence lawyers are squires. The technical victory goes to Sir Kettle, but after this Lady Alfreda 'gives equal guerdon' to the two knights, just as, in life, Buchanan won the case but was awarded negligible damages.[33]

This poem is noteworthy for being accompanied by a cartoon by the satirical illustrator Eugene Montagu ('Monty') Scott, entitled 'The Grand Pot and Kettle Tournament' (Figure 6).

The image combines a whole array of standard medievalist tropes with satiric idiosyncrasies, such as a squire rushing a bottle of beer or wine to the notoriously hard-drinking Buchanan. This conjunction of text and image reminds us of the importance of understanding these medievalist poems' relationship to what Julie Codell has described as the 'visuality' of the Victorian illustrated periodical as a medium of satire,[34] a point developed extensively in Marguerite Mahood's study *The Loaded Line: Australian Political Caricature 1788–1901*. Although Mahood does not single out medievalism as a visual idiom of satire, it certainly falls into the category she describes as 'allegorical satire'. The satiric mechanism of allegorical caricature, according to Mahood's succinct formulation, is that it 'brings the

[32] See A. W. Martin, 'Parkes, Sir Henry (1815–1896)', *Australian Dictionary of Biography*, V (1974), 399–406; and Bede Nairn, 'Robertson, Sir John (1816–1891)', *Australian Dictionary of Biography*, VI (1976), 38–46.

[33] See Martha Rutledge, 'Buchanan, David (1823?–1890)', *Australian Dictionary of Biography*, III (1969), 281–83.

[34] Julie Codell, 'Imperial Difference and Culture Clashes in Victorian Periodicals' Visuals: The Case of *Punch*', *Victorian Periodicals Review*, 39 (2006), 410–28.

Figure 6. Eugene Montagu ('Monty') Scott, 'The Grand Pot and Kettle Tournament', *Sydney Punch*, 25 August 1866.

magniloquence of legend, mythology, and history to a prosaic subject'.[35] And so it is with a profusion of satirical medievalist images found in the periodical press across the Australian colonies. Speaking of the waning use of classical allegory in political cartoons, Mahood argues:

> When, in the later years of the nineteenth century an Australian-born population, locally educated and concerned since childhood with material affairs, made up the greater proportion of the readership of illustrated colonial papers, the classical allegory grew rare. The politician was no longer Hercules with club and lion-skin, but a shearer collaring a refractory sheep, a grazier with a scabby run, or a miner disputing a claim with a rival politician — experiences which meant something to the new colonial generation.[36]

This observation cannot be extended to medievalist allegory. There were, it is true, periods of concentration — the Sydney press of the 1860s and 1870s, for instance, reflected Monty Scott's particular predilection for the joust as a metaphor — but over and over again, from publications throughout the entire second half of the nineteenth century and into the first decade of the twentieth, we continue to find

[35] Marguerite Mahood, *The Loaded Line: Australian Political Caricature 1788–1901* (Carlton: Melbourne University Press, 1973), p. 9.

[36] Mahood, *The Loaded Line*, p. 10.

images in which colonial public affairs and colonial politicians are presented as knights doing battle. Some, such as Scott's, are more specific in their reference, but others, such as Chinner's 'Both Determined' in *Quiz* (Figure 7), are broader in the scope of their social commentary. As a kind of subgenre of pictorial chivalric satire, the image that without argument was used most prolifically was that of St George slaying the dragon. The very icon of Victorian Anglophilic muscular Christianity, George was, as Andrew Lynch has recently demonstrated, ubiquitous in nineteenth-century Australia both within and beyond the colonial press.[37] Of the myriad of satirical uses to which this image was put, we can point again to political commentary (as just one example, see Figure 8), commentary on matters of public morality, and caricatures of the relationship between England and the colonial press, such as Scott's image of the editor of the Melbourne *Argus*, Edward Wilson, in which the dragon has been converted into 'the British lion' (Figure 9).

Figure 7. John Henry Chinner, 'Both Determined', *Quiz*, 12 September 1890.

[37] Andrew Lynch, '"Thingless Names"? The St George Legend in Australia', *The La Trobe Journal*, 81 (2008), 40–52.

Figure 8. John Henry Chinner, 'The Last of the Book Fiends', *Quiz*, 20 February 1891.

Figure 9. Eugene Montagu ('Monty') Scott, 'Awful Attack upon the British Lion', *Melbourne Punch*, 8 September 1864.

One of the best demonstrations of the symbiosis between the literary and the pictorial in medievalist satire can be found in the *Illustrated Sydney News*'s genuinely funny medievalist-Gothic confection, 'Ye Dolefule Ballade of Ye Vampyre & Ye Rayle to Wollongonge' (Figure 10).

Figure 10. Unknown artist, 'Ye Dolefule Ballade of Ye Vampyre & Ye Rayle to Wollongonge', *Illustrated Sydney News*, 24 June 1876.

As the title suggests, this poem's twelve sham-Middle English couplets and their accompanying cartoons narrate various politicians' unsuccessful attempts to lobby for an extension of the Sydney metropolitan rail network south to the coal-rich Illawarra region. Along with a range of New South Wales public figures, Henry Parkes, who was Premier at the time, again features as an object of satire, this time being described devilishly as 'Olde Harry' and portrayed as the 'vampyre' of the title, an image which at first seems mystifying, but is perhaps explained by the fact that Parkes, like the undead fiend that had taken nineteenth-century popular fiction by storm, had recently experienced yet another of his many career resurrections. Alternatively, Parkes's much-lampooned tendency to generate debt in the New South Wales treasury (recall that 'Light Verses' refers to him as 'bleed[ing] the poor public') might have been the inspiration of the image of him as a blood-sucking monster, although in the early 1870s the colony's coffers were uncustomarily full. The satire is dependent upon the relationship between the verbal and the visual, with the cartoons supplying explicitly what the mock-serious narrative voice omits. For instance, drawing on the popular ridicule of colonial heraldic ambitions, a number of seemingly earnest couplets are accompanied by images of local politicians with mock coats-of-arms that reflect their greedy natures. Plate VI is a perfect example of this. Couching a reference to Sir Thomas Dibbs, the then-manager of the Commercial Banking Company of Sydney, in creditable faux-Middle English, 'Thenne Dybbes, ye Croesus of ye Northe, / Doe teare hys shyrte and make hym wrothe', it then overlays the text with an image of Dibbs in front of a crest of arms embellished with devices of grasping hands and the words 'I WANT *ALLE*'. As with the poems and images discussed earlier, this image trades absolutely in the currency of knowingness, but is nevertheless extremely witty and penetrating in its gathering together of current affairs with the linguistic and visual tropes of medievalism.

What are we to make of the seemingly irreverent and even debasing use made of the Middle Ages in these poems and images? Do they, like the anti-feudal poems of *The Bulletin*, reflect a view that this period and those who clung to it were ridiculous and irrelevant in the context of colonial modernity? Codell's summary of the irreverent use of high art in the satirical images of London's *Punch* can be adapted virtually wholesale to our purposes here: 'they rudely take art [or the medieval period] off its pedestal and put it among the flotsam of current events motivated by social forces and power struggles in the realm of banality, chaos, momentary focus, and shifting worth'.[38] However, Codell's conclusions about the satiric mechanism of the London images cannot be readily extended to the

[38] Codell, 'Imperial Difference and Culture Clashes', pp. 423–24.

medievalism of their colonial counterparts. Her claim that *Punch*'s cartoons 'carnivalized the art world, turning high art into low humor, puns, and parody, while displaying the magazine's own knowledge of high art, and hailing readers as able to recognize the multiple dynamics of these allusions'[39] rightly recognizes the images' concessions both to knowledge and to its poor cousin, knowingness. But as attractive as the idea might be that these images playfully inverted high and low culture, much of the satiric medievalism in the Australian colonial press, despite initial appearances, preserved rather than deflated the gravitas of medieval chivalric culture. This gesture of preservation sprang principally out of their heavy and deliberate reliance on bathos, the mock-heroic technique famously described by Alexander Pope in which the very high (the idiom of chivalric honour) is brought into contact with the very low (the grubby world of colonial politics), with the intention that the incongruity should highlight the indignity of the low.[40] In order for these medievalist satires to expose the pettiness, pomposity, and corruption of the contemporary figures and situations being critiqued, they needed to maintain by contrast the dignity of medieval chivalry, medieval language, and medieval story. Henry Parkes and his colleagues looked ridiculous because they were not knights, despite their pretensions to noble bearings and, indeed, despite the fact that some of them had in fact received knighthoods.

There was, then, a kind of conservative crypto-nostalgia in the satirists' touch, a tacit respect for the medieval past that aligned them more closely not only with the drivellers' snatch-and-grab bid for historical depth but also, unexpectedly, with the po-faced medievalism of Gerontius. The genuine anti-medievalism of Socialist and nationalist verse was based on a belief in the superiority of the modern that put it out of step with the bulk of popular medievalist verse in colonial and newly federal Australia.

These poems were, with some marvellous exceptions, decidedly unsubtle, muddled in conception and crude in execution. Yet it is their wildcard quality — their unpredictable and improbable combinations, their divided cultural allegiances, their sudden humour — that makes them so compelling a barometer of the many registers and tensions in colonial versifiers' attitudes toward the Middle Ages. Together with the images that surrounded them, these poems are also testament to the frequency with which the Australian reading public looked into their newspapers and saw themselves reflected back, whether in shards or full-length mirrors, in medieval dress.

[39] Codell, 'Imperial Difference and Culture Clashes', p. 423.

[40] Alexander Pope, 'Peri Bathous, or the Art of Sinking in Poetry', in *Alexander Pope: The Major Works*, ed. by Pat Rogers (Oxford: Oxford University Press, 2006), pp. 195–238.

Chapter 5

# The Round Table and Other Furniture: Medievalism on the Colonial Australian Stage

On 29 August 1866, the Melbourne *Age* theatre reviewer remarked upon 'the exorbitant desire recently manifested by the Melbourne public for the romantic, the historical'.[1] The performance that prompted this comment was *Ivanhoe, or the Trial by Battle*, a theatrical adaptation of Sir Walter Scott's medievalist novel *Ivanhoe*. Premiering at the Theatre Royal on 25 August 1866, the play was an amalgamation of the two best-known adaptations of Scott's novel, W. H. Murray's *Ivanhoe* and Thomas Dibdin's *Ivanhoe, or the Jew's Daughter*.[2] Although the opening-night performances garnered tepid reviews from both *Argus* and *Age* reviewers, the scenery was unanimously praised for its historical verisimilitude and 'minute care in the details'[3]. The *Argus* reviewer enthused:

> the various portions of Sherwood Forest are shown with an appearance of reality which, combined with the foresters carrying their bows and their javelins, and the sound of the 'brisk horn', takes the imagination vividly back to the old feudal time.[4]

The scene depicting 'the conflagration and destruction of Torquilstone Castle and the abduction of the Jewish maiden' was especially singled out in both newspapers for its spectacular scenic effects. That this production of *Ivanhoe* continued to be part of public consciousness for some time afterwards is evident in the noticeable

[1] *The Age*, 29 August 1866.

[2] See *The Argus*, 27 August 1866. See also James C. Corson, 'Scott's Novels: Dramatized Versions', *Notes and Queries*, 189 (1945), 17–18. My thanks to Anne McKendry for drawing my attention to this production of *Ivanhoe.*

[3] The *Age*, 28 August 1866.

[4] The *Argus*, 27 August 1866.

presence of *Ivanhoe*-themed costumes at the Mayor's Fancy Ball held in Melbourne's New Exhibition building on Thursday, 20 September 1866. According to the list of guests' costumes published in *The Argus*, Melbourne's great and good chose to embody a number of the play's Scottian *dramatis personae:* Mr John Bruce came as Wilfred of Ivanhoe, Mr W. C. Biddle as the brooding Templar Brian de Bois Guilbert, Mr Thomas Drysdale as Robin Hood, and Messrs Samuel Brush and Richard Goldsbrough as Friar Tuck. Furthermore, no fewer than four gentlemen of Melbourne society donned the distinctive garb of the Knights Templar, and another two came as 'jolly friars', costumes which more obliquely but unmistakably referenced *Ivanhoe.* Among the ladies we find Mrs W. M. Kilpatrick and Mrs Joseph Wilkie evoking the world of *Ivanhoe* by coming, respectively, as 'a Norman lady' and 'a lady of the court of Richard Coeur de Lion'. The costumes at this ball were not limited to medieval personages, or indeed to figures from European or English history. Nevertheless, the imaginative appeal of the medieval period is strongly in evidence: those *Ivanhoe*-esque characters kept company with numerous others inspired by the Middle Ages, including monks, hermits, friars, knights, a troubadour, noblemen and noblewomen, and peasants.[5]

It is true that the Melbourne *Ivanhoe* was performed at a moment when Australian audiences, along with their British and American peers, had found what Eric Irvin has called a 'new god to worship — sensationalism', and that this sensationalism was at least as appealing as its medievalism to its audiences.[6] Indeed its conflagration scene was in many respects a typical sensation scene that catered directly to the current thirst, cultivated in the wake of the sensational melodramas of Dion Boucicault, for elaborately staged 'natural' disasters in the form of floods, fires, and avalanches, courtesy of the latest developments in stage technology.[7] What was significant about this production, however, with its combination of pyrotechnics and a detailed evocation of 'feudal times', was that it reflected another contemporary taste among colonial audiences, which will be the subject of this chapter: that is, the combination of early European history with state-of-the-art stage spectacle. *Ivanhoe* may have been a particularly timely production, coinciding

[5] *The Argus*, 21 September 1866.

[6] Eric Irvin, *Australian Melodrama: Eighty Years of Popular Theatre* (Sydney: Hale & Iremonger, 1981), p. 27.

[7] For the reaction of London audiences to Boucicault's 1863 adaptation of one of Scott's *Waverley* novels (*The Trial of Effie Deans*, from Scott's *The Heart of Midlothian*) see Lynn M. Voskuil, 'Feeling Public: Sensation Theater, Commodity Culture, and the Victorian Public Sphere', *Victorian Studies*, 44 (2002), 245–74.

as it did with Melbourne's great Gothic Revival cathedral projects and premiering just before the opening of the city's Intercolonial Exhibition, which was to include the much-fêted Gothic-style Mediaeval Court discussed in this book's Introduction.[8] But this production was far from alone in channelling the colonial Australian public's taste for melodrama and sensation in the direction of historical pictorialism, a pictorialism in which the medieval past enjoyed a privileged place. When we examine the theatrical offerings in the Australian colonies from at least 1840 to 1910 and beyond, we find that an entire spectrum of stage genres placed before local audiences vivid reconstructions of the European — and arguably most importantly, the English — Middle Ages.

If we were to consider theatre for its contribution to a local culture of creative originality — already a problematic concept, as we have seen, when it comes to colonial Australian medievalism — its role would have to be supplementary, as there are fewer examples of locally written medievalist theatre than there are novels or, especially, poems. But when considered as a popular cultural form, theatre is an indispensable counterpart to the serialized literature and periodical poetry of colonial and newly Federated Australia. Richard Fotheringham sums up the views of the majority of theatre historians, as well as historians of Victorian popular culture, when he says:

> For nearly all the 1832–1930 period [...] live theatre was *the* major public entertainment industry in Australia [...] any history of Australia in the period to 1930 written as if such cultural institutions did not exist or were marginal to more serious subjects is missing major sites of public activity, discourse and display.[9]

It is vital, then, to include medievalist theatre alongside the popular writings discussed in this book, as a creative form of medievalism located at the cusp of literary art, material culture, and popular entertainment.

Despite the strong presence of medievalist drama on the colonial Australian stage, it has fared ill in the historiography of Australian theatre. Virtually no work has been devoted to it, with the exception of an essay by Margaret Rogerson on a 1905 production of the medieval morality play *Everyman* and an article by Veronica Kelly on the 1906 production of the idiosyncratic Australian-authored

[8] See D'Arcens, '"The Last Thing One Might Expect": The Mediaeval Court at the 1866 Intercolonial Exhibition', *The La Trobe Journal*, 81 (2008), 26–39.

[9] *Australian Plays for the Colonial Stage 1834–1899*, ed. by Richard Fotheringham (St Lucia: University of Queensland Press, 2006), p. xxiii.

play *Parsifal: or The Redemption of Kundry.*[10] While plenty has been said about the tendency of early Australian theatre to reproduce or adapt English plays, many of which were themselves adaptations of European plays, little has been said about the cultural meanings of these plays in the Australian context, beyond a reductive assumption that they reflected a slavish colonial attempt to replicate British theatrical styles and fashions. This is also been the case with plays that had early European or English settings. These, with the notable exception of Kelly's powerful analysis of *Parsifal*, have generally been regarded as not meriting analysis as vehicles for the exploration of local issues and preoccupations. Within a critical paradigm that sometimes too easily assumes that 'properly' Australian theatre will feature Australian settings, events, and characters, Australian theatrical medievalism has implicitly been consigned to the realm of escapism from the Real. In this respect its fate echoes the fate of Rolf Boldrewood's Anglo-Saxonist writings, which have been eclipsed by his highly sensational but conspicuously Australian bushranging novel *Robbery Under Arms* (which itself inspired numerous theatrical adaptations), and the fate of Gordon's medievalist poems, which, until Ackland's interventions, were dismissed as the effete, escapist poor cousins to his robust bush ballads.

A recent case in point can be found in Fotheringham's introduction to his *Australian Plays for the Colonial Stage, 1834–1899* (2006). Emphasizing the impact of stage realism on colonial audiences, Fotheringham states that '[t]he greatest praise for acting and for stage setting were for them to be "realistic"'. Yet despite his passing concession that other times and places were 'considered representable by actors in a "realistic" way', he explicitly links the Real with the local and the current, and relegates historical genres to the realm of the unreal:

> At the other extreme were the attempts to close off theatre from issues of measurable representation entirely, as a historical romance, or a J. C. Williamson fantasy musical or pantomime attempted to do, toying with the local and recognizable from the safe vantage point of another time, place, and world.[11]

Fotheringham's alignment of historical romances with the rejection of realism is especially notable here, and especially questionable, when we remind ourselves that the *Argus* review of *Ivanhoe* reserved its warmest praise for the 'appearance of reality' achieved in the play's set. What this review discloses, along with other

[10] Margaret Rogerson, 'Australian "Everymans": Post-Medieval Spiritual Adventurers', in *Medievalism and the Gothic in Australian Culture*, ed. by Trigg, pp. 81–97; and Veronica Kelly, 'J. C. Williamson Produces *Parsifal, or the Redemption of Kundry:* Wagnerism, Religion, and Sexuality', *Theatre History Studies*, 15 (1995), 161–81.

[11] Fotheringham, *Australian Plays for the Colonial Stage*, p. xlviii.

reviews of medievalist plays, is that colonial Australian audiences' enthusiasm for realism was extended not just to plays that strove to represent life in the Australian colonies but also to plays with historical settings. In an age fascinated by antiquarian recovery and reconstruction, the historical past, including and in some cases especially the medieval past, was a category of the Real that people were experiencing as increasingly knowable and representable. Even if, as the *Ivanhoe* review suggests, the medieval past was experienced principally via the audiences' collective historical imagination, there was a clear sense that this past was real and could be re-experienced in the here-and-now through the agency of evocative stage representation.

Paying particular tribute to the role of colonial Australia's accomplished scene painters in generating meticulous reconstructions of the past, Harold Love remarks that their work bears 'excellent testimony to the prevailing trend to historicism in stage design', a trend that reached its apotheosis in John Hennings's use of archaeological accounts and reconstructions to create historically correct scenery.[12] Far from 'attempt[ing] to close off theatre from issues of measurable representation', Hennings created representations of the past, such as late medieval Switzerland in Rossini's *William Tell*, that Love describes as 'images which took on a being of their own and became a living participant in the action'.[13] Love also singles out medievalism as the form of stage historicism that generated particular expectations of historical verisimilitude and 'impatience with many time-sanctioned anachronisms':

> The appearance of nigger [sic] minstrels in *Gustavus III*, the peasants with elastic-sided boots in *William Tell*, and monks with moustaches and an infernal spirit in a tutu in *Robert le Diable* led to sternly disapproving comments from the press.[14]

This sense of the presence of the medieval past, as with a number of the other forms of medievalism examined in previous chapters, offers yet another challenge to the

[12] Harold Love, *The Golden Age of Australian Opera: W. S. Lyster and his Companies 1861–1880* (Sydney: Currency, 1981), p. 107. The production to which Love refers is an 1866 Sydney production of Rossini's *Semiramide* for which Hennings painted the scenery. Alec Bagot's *Coppin the Great: Father of the Australian Theatre* (Carlton: University of Melbourne Press; London: Cambridge University Press, 1965) also points to the key importance of Coppin's scene illustrator and 'most valuable assistant' (p. 90), Edward Opie.

[13] Love, *The Golden Age of Australian Opera*, p. 106. The Melbourne *William Tell* production, from December 1867, is mentioned on p. 108.

[14] Love, *The Golden Ages of Australian Opera*, p. 111.

binary opposition in which realism (aligned with the contemporary) and escapism (aligned with the past) are pitted straightforwardly against one another.

The fact, moreover, that the Middle Ages might have provided a distant vantage point for certain Australian-authored plays' treatments of local concerns should not lead us to assume that this distance automatically guaranteed, as Fotheringham suggests, a desultory, remote, or 'safe' engagement with the local. Even in cases where the ancient setting provided a strategic setting for dealing with controversial local topics, we should not assume that the engagement was mere 'toying', with no genuine element of social commentary attached to it. Fotheringham quite rightly states:

> [...] it is essential, if we are to try to understand something of the power of stories seen and heard on the colonial stage, to consider more fully the ways in which representers and representations were interpreted in relation to what audiences understood as real life.[15]

If we are to follow this injunction, then we must include the historical past within the Real for these audiences. An analysis of medievalism in colonial theatre thus supplements and questions the dominant narrative in which the development of an authentic Australian drama is synonymous with conspicuously Australian settings and themes.

The dominance of the narrative of slavish colonial consumption is, nevertheless, understandable; for as with the colonial literary culture of the period, much of what was consumed by the theatre-going public in the Australian colonies was imported from elsewhere, especially Britain, either wholesale or in superficially localized form. A widely cited example of superficial localization is the incorporation of 'local allusions' and an aboriginal corroboree scene into an 1856 Melbourne production of the pantomime Harlequin *King Blear and his Three Daughters.*[16] But this largely British provenance should not lead us to regard medievalist plays staged in colonial Australia as simple equivalents of, say, Scott's novels or Tennyson's poems, which appeared in the identical form whether read in London, St Louis, or Hobart. Rather, the unique nature of theatre as a medium, in particular its dependence on the creativity of local stage painters, costumiers, actors, stage managers, musicians, and so on, meant that even if the written script were performed exactly as written, these plays were not facsimiles of British or European productions. Thus Australian

[15] Fotheringham, *Australian Plays for the Colonial Stage*, p. xlvii.

[16] See Veronica Kelly, with Mary Ann Hunter and Sue Cullen, 'File 2, Plays', *Annotated Calendar of Plays Premiered in Australia, 1850–1869*, 4 files (School of English, Media Studies, and Art History, University of Queensland: ePrints@UQ, 1995 and 2004), p. 5.

theatrical medievalism begs to be considered on different terms from literary medievalism. It is more apt to regard such local medievalist productions as *Ivanhoe* or *Robin Hood*, to take just two examples, as equivalent to those local adaptations of British medievalist fiction and poetry discussed in earlier chapters, where a largely derivative tendency sits, sometimes happily, sometimes under considerable strain, alongside elements that reflect an engagement with local events, scenes, and audience tastes.

Furthermore, as will be discussed later in this chapter, there were also some locally written examples of medievalist drama that are significant for their use of medieval settings as vehicles for exploring a range of 'hot' colonial topics, such as the value of harsh penal codes — a topic of natural interest in colonies whose foundations were intimately bound up with convict transportation — the trials of expatriation, the treachery of subjugated races, the protocols of imperial rule, and, increasingly, themes such as emergent nationhood. Kelly, speaking of early Shakespeare productions in Australia, has described

> the situated and local meanings of these various productions as they linked with the realities of colonial politics and local knowledge which subverts, appropriates and familiarises the remote and antique, refusing the positions of colonial deferral and historical supplementarity which can only conclude: 'we lack all this'.[17]

As will be shown, a comparable argument can be made about the often intensely local nature of Australian theatrical medievalism.

So what did the Middle Ages look and sound like on colonial Australian stages? In its broadest contours, the main trends of medievalist theatrical representation corresponded with, indeed closely shadowed, the main trends appearing on the British and American stages.[18] These included Gothic dramas such as Matthew

[17] Veronica Kelly, 'Shakespeare in Settler-built Spaces: Oscar Asche's 'Recitals' of Julius Caesar in the Melbourne and Sydney Town Halls', *Contemporary Theatre Review*, 19 (2009), 353–66 (p. 365).

[18] This discussion of medievalist plays in Australia is compiled from a range of sources: F. C. Brewer, *The Drama and Music in New South Wales* (Sydney: Charles Potter, Government Printer, 1892); Katharine Brisbane, *Entertaining Australia: An Illustrated History* (Sydney: Currency, 1991); Veronica Kelly, with Mary Ann Hunter and Sue Cullen, 'File 2, Plays'; Harold Love, *The Australian Stage: A Documentary History* (Kensington: University of New South Wales Press, 1984); 'Osric' (Humphrey Hall and Alred John Cripps), *The Romance of the Sydney Stage* (Sydney: Currency in association with National Library of Australia, 1996); John R. Spring, *A Frequency List of Dramatic Performances Advertised in the Melbourne* Argus *between January 1860 and December 1869* (Melbourne: Monash University, English Dept., 1977); and *The Companion to Theatre in Australia*, ed. by P. Parsons (Sydney: Currency in association with Cambridge University Press, 1995).

Gregory ('Monk') Lewis's *The Castle Spectre and The Tower of Nesle*, and Charles Robert Maturin's *Bertram, or, The Castle of St Aldobrand*, which tapped into the popular fascination with 'medieval' gloom, horror, and irrationality.[19] There were also a considerable number of plays whose action was based on historical events from the Middle Ages, especially the English Middle Ages. To take just two examples, we find such plays as Robert Taylor Conrad's 1835 *Aylmere, or the Kentish Rebellion* performed in 1855 at the Prince of Wales, Sydney, while John Braham and Thomas Dibdin's Napoleonic wartime 'historical comic opera' *The English Fleet in 1342* was performed in 1848 in Sydney's Victoria Theatre. Despite being performed in Australia more than thirty years after the cessation of the Napoleonic wars, its patriotic message about the medieval antecedents of contemporary British naval dominance still pertained, and it is not hard to understand its appeal for colonial audiences, whose lives as settlers had been shaped in so many ways by British seafaring.

One of the more idiosyncratic medieval episodes revived in heavily fictionalized form appears in *The Forest of Bondy or the Dog of Montargis*, an English translation of the hugely successful 1814 play *Le Chien de Montargis, ou la Forêt de Bondy* by the French melodramatist René Charles Guilbert de Pixérécourt. This play, which was performed at Sydney's Victoria Theatre in 1841, was adapted from a legend about a trial-by-combat allegedly organized by the French king Charles V in the early 1360s, in which the loyal dog of Charles's murdered courtier Aubry de Montdidier fought and defeated his owner's killer, Robert Macaire. Macaire's name became synonymous in French melodrama with villainy, although it became detached from the medieval character: in *Robert Macaire*, performed at the Victoria Theatre in 1855, and *The Two Prisoners of Lyons, or the Duplicate Keys,* performed at the Olympic Theatre in 1842, both English adaptations of French originals, he is villainous but no longer medieval. The popularity of *The Dog of Bondy* undoubtedly owed much to the novelty of featuring a trained dog in the lead role and to its transformation of the legend into canine detective drama; but it is not unreasonable to surmise that the medieval setting, by evoking an alien world in which justice was pursued through seemingly irrational paths, would have added historical piquancy to the eccentric story.

Other plays, while dramatizing episodes from the Middle Ages, were focused more intently on exploring the historical figures at their centre. Apart from the late

[19] See Anastasia Nikolopoulou, 'Medievalism and Historicity in the English Gothic Melodrama: Maturin's *Bertram: or, The Castle of St Aldobrand*', *Poetica: An International Journal of Linguistic Literary Studies*, 39–40 (1994), 139–53.

medieval English and French monarchs depicted in Shakespeare's chronicle plays, which were regularly mounted in colonial theatres throughout the late nineteenth and early twentieth centuries, colonial Australian audiences encountered such heroic figures as Joan of Arc and Jack Cade, leader of the 1450 Kentish rebellion, along with a gallery of medieval monarchs and nobles that included Louis XI of France (in Dion Boucicault's play of that name), Richard Coeur de Lion, James III of Scotland, Robert the Bruce, the Merovingian king Chilperic, after whom Hervé named his 1868 operetta, and William the Conqueror's father Robert Duke of Normandy, who was the central character in Giacomo Meyerbeer's much-performed opera *Robert le Diable.* Also prominent were dramas developed out of medieval literary-historical figures such as Robin Hood and King Arthur, Parsifal, and William Tell. Audiences were introduced to the most famous author of trecento Florence, Giovanni Boccaccio, through Franz von Suppé's operetta *Boccaccio*, in which the writer is the central character.

There were also numerous plays inspired by nineteenth-century medievalist literature. Among these, three particularly powerful influences can be singled out. The first is Victor Hugo's novel *The Hunchback of Notre Dame* (1831), set in fifteenth-century Paris. Of the many stage derivatives from Hugo's novel, the most performed across the Australian colonies appear to be a range of plays with the title *Esmeralda*,[20] and James Sheridan Knowles's much-revived *The Hunchback* (1832), performed repeatedly in Melbourne, Sydney, and Adelaide from the 1840s to the 1880s. There were also other, more satiric performances based on the same story, such as Fredrick Hobson Leslie's *Miss Esmeralda*, which played at Melbourne's Princess Theatre in 1888. The second major text to receive multiple stage adaptations was Goethe's poetic masterpiece *Faust.* This was most famously dramatized in operatic form, first in Lutz's 1855 grand opera *Faust and Marguerite*, which was first performed in Sydney, at least in part, the same year it was written and soon after in Gounod's 1859 *Faust*, performed in Sydney and Melbourne throughout the 1860s, 1870s, and 1880s. Interestingly, satires of the Faust story were circulating in colonial theatres even prior to the operatic treatments, William Leman Rede's

[20] The details on these are unclear, but these *Esmeraldas* could variously have been adaptations or selections from, among others, the 1836 opera *La Esmeralda* written by Hugo himself with Louise Bertin, or the 1838 opera *Esmeralda* by Alberto Mazzucato, or the 1844 ballet *La Esmeralda* by Cesare Pugni, or the 1847 opera *Esmeralda* by Alexander Dargomyzhsky, or the 1869 opera *Esmeralda* by Fabio Campana, the 1851 opera *Esmeralda* by Vincenzo Battista, or, as is most likely after 1883, the hugely popular opera *Esmeralda* by A. T. Thomas.

burletta *The Devil and Dr Faustus* being performed in Sydney in 1853. This satiric strain was, moreover, still finding audiences well after the peak of *Faust*omania in the Australian colonies; in 1892 the burlesque 'Faust Up To Date', also written by Lutz, was performed in Sydney by the touring London Gaeity company. *Faust*'s status as a performative mainstay on the colonial stage is evident in the numerous visual representations in the press featuring its characters, particularly Mephistopheles. For instance, Phil May produced a cartoon for *The Bulletin* on 13 October 1886, in which he made a diabolical pun on the name of 'Alfred Dam(n)pier', whose long-time association with the role had most recently been manifested in a

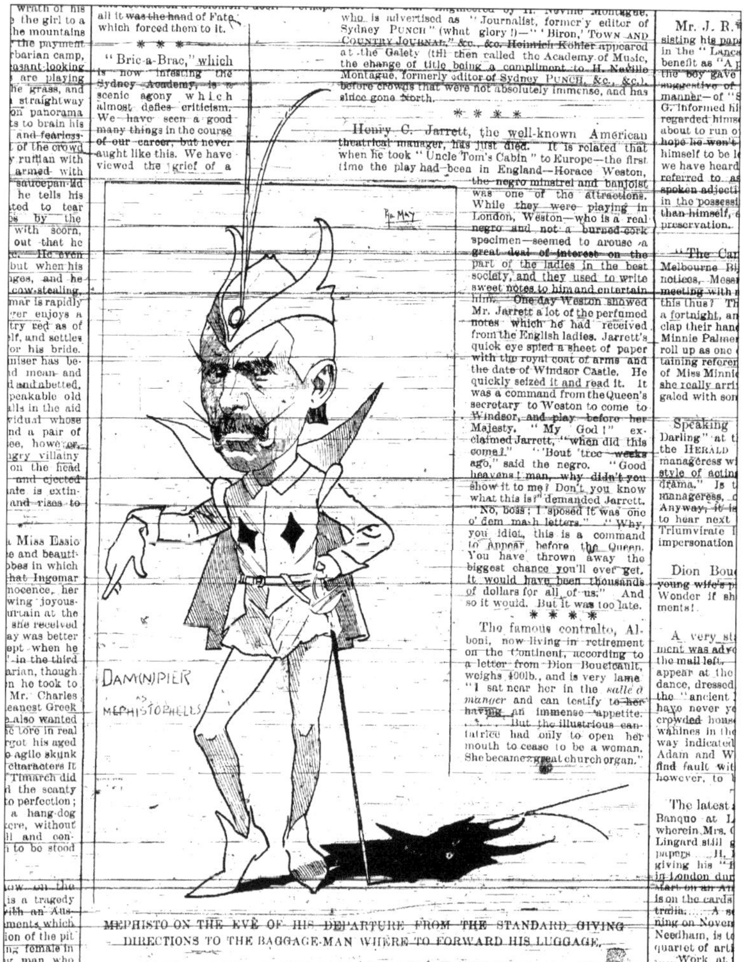


Figure 11. Phil May, 'Dam(n)pier as Mephistopheles', *The Bulletin*, 13 October 1886.

performance at Sydney's Royal Standard Theatre (Figure 11). Two years later, the *Sydney Illustrated News* contained sketches of the production at Her Majesty's

Figure 12. Unknown artist, 'George Rignold as Mephistopheles', *Sydney Illustrated News*, 26 April 1888.

Theatre starring George Rignold as Mephistopheles (Figure 12). This locally written production, from the pen of Gilbert Parker, the Canadian-born then-editor of the *Sydney Morning Herald*, is important for reminding us that we should not assume that the myriad colonial productions of *Faust* were always necessarily Gounod's or Lutz's. The legend had captured the theatrical imaginations of the local writers as well.

Finally, the medievalist novels of Walter Scott, in particular *Ivanhoe* and his Crusader novels, spawned a small industry of theatrical presentation. *Ivanhoe* gave rise to a rash of theatrical versions, as well as numerous medieval Jewry spin-offs, including W. Moncrieff's *The Jewess, or the Council of Constance*, performed in Sydney and Adelaide in the 1830s and 1840s, and Fromental Halévy's grand opera *La Juive* (1835), which was later performed to local acclaim by G. S. Lyster's opera company in 1874. Scott novels set during the crusades, such as *The Talisman* and *Count Robert of Paris*, also inspired a tenacious fad that led to a number of medievalist-orientalist dramas, such as the spectacle *The Moors of Spain*, performed in 1856, George Colman's historical musical drama *The Mountaineers*, about the fifteenth-century siege of Granada, which had two seasons at the Victoria Theatre in 1856, and *Tancredi*, also performed at the Victoria in 1856 and probably adapted from Rossini's admired 1813 opera of the same name. The most 'local' of these productions was the revenge tragedy *Salalthiel or the Jewish Chieftain*, adapted by the Sydney playwright Conrad Knowles from Edward Bulwer-Lytton's novel *Leila: or the Siege of Granada.*

In many cases, audiences encountered representations of medieval societies that were loosely regionalized. Along with the above-mentioned English and Hispanic-Oriental settings, a loosely conceived 'Italianate' Middle Ages featured particularly in operatic productions: Guiseppe Verdi's medievalist offerings included *I Lombardi*, which Italianized the medieval Crusades genre; *I Vespri Siciliani*, set in thirteenth-century Palermo; *I due Foscari*, set in fifteenth-century Venice; and Suppé's *Boccaccio*, set in fourteenth-century Florence. A loosely 'Ibero-Latinate' Middle Age took the stage in Verdi's *Il Trovatore*, set in fifteenth-century Spain, and Donizetti's *La Favorita*, set in fourteenth-century Castile. A fictionalized 'ould Ireland' was the setting of the three Sydney-authored dramas *The Hibernian Father* by Edward Geoghegan, *The Outcast, or the Irish Maniac* by Francis Belfield, and the final Act of *Lough Deargh's Shrine* by George Ferrers Pickering. And, of course, there was the mytho-Teutonic medievalism of William Vincent Wallace's hugely popular and famously spectacular opera *Lurline*, and later of Wagner's operas, which were performed in Australia from 1877 on, with a first full season occurring in 1907. An arresting and anomalous instance of Australian-authored mytho-

Teutonism was J. C. Williamson's 1906–07 *succès de scandale*, the religious drama *Parsifal, or the Redemption of Kundry*, written by the Rev. T. Hilhouse Taylor. Kelly has anatomized *Parsifal*'s compelling combination of portentous Teutonic Arthurianism, Orientalism, muscular Christianity, prurient (but redeemed) female sexuality, and state-of-the art scenic effects. What is of particular interest here is that Kelly's suggestion that the play is perhaps best not regarded as an example of medievalism. She argues that, despite its 'ahistoric mediaeval setting', the mythic and moral emphases of this religious drama align it more closely to the genre of the improving 'toga play', such as Wilson Barrett's *The Sign of the Cross* or the Rev. George Walters's *Joseph of Canaan*, which had been popular for the past twenty-five years and which were profitable vehicles for attract non-conformist audiences who ordinarily shunned theatrical entertainment.[21] Kelly is right to point to both the play's unstable genre and to the mythic non-specificity of its setting; but, as the many plays explored throughout this chapter illustrate, neither of these precludes the play from being medievalist. Indeed, their eclecticism is very much of a piece with nineteenth-century medievalism in general, and theatrical medievalism in particular. Furthermore, the play's reliance upon popular understandings of the Grail romances, especially as channelled through Wagner, situates medievalism at the heart of the play.

The fairy transformation scenes that cropped up in innumerable pantomimes, burlesques, and stage spectaculars, including such later iterations as Gilbert and Sullivan's *Iolanthe*, can also be described as a variety of stage medievalism. There is no doubt that these scenes were, in performance (and commercial) terms, valued more for the opportunity they provided to combine spectacular scenery and stage machinery with diaphanous costumes and 'leg shows'. But their fairy grottoes and other-worldly *dramatis personae* clearly drew upon the idiom of nineteenth-century romantic medievalism, with its fascination for the folkloric world of faëry.[22] This kind of fantastic, generalized depiction of pre-modern pastness did not necessarily sit at odds with more historical representations. Both the cross-genre emphasis on

[21] Kelly, 'J. C. Williamson Produces *Parsifal*', p. 170.

[22] Paul Buczkowski's discussion of James Robinson Planché, that father of British fairy extravaganza, emphasizes his heavy reliance on the French tales of Marie-Catherine d'Aulnoy, which he translated into English and made the basis of many of his extravaganzas. Planche's translation of Charles Perrault's fairy tales also expresses the intimate link between fairy extravaganza and the popular antiquarian interest in fairy tales. See Paul Buczkowski, 'J. R. Planché, Frederick Robson, and the Fairy Extravaganza', *Marvels and Tales: Journal of Fairy-Tale Studies*, 15 (2001), 42–65.

spectacle and the sheer rapidity with which plays succeeded one another in a single season joined them with historical plays to generate a kind of non-specific theatrical Middle Ages. The archives of local impresario, George Selth Coppin, for instance, show how in a period of less than six months in 1845 no fewer than six medieval-themed plays were performed in Melbourne, each featuring a different Middle Ages. The same archive regularly lists at least three differing medievalist productions per year in most years across the 1840s to the 1880s, with the 1870s being particularly rich in medievalist representation.[23] These productions often followed closely on one another, so that regular theatre-goers in metropolitan centres, much like the readers of the verse published in local periodicals, were frequently bombarded in a short space of time with widely divergent depictions of the medieval era.

As this selected list shows, just as these productions ranged freely across the medieval period, so too they ranged from serious or 'legitimate' genres, such as historical dramas and chronicle plays, across more populist modes, such as melodramas and historical romances, operas and opéras-bouffes or operettas, and through to such unabashedly frivolous and ephemeral entertainments as comediettas, burlesques, fairy extravaganzas, and pantomimes. This breadth of genre led to the medieval past being represented on a sliding scale from antiquarian exactitude to mythic spectacle. And yet, despite their widely divergent creative commitments and motives, which ranged from cultural edification to financial profit, these representations had in common an ability to render this remote period vividly immediate for colonial audiences. In whatever genre, nineteenth-century Australian theatrical medievalism was significant for its very nature as a representational medium; for the stage had the singular capacity to offer a simultaneously physical and spatio-temporal embodiment of the Middle Ages, and of medieval people, that was unavailable to all other representational forms. Medievalist theatre was thus not simply part of the larger nineteenth-century antiquarian project: rather, in agreement with Richard Schoch, we can see that theatre was arguably the most successful iteration of medievalist antiquarianism, as it animated and presented — as in literally made present — personages, events, and scenes from the Middle Ages.

Theatre was, moreover, a particularly charged medium of popular medievalism in an era in which spectacular stage effects and historical pictorialism coalesced with

[23] George Selth Coppin Archive, Box 12, Folders 3 and 4, held in the National Library of Australia.

contemporary convictions about the meaning of the distant past for the present. Whether medievalist productions reflected and promoted a belief in the continuity between the Middle Ages and the present, or whether they were concerned with actively attempting to 'reconstruct' medieval culture in the present, they frequently, if inadvertently, had a deeply ideological dimension. This can be seen, as will be discussed later, not only in the more self-avowedly edifying 'historical' productions but even, or perhaps especially, in some of the most seemingly frivolous light entertainments with medieval themes and settings. While theatre historians have rightly emphasized the commercial imperatives driving the often-struggling playwrights, actors, and companies of nineteenth-century Australian theatre (attracting an audience, recouping one's costs, and so on), this does not preclude an ideological substratum within their productions. Fotheringham suggests that the 'mass' nature of theatre as a medium of entertainment gave it weight within the public imaginary as a space where a communal sensibility could be forged:

> Because [plays] were where people from different classes and walks of life were seen in close proximity at the same time, they in turn became the dominant metaphors of a society trying to imagine itself as a diverse yet unified community that shared common interests and concerns.[24]

The sense of community was not just aimed at generating cohesive identity within colonial society; theatre was also instrumental in forging Australia's sense of its place within a larger imperial orbit. Bill Dunstone, discussing Wilson Barrett's visit to Perth during his tour of 1898, argues for the importance of seeing Barrett's performances of Shakespeare as strategic and rhetorical declarations of 'the culture of empire', arguing that:

> Barrett's lavish settings and costumes were intended to 'restage' a theatrical trace of imperial London within the closed walls of Perth's Theatre Royal, designating the Royal's stage as a threshold across which two nominally 'British' cultures could act out a supposedly common identity.[25]

To this can be added Schoch's more specific contention about the ideological significance of medievalist theatre in this period. Schoch argues that '"performing the Middle Ages" was itself a political event because it strove to construct and express a national identity through the display of historical relics and historical

[24] Fotheringham, *Australian Plays for the Colonial Stage*, pp. xxiii–xxiv.

[25] Bill Dunstone, 'Dinkum Shakespeare? Perth, Empire and the Bard', in *O Brave New World: Two Centuries of Shakespeare on the Australian Stage*, ed. by John Golder and Richard Madelaine (Sydney: Currency, 2001), pp. 163–79, notes 275–76 (p. 165).

bodies'.[26] Schoch's comments refer to the stages of Victorian England, but, as can be seen in this chapter, medievalist theatre played a crucial role in placing before colonial Australian audiences historical scenes of nation formation and governance whose entertainment value underwrote their force as spectacles of instruction on attitudes to empire.

Medievalism in the Australian colonial theatre is an uneven story, and it is impossible to speak in detail about all the plays performed across the nineteenth century. Unsurprisingly, there was a strong Sydney-Melbourne dominance in the mid-to-later nineteenth century; and indeed, this dominance continues today. But there is also evidence of the staging of numerous medievalist performances in other colonial cities, such as Adelaide, Brisbane, Hobart, and, later, Perth, and in larger regional settlements, particularly gold, coal, and mineral mining towns, which included Ballarat on the Victorian goldfields, Maitland and Gulgong in New South Wales, Launceston in Tasmania, Rockhampton in Queensland, and, later, Coolgardie in the Western Australian goldfields. But apart from the anomalous *Parsifal* discussed earlier, the two 'flash points' of theatrical medievalism that can with full justification be called local came in 1840s Sydney, which witnessed a cluster of medievalist dramas, and the 1860s and 1870s when Melbourne played host to a number of locally penned medieval-themed burlesques.

The 1840s in Sydney is unique for having left us records of several entirely local melodramas with medieval settings. The content of some of these, such as Belfield's *The Outcast, or the Irish Maniac*, is known to us only through review synopses,[27] but the manuscripts of a number are now lodged in the New South Wales State Records Office, within the correspondence of the colonial secretary, who, like his British counterpart the lord chamberlain, was in charge of approving and licensing plays in the colony. While far from comprehensive, this record is described by Janette Pelosi as 'remarkable' as an archive of plays that managed to survive the fires that destroyed so many of the manuscripts housed in individual theatres throughout colonial Australia.[28] Even more remarkable is the fact that in this single record we find no fewer than four medieval dramas written in the 1840s: *Lough Deargh's Shrine, or, The Cave of Penance* by George Ferrers Pickering; *The Hibernian Father* by Edward Geoghegan, who was at that stage still serving out his sentence as a

[26] Schoch, *Shakespeare's Victorian Stage*, p. 116.

[27] A full plot outline of Belfield's play was published in *Bell's Life in Sydney and Sporting Reviewer*, 10 July 1852, p. 2.

[28] Janette Pelosi, 'Colonial Drama Revealed, or Plays Submitted for Approval', *MARGIN: Life and Letters in Early Australia*, 60 (2003), 21–34.

transported convict; *Raymond, Lord of Milan: A Tragedy of the 13th Century* by Edward Reeve; and *Salathiel, or The Jewish Chieftain* by Conrad Knowles, although the latter was adapted practically verbatim from Edward Bulwer-Lytton's 1838 novel *Leila: or the Siege of Granada.* Just as Boldrewood's novels were only one example of locally adapted medievalism in a sea of imported product, and are no less significant for that, so too these plays constitute a small but revealing cluster pointing to local playwrights' taste for medievalist melodrama. Their significance should not be taken, however, to be synonymous with their popularity or impact. Most of these plays enjoyed only extremely brief runs, being performed for a few nights at most. Many attracted only brief critical notices, and some of them no notices at all; some exist only as single unpublished manuscripts lodged in bureaucratic archives; almost none, with the exception of *The Hibernian Father*, has been revived for subsequent performance. Their significance lies, rather, in what they reflect of the colonial attempt to interpret and adapt the medieval past for local audiences. Even if many of them fell wide of the mark, the assumption that their authors believed these plays would appeal to colonial audiences (nineteenth-century playwrights needed hits more urgently than their contemporary equivalents) provides us with a starting point for considering how the Middle Ages might have been 'Australianized' by the pens of colonial dramatists.

In her discussion of the plays in the colonial secretary's correspondence, Margaret Williams directly attributes 'the very large number of [...] dramas set in nineteenth-century Ruritanias or historical settings' to the colonial secretary's censorship of plays that were construed as offering commentary on social, political, or sectarian matters within the colony. Her argument that '[a]ny form of radical thought or comment on social issues [in plays by local authors] was camouflaged by remote historical settings or romantic nowheres as far as possible from the less creditable realities of the colony' is especially relevant to a consideration of the valency of Australian medievalist dramas within their contemporary contexts, as it acknowledges the possibility that these plays were directing themselves at the local via the medieval.[29] While this argument bears a partial correspondence with Fotheringham's argument that historical plays 'toy[ed] with the local and recognizable from the safe vantage point of another time, place, and world', Williams's assessment is rather less dismissive, crediting these plays with attempting (albeit with varying success) to engage seriously with local issues in a way that reached beyond 'toying safely'. Acknowledging these plays' topicality need not lead

[29] Margaret Williams, *Australia on the Popular Stage 1829–1929: An Historical Entertainment in Six Acts* (Melbourne: Oxford University Press, 1983), p. 20.

us to any inflated claims about their radicality or their profundity; their authors' combination of exotic setting with topical issues was, after all, as Williams emphasizes, a fundamentally commercial exercise.[30] But it does allow us to move beyond any short-changing notions of Australian-authored medievalist dramas as merely escapist curios or botched imitations of British and European plays.

Of the medievalist plays found in the colonial secretary's papers, Knowles's *Salathiel* is, on first inspection, the least conspicuously linked to the concerns of colonial Sydney. Set in Moorish Granada during the pitch of the Christian King Ferdinand's *reconquista* of that city, the play's central plot revolves around the Jewish chieftain Salathiel's tireless, bloodthirsty, and ultimately self-destructive pursuit of revenge against both Moors and Christians for their persecution of Jews over many centuries.[31] This plot is further complicated by the play's ultimately abortive love story between Salathiel's daughter Salome and her beloved, Agib Muza, a Moorish chieftain. Along with the interfaith titillation offered by this love story, which had been in fashion ever since Walter Scott's Rebecca cast her Sephardic spell over Wilfred of Ivanhoe, the play's aesthetic appeal is not difficult to discern: its Moorish fortresses and palaces, complete with fountains and ornate gateways, offered a scenic artist the opportunity to recreate full-scale medieval-oriental exotica. Alongside these dramatic and scenic elements, though, the play would have had a more sober thematic significance for the settler theatregoers of Sydney. Apart from the troubling spectre of anti-Semitism in the characterization of Salathiel, by dramatizing the vengeful resentment of a former chieftain against those he believed to be occupiers and usurpers, the play arguably spoke pointedly, though obliquely, to settler audiences whose fears about aboriginal reprisals had been nourished by a solid diet of news stories and explorers' journals featuring frontier violence and attacks on European settlers.[32] The play's conclusion, however, ultimately offered comfort to the anxious settler psyche; for although Salathiel's rage offers a menacing spectacle of subaltern unrest and retaliation, it also

[30] Williams, *Australia on the Popular Stage*, p. 21.

[31] Conrad Knowles, *Salathiel, or the Jewish Chieftain*, [SZ 64], Colonial Secretary CGS 908, *Plays submitted for approval prior to being performed, 1842–52*, New South Wales State Records.

[32] In Henry Reynolds, *Dispossession: Black Australians and White Invaders* (St Leonards, NSW: Allen and Unwin, 1989), a compilation of primary sources detailing early settlers' views of indigenous Australians, Reynolds points out that while few colonists had experience of frontier life and its attendant conflicts, their consumption of newspapers, and in particular illustrated periodicals, exposed them to these events (p. 32). He also reproduces passages from published versions of explorers' journals that were part of the fare of the colonial reading public.

leads to his increasing isolation and final self-immolation. As we saw in Chapter 1, the equivalence between medieval Jewry and Australian aborigines, as races threatened by but also threatening to the English/Australian polity, was also evoked obliquely by Rolf Boldrewood in *A Sydney-Side Saxon*. Here, as in Boldrewood's novel, the equivalence is not overtly registered within the text, but is left to the audience to recognize. The play received a long preliminary notice as a 'great novelty' in the *Sydney Morning Herald* on 4 August 1842, and was positively reviewed on 6 August, although the reviewer did note that the actor playing Agib Muza, Francis Nesbitt, had been replaced at the last minute due to his drunkenness.[33]

It is easier to surmise the appeal for colonial audiences of *Lough Deargh's Shrine* and *The Hibernian Father*, with their prominent shared themes of punishment and clemency.[34] Written in the years immediately after the cessation of convict transportation to New South Wales in 1840, they can both be regarded as historically displaced 'post mortems' on convictism and the penal system. Both feature authority figures — Raymond, Viscount Peuilleaux in *Lough Deargh's Shrine* and Walter Lynch in The *Hibernian Father* — whose application of the law is either intemperate and inconsistent (Raymond), or rigid and misguided (Walter Lynch). As both plays use the revenge tragedy genre as the vehicle for their exploration of law, their later stages both culminate in a scene in which a wronged character confronts his judge or oppressor, either to reclaim justice or to have cruel justice meted out to him. While these plays do not parade their equivalence to the themes of such genres as convict narrative and criminal autobiography, it is difficult to avoid their resonance with such stories, and it does not seem a stretch to suggest that these themes would have been interesting to audiences whose lives had been touched by convictism, either directly or indirectly. Fotheringham argues '[g]iven its convict origins, colonial European Australia was more than usually sensitive to what was in any case one of the era's great obsessions: crime and punishment', and singles out 'testing of evidence and pleas in mitigation' as two particular narrative preoccupations that found favour with colonial audiences.[35] This same set of interests would later lead audiences from the early 1870s on to read Marcus Clarke's landmark convict romance *His Natural Life*, which was repeatedly adapted for the

[33] *Sydney Morning Herald*, 6 August 1852, p. 2.

[34] Edward Geoghegan, *The Hibernian Father*, [SZ 58], Colonial Secretary CGS 908, and *Lough Deargh's Shrine*, [SZ 57], Colonial Secretary CSIL 47/1720), both in *Plays submitted for approval prior to being performed, 1842–52*, New South Wales State Records.

[35] Fotheringham, *Australian Plays for the Colonial Stage*, p. lxxiv.

stage in the 1880s. Just as these plays make no explicit reference to convictism, conversely Clarke's novel makes no explicit reference to the Middle Ages; yet it shares with these plays not only a trademark Gothic gloom but also a number of key motifs typical of convict romances: wrongful conviction, mistaken identity, a return to the source/confrontation with justice, and a commentary, via narrative, on the rational application of law.

Pickering's *Lough Deargh's Shrine*,[36] despite a highly convoluted plot that bears some echoes of *Othello*, is the less complex work of the two. Its Irish name is rather misleading, given that it is mainly set in the citadel of Rhodes and in the castle of Raymond, who is general of the Italian army stationed there; the visit to the eponymous Irish shrine does not take place until the fourth and final act. In many ways this play's medievalism is almost incidental. Despite its setting in medieval Rhodes, an important outpost of Christian-Saracen conflict, this is only gesturally alluded to in the play's opening scene, when Raymond enters celebrating the return of 'our tattered banners [...] [c]rimsoned with Moslem gore' (Act I scene 1). Other than this, and one later description in Act II scene 1 of a dream bristling with medievalist commonplaces ('gallant warriors in polished mail,/ With crimson plumes and breastplates fretted o'er / with links of virgin gold' and so on), there is little to distinguish the play from other Jacobean-esque Italianate revenge-tragedies. Its historical setting retreats into the background as the personal animus between Raymond and Sir Ugolino di Castella, and the star-crossed love between Ugolino and Raymond's sister Madoline, take centre stage. But there is one other brief but curious medievalist detail in the play that warrants attention, for it arguably links the play back to its context of performance. In Act II scene 2, we learn of Raymond's remorse at having slain Madoline out of rage over her love for Ugolino, and his determination to undertake penance for this crime. It is at this point that we also learn that he has been granted safe passage to the penitential site on the Irish lake Lough Deargh by the English king, an unspecified Richard but presumably Richard Coeur de Lion, who had visited Rhodes in 1191. This is an arrestingly incongruous detail. Raymond, his French name notwithstanding, is Italian, and up until this point there has been nothing linking him to England or to Richard. Furthermore, although the timeframe of the action is non-specific, the Rhodes of Pickering's play is either a Byzantine territory or a stronghold of the order of the Knights Hospitaller, a fact which makes Richard's intervention even more specious. But we can also read this scene as a revealing instance of different Middle Ages being wilfully amalgamated to service the play's topical concerns. When we

[36] Performed at the Royal Victoria Theatre, Sydney on 13 December 1847.

consider the play's colonial context, this detail arguably makes more sense, as this scene offers its colonial audience the spectacle of a confessed criminal and sinner being granted the opportunity by the English king to atone in a faraway English colony.[37] It is difficult to discern whether the Lough Deargh cave operates in the play as an analogue for penal servitude or an alternative to it, in that a character inhabiting a far-flung and violent border territory is given leave to return to the bosom of Christianity. In any case, the politics of penality is ultimately overwhelmed by the revenge plot, as Ugolino, disguised as a monk, follows Raymond to the penitential cave, killing him and then himself.

Adapted from Irish legend, Edward Geoghegan's The *Hibernian Father* premiered at The Royal Victoria Theatre, Sydney, on 6 May 1844. Set in fifteenth-century Galway, the play tells the story of Walter Lynch, the recently appointed Warden of Galway, whose son Oscar returns from two hedonistic 'years of absence passed 'neath southern skies' (Act I scene 3) and is arrested for the drowning murder of his erstwhile friend and rival in love, the Spaniard Alonzo. After five acts of mounting intrigue, which includes the discovery that Alonzo has survived his overboard ordeal and has been advised in a dream to speed to Galway to save his friend, the play reaches its shocking conclusion, in which Walter not only tries and condemns his son but also dispatches him with his own hands when the executioners refuse to carry out the sentence. *The Hibernian Father*'s place in colonial theatrical history has owed much to the early controversy that surrounded its apparent plagiarism of the 1832 Irish play *The Warden of Galway* by the Rev. Edward Groves. Whilst Williams concludes that the plagiarism charges were merited, she nevertheless argues for the superiority of Geoghegan's play over Groves's, and for the singularity of Geoghegan's treatment of his subject: '[t]he political questions raised by *The Hibernian Father* are surprisingly complex, especially in a penal colony such as New South Wales in 1844. In whom is the law embodied? [...] Flawed as it is, plagiarism or no, *The Hibernian Father* is a remarkable play for a convict author to have produced as his first work for the theatre'.[38] Williams's comment indicates the other major reason why this medievalist play, which was well received in its own time, deserves our attention today. *The Hibernian Father*'s narrative clearly positions itself against capital punishment, and more generally against the bloody-minded implementation of the rule of law at all costs. As with the other plays in the colonial secretary's register, it uses its medieval setting, with all of that period's attendant connotations of irrationality and

[37] Ireland had become an English colony under Richard's father, Henry II.

[38] Williams, *Australia on the Popular Stage*, p. 29.

brutality, to offer a displaced commentary on the irrationality and brutality of modern convictism. In this respect the play is more accomplished than *Lough Deargh's Shrine*. Both plays are highly melodramatic, but Geoghegan's examination of punishment and clemency is more successful than Pickering's because his play's thematic concerns dovetail with its plot rather than being overtaken by the demands of revenge tragedy. The condemnation and execution of son by father, flying in the face of the revered paternal-filial bond, offers a parable into which we can read the particular tragedy of colonial convicts' severance from the parent culture. At the time *The Hibernian Father* was written, according to Willliams, there was a 'particular ban on the depiction of the criminal as hero in a colony still largely composed of convicted criminals',[39] with the colonial secretary being particularly cognizant of New South Wales' convict history as an issue to be side-stepped in theatrical representation. *The Hibernian Father* demonstrates, through its use of Oscar, the Auld Irish faux-criminal hero, one way in which this ban effectively could be side-stepped, to allow for the exploration of the highly contentious topic of convictism.

*The Hibernian Father* and *Lough Deargh's Shrine* are not alone among medievalist plays in dealing with Australia's convict history. Several decades later, in 1907, we find another example in which the link between medieval and Australian penal codes and criminality was openly recognized. A highly popular Sydney production of *Robin Hood* attracted reviews that likened the medieval outlaw to nineteenth-century Australia's own most legendary outlaw, the bushranger Ned Kelly (1855–80). With penetrating humour not only about the romanticizing of Robin Hood as an outlaw-hero, but also about the related contemporary melodramatic fetish for bush-ranging tales and the emerging romantic cult of Kelly, the *Bulletin*'s reviewer of *Robin Hood* on March 7 remarked: 'it has taken us only twenty-five years to make Ned Kelly the perfect gentleman who takes off his hat ten times a day to a lady and is a lamb with children, and the world has had about thirty times twenty-five years to put a polish on the Sherwood bushranger'.[40]

Another medievalist treatment of topical issues that emerged out of the early theatrical scene in Sydney was Edward Reeve's *Raymond of Milan: A Tragedy of the 13th Century*, the script of which was published in 1851.[41] Dramatizing the demise

[39] Williams, *Australia on the Popular Stage*, p. 20.

[40] Irvin also cites this review in *Australian Melodrama*, p. 85.

[41] Edward Reeve, *Raymond, Lord of Milan: A Tragedy in the 13th Century* (Sydney: Hawksley & Cunninghame, 1851). Number in the archives of the Colonial Secretary's correspondence: [SZ 103].

of the Milanese Della Torre dynasty, whose fortunes are captured in the tragic figure of Raymond, this play, yet again, could not seem further from the concerns of colonial Sydney. Reeve advertises *Raymond*'s antiquarian credentials by prefacing his manuscript with a document called 'Facts from History for the Tragedy of Raymond, Lord of Milan', in which he claims that the play is sourced from no fewer than seven scholarly references. Yet it is clear, historicist aspirations notwithstanding, that the play is determinedly contemporary in its focus. As well as sharing the previous two plays' interest in the merits of punishment and clemency, *Raymond* evinces a strong thematic concern with good governance that dwells specifically on how a subordinate state under an imperial power should conduct itself in relation to its imperial master. Much of the political intrigue that drives its plot emerges out of Raymond's decision to rebel as civic Lord against the imperial rule of the sovereignty of the Holy Roman Empire, a decision that generates divided loyalties in his followers that eventually lead to his assassination. The play is laden with lengthy stentorian speeches in which Raymond proclaims the virtues of political independence, urging his subjects not to

> pluck off the laurels earned by sweat and blood,
> Teach your free lips to lisp in adulation,
> And whisper slavish words of deference,
> For Richard, Emperor of all Germany,
> Demands it. (p. 13)

The play's 1851 publication date strongly suggests that Reeve was inspired by contemporary Italian politics, in particular the 1848 Milanese uprising against Hapsburg rule. The fact that the medieval Imperial rulers are called 'Austrians' exposes its nineteenth-century reference point, although there is later one medieval-inflected allusion to them as 'haughty Swabians'. It is also significant that, after over a decade of total neglect, the play was finally dusted off and performed in 1863, soon after the unification of Italy. Yet Reeve's engagement with the psychology of colonial submission, and with the formation of sovereign nationhood and political self-determination, has a broader sweep that would have appealed to those in his home colony who were interested in (or at least dreaming of) a future marked by Australian national sovereignty. Particularly intriguing in this respect is the play's ambivalent exploration of the need for imperial submission to be replaced, at least in the short term, by home-grown autocratic rule. Having defied imperial rule, Raymond opines to his subjects:

> Milan is free but must be ruled,
> Else the reaction of past servitude
> Will generate license, — license anarchy,

> And anarchy (as ever) resolve itself
> Back again into slavery. — — Young nations must be taught
> The wholesome bitter duties of obedience.
> Walk ere they can run — learn ere they can dictate,
> For trust me states that cannot rule themselves
> Will never govern others. (p. 26)

The resonances for colonial Australia are tantalizing, but inconclusive. For all the force of Raymond's political vision — many resist it but few can withstand it — he is murdered; and while he is noble in death, cut down by enemies motivated as much by sexual jealousy as civic pride, his dying speech seems to scotch any future prospects of an independent state. Whatever conclusion audiences might have reached from the play's ending, the portrayal of Milan as a city whose past prosperity is inseparable from its imperial submission, but whose future prosperity might lie in self-determination, would not have seemed as historically remote to colonial Australian audiences as might initially appear.

Of course, as outlined earlier, these plays need to be considered within the larger context of the many 'foreign' medievalist plays and operas performed in colonial Australia. One especially important inclusion in this respect is the mass of local productions of Shakespeare. Just as Scott and Tennyson exerted a huge influence on Australian novelists and poets, Shakespeare productions gave local authors a taste for historico-tragic themes, as suggested by *Shrine at Lough Deargh* and *The Hibernian Father*, and *Raymond, Lord of Milan*. Their self-conscious use of 'Elizabethanese' has led to what Williams regards as a misapprehension of them as 'the closet efforts of literary gentleman [sic] writing pretentiously in imitation of Shakespeare and the classics with little understanding of the theatre'.[42] Over the past decade more has been written about the performance of Shakespeare in Australia, with a particularly significant contribution made by John Golder and Richard Madelaine's edited volume *O Brave New World: Two Centuries of Shakespeare on the Australian Stage* (2001). But, again, within this scholarship there is almost no acknowledgement of the significance or frequency of Shakespeare as a vehicle of medievalism, despite Schoch's assertion that '[o]ne of the inherent complications of Victorian theatrical medievalism was its unavoidable reliance on Renaissance dramatic texts [...] [a] Shakespearian past inevitably ghosts or haunts [Victorian] theatrical representations of the medieval past'.[43] From the earliest years of settlement there was a tradition of unadorned Shakespeare readings, abridged

[42] Williams, *Australia on the Popular Stage*, p. 21.

[43] Schoch, *Shakespeare's Victorian Stage*, p. 10.

versions of plays, and performances of individual scenes or speeches, but between the mid- and late nineteenth century, Shakespeare as dramatic spectacle also became an abiding means by which the medieval past was brought to life before Australian audiences, whether in the violent, tragic manifestation of *Macbeth, King Lear*, or *Hamlet*, the romantic guise of *Romeo and Juliet*, or the historical, martial form of *Henry IV*, *Henry V*, *Richard III*, or *King John*.

Medievalist Shakespeare in colonial Australia is far too large a subject to be given full treatment here. Its increased popularity was, however, in large part due to the influx of international acts who toured in the wake of the gold rushes. Of these, perhaps the best known in the 1850s was Gustavus Vaughan Brooke, whose most memorable medievalist roles were his Macbeth, Henry IV, and Richard III. The presence of touring Shakespearean stars continued into the 1860s. Among these, one visit in particular deserves honourable mention: between October 1863 and June 1864, Melbourne and its environs, and Sydney, witnessed two theatrical seasons of the renowned English Shakespearean actors Charles and Ellen Kean, who had come to Australia under the management of George Coppin. The Keans, who by the time of their Australian tour were some years past their prime, had built their reputation on their exhaustively researched, grandiose stage sets and fastidiously correct period costumes. Although their antiquarian ambitions extended broadly across history, they arguably reached their apotheosis in the reproduction of the English Middle Ages via Shakespeare's chronicle plays. As dramatizations of English history, Kean's productions of Shakespeare's chronicles were significant for their deployment of an antiquarian aesthetic in the service of a nationalist theatrical pedagogy. These plays were regarded as historical records, and Shakespeare as a vehicle for teaching English history to the English and, by extension, the colonial public. Such was the historical exactness of the Keans's 'upholstered Shakespeare' that Charles Kean, arguably more fêted for his research than his acting, was made a Fellow of the Society of Antiquaries in 1857.

Letters exchanged between the actor and his Australian manager suggest, however, that the Melbourne productions were less lavishly antiquarian than those the Keans had staged in England.[44] In fact, the ageing Kean's plan had been to give scene readings in Australia, and he relented only grudgingly when Coppin stressed the financial risk involved in offering Shakespeare to the sensation-addicted

[44] Letters from Coppin to Kean, 22 October 1862, and from Kean to Coppin, 25 February 1863, in J. M. D. Hardwick, *Emigrant in Motley: The Journey of Charles and Ellen Kean in quest of theatrical fortune in Australia and America, as told in their hitherto unpublished letters* (London: Rockliff, 1954), pp. 51 and 55.

Australian public without the theatrical spectacle for which Kean was renowned.[45] Reviews of the Keans's Melbourne performances in late 1863 suggest that actor and manager struck a compromise. For while there are mentions of splendid costumes,[46] and handsomely mounted individual scenes, the Melbourne stage was, it seems, comparatively bare. The *Age* review of their *Henry VIII*, despite its reminiscence about the 'unrivalled splendour' of the Keans's London performances of this play, admits that the Melbourne version is 'divested [...] of [...] many of its original accessories' and 'not splendidly illustrated in [its] theatrical furnishings and scenery'.[47]

Nevertheless, these reviews disclose the reviewers' determination to treat these relatively austere performances as instances of the Keans's antiquarian art. Melbourne audiences were urged to see history alive before them not in the distractions afforded by 'the "upholstery" of Oxford street'[48] but in the performers' meticulous embodiment of historical personages. This displacement of the antiquarian impulse from the scenery to the acting is perhaps best illustrated in *The Age* review of their performance of Dion Boucicault's play *Louis XI*, which describes Charles Kean's enactment of the fifteenth-century monarch as 'a pre-Raphaelite picture, finished with scrupulous accuracy of detail [...] we quite forget about the actor and the stage — we have laid open before us a stirring page in the history of France'.[49]

The Keans might have been forced to travel light, but they demonstrated the historical genius of their acting in a whole suite of mostly Shakespearean medievalist plays, including *Richard III*, *King John*, *Louis XI*, *Macbeth*, *King Lear*, and *Henry VIII*. Moreover, their presence in Melbourne managed to generate some rather more spectacular antiquarian Shakespeare. In a fierce rivalry that became the stuff of local satire,[50] the actor Barry Sullivan, incumbent at the Theatre Royal between 1862 and 1866, mounted his own more lavish productions, often of the identical plays being performed by the Keans. The *Age* review of his *Richard III*,

[45] Coppin to Kean, 22 October 1862, in *Emigrant in Motley*, p. 50.

[46] That the Keans did bring some costly period costumes with them is suggested by an article in the *Argus* on 12 April 1864, p. 5, which mentions that the Keans's costumes were seized as collateral against a debt owed by the insolvent manager of the Haymarket Theatre.

[47] *The Age*, 27 October 1863.

[48] *The Age*, 27 October 1863.

[49] *The Age*, 26 October 1863.

[50] The *Melbourne Punch* made repeated sport of the Kean/Sullivan rivalry throughout late 1863. This rivalry, and the 'unscrupulous, wicked tricks' of the 'madly jealous' Barry, is discussed by an incensed Ellen Kean in a letter to her daughter Mary, dated 20 November 1863. See *Emigrant in Motley*, pp. 97–100.

which in November 1863 he staged in direct competition with the Keans's production of the same play, describes the performance as '[p]roduced with beautiful scenery and splendid appointments'.[51] Sullivan's particular advantage over the Keans was that he had at his disposal the valuable services of John Hennings, whose painted historical backdrops were widely hailed as equal to those seen by London audiences, the highest praise imaginable for a colonial artist.

After the Keans, the colonies witnessed the arts of numerous other antiquarian Shakespeareans, again mostly touring actors from Britain and America, but also some local talent, such that audiences in the Australian colonies became accustomed to this aesthetic. One of the best-known purveyors of spectacular historical Shakespeare through the 1880s and 1890s was George Rignold. After an acclaimed initial tour in 1876, of which the jewel was his lavish, tableau-driven (complete with teeming horseback battle scenes) rendition of *Henry V*,[52] Rignold returned to Sydney, where he was to become so synonymous with his popular portrayal of Henry V at Her Majesty's Theatre, Sydney, that he would fly the Plantagenet monarch's standard at his home whenever he was resident there.[53] An 18 March 1883 *Illustrated Sydney News* review of Rignold in this role admired his acting, but was almost entirely preoccupied with the visual spectacle of the staging. Several photographs survive of Rignold in his various serial embodiments of this signature role, and in them we can observe an attempt at verisimilitude, especially of costume (Figure 13).

Rignold's productions also, as Richard Fotheringham points out, appealed directly to audiences' Anglophilic interest in dynastic history, thereby perpetuating the nationalist-imperialist agenda of the Kean productions. Later, the locally born but London-trained Oscar Asche and his wife Lily Brayton undertook tours to Australia in 1910 and 1912–13. These tours, in which Asche was, according to Richard Madelaine, 'praised for presenting Shakespeare with the accuracy of detail and scholarly earnestness that made his productions the equivalent of history

[51] *The Age*, 16 November 1863.

[52] See Richard Fotheringham's description of this production in his entry on Rignold in *The Companion to Theatre in Australia*, ed. by Parsons, p. 502.

[53] Helen M. van der Poorten, 'Rignall, George Richard (1839–1912)', *Australian Dictionary of Biography*, VI (1976), 30. 'Rignold' was Rignall's stage name.

lessons',[54] are regarded by critics as the last hoorah for Victorian-style pictorial Shakespeare in Australia (Figure 14).

So pervasive was the Shakespearean medievalist idiom that it was reflected in other popular media. Again, the political cartoon is an index of the absorption of medievalist Shakespeare into colonial satirical self-understanding. In *The Bulletin* on 4 March 1893, we see Livingston Hopkins using the comic confrontation from *Henry V* Act V scene 1, in which the Welshman Fluellen humiliates Pistol by forcing him to eat his leek, to depict the recent appointment of the New South Wales governor Sir Robert Duff by the British Prime Minister Gladstone (Figure 15).

In this cartoon, 'John Bull', in the character of Fluellen, forces a leek with Duff's name on it into the mouth of the New South Wales premier, who, captioned beneath as 'Premier G. Republican Dibbs', protests that the name of the new governor be submitted to parliament. At one level, readers could take pleasure in the irony of Shakespeare's medieval dynastic drama being used to service an anti-imperialist commentary. Although Dibbs was himself cautious of the *Bulletin*'s cherished goal of federation, and had accepted a knighthood the year before, he had for some years generally enjoyed the *Bulletin*'s good opinion. More central to the current discussion, however, is the fact that the cartoon assumes its readership's familiarity with this scene — a familiarity that was more likely, given the many recent productions of *Henry V*, to have come from theatrical exposure than from careful private conning of the Shakespearean text.

This comic approach to the Middle Ages was not, as indicated earlier, limited to newspaper illustrations, but had a solid presence within theatrical representation. This is particularly the case with the burlesque, which was an enormously popular comic vehicle for presenting medieval legend to Australian audiences. Eric Irvin says of it:

> It is not necessary to recount the plots of these burlesques. Their titles tell us all we need to know. They were beautifully mounted; superbly costumed; set to bright, catchy music; housed in a series of finely painted stage pictures; and replete with the atrocious puns so much enjoyed by audiences of the time.[55]

[54] Richard Madelaine, 'Substantial Pageant: Oscar Asche, Latter-Day Pictorialism, and Australian Audiences, 1909–24', in *O Brave New World*, ed. by Golder and Madelaine, pp. 103–20 (p. 104). Veronica Kelly has more recently reminded us that 'detailed historical pictorialism is as consistent with the positivist and scientific impulses of theatrical modernism', and argues that Asche was also interested in modernist staging. See Kelly, 'Shakespeare in Settler-built Spaces', p. 362.

[55] Irvin, *Australian Melodrama*, p. 21.

Figure 13. Napoleon Sarony, 'Photograph of George Rignold as Henry V', Canberra, National Library of Australia, 1875. Reproduced with permission of the National Library of Australia.

Figure 14. 'Postcard of Miss Lily Brayton as "Queen" in Richard II', London, J. Beagles & Co., Canberra National Library of Australia. Reproduced with permission of the National Library of Australia.

Figure 15. Livingston York Hopkins ('Hop'), 'Eating the Leek (Henry V, Act V, scene i)', *The Bulletin*, 4 March 1893. Reproduced with permission of the National Library of Australia.

No-one would cavil at Irvin's description of the burlesques' use of populist spectacle; but are we to accept his assessment of them as so banal as to be essentially content-free diversions? Were these plays, in defiance of nineteenth-century medievalist practice, able to evacuate their medieval legends of all historical and cultural meaning for their colonial audiences? Looking at Australian medievalist burlesque, we find that they can be seen to be poised uneasily between imperialist triumphalism and the throwaway approach to premodern legend and history described by Irvin. Furthermore, it can be argued that their ambivalent use of medieval English source material dramatizes a cultural tension in which a nostalgic reiteration of shared origins with England rubs shoulders with the proleptic staging of separate Australian nationhood.

Veronica Kelly has noted the 'prevalence of [...] historical themes' in the Australian burlesque.[56] Because of its parodic nature, burlesque was what can be called a particularly voracious, even predatory, genre, ranging widely across history and across cultures for satiric quarry. No historical event or figure, no serious drama, no piece of high literature, was safe from its cannibilizing clutches. As such, colonial audiences were likely to see burlesque treatments of Homeric legend, orientalist tale, the Latin-American *conquista*, or even contemporary Australian society rubbing shoulders fairly indiscriminately with medievalist burlesque. Sometimes this cross-historical cannibalizing even took place within a single play, as in William Mower Akhurst's adaptation of a burlesque based on the Carolingian romance *Valentine and Orson*.[57] According to the *Argus* review of the play, scenes featuring the château of King Pepin, the Gothic interior of 'The Castle of the Green Knight', and the medieval city of Orléans were interspersed with scenes in an Egyptian temple, a vista of classical Athens, and 'the Frozen Regions', and finally culminated in a tableau featuring an 'equestrian statue' of Melbourne's adopted son, the recently perished explorer Burke.[58] Despite the broad historical net cast by burlesque, events and legends from the Middle Ages, and their nineteenth-century nostalgic reworkings, were deemed particularly ripe for travesty and were regular targets of the burlesquers' pens, including those of local theatre writers. Most of these burlesques took the form of minimally localized British hits and, as such, can only be taken to be 'Australian' under the broad definition outlined earlier in this chapter. A small number of them, however, can be more readily described as intrinsically and revealingly reflective of their colonial Australian provenance.

[56] Kelly, 'Burlesque', in *The Companion to Theatre in Australia*, p. 115.

[57] *Harlequin Valentine and Orson*, performed at the Theatre Royal, Melbourne, 1861.

[58] *The Argus*, 27 December 1861.

Of the medievalist burlesques either written in Australia or adapted for Australian audiences, three can be singled out for particular attention. These are Akhurst's *King Arthur; Or, Launcelot the Loose, Gin-ever the Square, and the Knights of the Round Table and Other Furniture*[59] as well as his 1869 *The Battle of Hastings; Or the Duke, the Earl, the Witch, the Why and the Wherefore*[60] and Marcus Clarke and Henry Keiley's more modestly titled fairy extravaganza *Alfred the Great.*[61] Apart from the fact that these are the only medievalist burlesques whose libretti are still available (unlike, for instance, Akhurst's 1858–59 play *Harlequin Robin Hood,* for which no text survives) all three plays claim our attention for their lampooning of significant 'nation-making' figures or events from English medieval legend and history. In this respect they offer useful test cases to determine the ideological 'work' done by medievalist burlesque as performed in colonial Australia.

They were, furthermore, each very popular. Reviews routinely mention capacity crowds at their performances. Irvin credits Akhurst with being the pioneer of the long theatrical run in Australia,[62] and *Alfred the Great* was among Clarke's most popular plays.[63] It is true that, looked at alone, the libretti offer incomplete evidence of the audiences' experience of these plays, as burlesque was an uncommonly protean genre, responding in each performance not only to changing audience demands but also to the news of the day.[64] Indeed, the reviews in *The Argus* from the first two weeks of *Alfred the Great*'s run track a virtual overhaul of sections of the play, with some scenes rewritten, others removed and later restored, and the whole play generally renovated in response to its lukewarm opening night review.[65] Nevertheless, the libretti, for all their betrayal of this performative mutability, allow

[59] Premiered 31 October 1868 at the Theatre Royal, Melbourne.

[60] Premiered 29 March 1869 at the Theatre Royal, Melbourne.

[61] Premiered 24 December 1878 at the Academy of Music, Melbourne.

[62] Irvin, *Australian Melodrama*, p. 20. Spring's *A Frequency List of Dramatic Performances in the Melbourne* Argus *between January 1860 and December 1869* calculates an impressive thirty-three performances for *King Arthur*, while *The Battle of Hastings* had a run of eleven performances.

[63] Kelly says it 'achieved a good run', in her entry 'Marcus Clarke', in *The Companion to Theatre in Australia*, p. 147.

[64] On this, see Richard Schoch, *Victorian Theatrical Burlesques* (Cambridge: Cambridge University Press, 2003), pp. xxii–xxvi.

[65] A review in the *Argus* from 31 December 1878 mentions alterations to dialogues and the final transformation scene (p. 5), while the same paper notes on 2 January 1879 that a scene that had been removed from the production had again been restored (p. 5).

us to analyse the content of at least one version of these plays and to discover details that are only alluded to, or indeed completely passed over, in review notices.

The term 'medievalist burlesque' refers here to plays whose plots travestied grandiose events and personages from medieval history and legend. Despite their pre-modern settings, these plays' dialogue was peppered with local and topical references, was typically written in rhyming couplets, and was heavily seasoned with excruciating puns. As Irvin's comments indicate, they were visually and aurally sumptuous, with spectacular transformation scenes, fairy spectacles, and ballet interludes. Richard Schoch, who has spearheaded the recent rehabilitation of this maligned Victorian genre, argues that the burlesques' 'inherently metadramatic' nature — that is, their status as populist comedic plays that travesty recognizable 'legitimate' dramas — makes them uniquely telling instances of popular culture's response to the development of Victorian theatre.[66] In the Australian context, the medievalist burlesques do not seem quite so centrally driven by the metadramatic impetus; but they do reflect Schoch's more general contention that burlesques by their very nature implicate themselves in that which lies outside them, including other texts and performances, and their cultural-historical contexts.[67] In this respect they seem a particularly apposite genre for treating medievalist themes, for their referentiality echoes and reinforces the appropriative impetus at the heart of medievalism. Akhurst's *King Arthur* seems, for instance, not to have been heavily influenced by Arthurian theatre; according to the chronology traced by Alan Lupack, the avalanche of Arthur plays was still two decades off.[68] Rather, the play's focus on Guinevere, Elaine, and Vivien, and direct references to Tennyson and Gustav Doré, suggest the more immediate influence of the first four of the *Idylls of the King*, which had been published nine years earlier, and of Doré's illustrations of them, which had been published earlier that year.[69] *The Battle of Hastings* appears to be lampooning the ponderous mock-Norse of Edward Bulwer-Lytton's 1848 novel *Harold, or the Last of the Saxon Kings*, but it is also very likely to have been inspired more generally by the exhaustive commemoration of the Battle of Hastings

[66] Schoch, *Victorian Theatrical Burlesques*, p. xii.

[67] Richard Schoch, *Not Shakespeare: Bardolatry and Burlesque in the Nineteenth Century* (Cambridge: Cambridge University Press, 2002), p. 30.

[68] See Alan Lupack, *Arthurian Drama: An Anthology* (New York: Garland, 1991), pp. xvii–xxxiv, 311–22. See also Jerome V. Reel, Jr, 'The Music of Arthur: A Listing', on the *Arthuriana* website: <http://www.lib.rochester.edu/camelot/acpbibs/reel.htm>.

[69] W. M. Akhurst, *King Arthur; Or, Launcelot the Loose, Gin-ever the Square, and the Knights of the Round Table and Other Furniture: A Burlesque Extravaganza* (Melbourne: Bell, 1868), p. 30.

two years earlier in 1866, the eight-hundredth anniversary of the Norman Invasions.[70] Finally, *Alfred the Great* may perhaps have had a loose theatrical model, given that the prolific Victorian literature on Alfred included a number of plays and even burlesques,[71] including one performed in Melbourne in the 1860s, but it too was very probably inspired by the recent millennial commemoration of Alfred's victory over the Viking invader Guthrum in 878.

The particular importance of the burlesques selected here lies in the contradictory combination of their physical medium and their facetious representations of the English medieval past. Irvin treated the mismatch of form and content as grounds for dismissal, but it is actually vital to understanding the burlesques' theatrical, ideological, and historical value. As examples of medievalist theatre, the Australian burlesques sat incongruously at the cusp of antiquarian fetishism and populist anachronism. In harbouring this incongruity, these plays reflected the ambivalence at the heart of Australian medievalism. Their physical splendour reflected the antiquarian desire to reanimate the nationalist high points of English medieval history, and their fast-and-loose verbal and performative treatment of their material reflected an apparently more irreverent attitude toward this illustrious past.

Their satiric treatment notwithstanding, the burlesque writers, performers, and stage artists clearly revelled in vividly recreating such weighty historical moments as Alfred's victory over Guthrum or Arthur's mortal combat with Mordred. As with the melodramatic, sensational, and also the 'legitimate' genres discussed earlier, this antiquarian impulse was most visible in the burlesques' use of scenery, costume, and staging. In the context of the medievalist burlesques written by Akhurst, the libretti indicate that the medievalist *mise-en-scène* was produced by the celebrated John Hennings, who had been responsible for the scenery in so many 'legitimate' productions.[72] In the libretto of *The Battle of Hastings*, the 'magnificent scenery' is

[70] On Victorian representations of the Norman conquest, see Clare Simmons, *Reversing the Conquest;* for a more focused discussion of the 1866 commemorations of the Battle of Hastings, see Asa Briggs, 'Saxons, Normans and Victorians', pp. 215–35.

[71] For a discussion of nineteenth-century theatrical representations of Alfred, see Donald Scragg's 'Introduction: The Anglo-Saxons, Fact and Fiction', in *Literary Appropriations of the Anglo-Saxons from the Thirteenth to the Twentieth Centuries*, ed. by Scragg and Carole Weinberg (Cambridge: Cambridge University Press, 2000), pp. 1–21 (pp. 15–20).

[72] Hennings's career is discussed at length by Mimi Colligan in *Canvas Documentaries: Panoramic Entertainments in Nineteenth-Century Australia and New Zealand* (Carlton: Melbourne University Press, 2002); and by Anita Callaway in *Visual Ephemera: Theatrical Art in Nineteenth-Century Australia* (Sydney: University of New South Wales Press, 2000).

listed as created by Hennings 'from historical sketches', and the setting notes mention such historically specific scenes as 'a half-ruined Roman villa restored in the Anglo-Saxon style'.[73] One review of Akhurst's classicist burlesque *The Siege of Troy* praised Hennings's scenery for improving the taste of the viewer and, in doing so, mercifully eclipsing the author's tawdry efforts.[74]

In an influential argument about the relationship between Victorian pictorial and performative arts, Martin Meisel claims that the pictorialism of nineteenth-century drama was not limited to its *mise-en-scène* but extended rather to the dramaturgy itself.[75] This observation is certainly borne out, indeed epitomized, in the pictorialized Shakespeare of George Rignold, with its tendency to organize the plays into a series of highly spectacular tableaux and set-pieces. While Meisel takes melodrama as his example, his argument is also applicable to burlesque, which built spectacle and pictorial elements such as *tableaux vivants* firmly into the development of the plot. To take just one instance, at the end of scene 3 of *King Arthur*, immediately after Arthur's coronation, we find a stage direction calling upon the Round Table Knights to engage in a series of *poses plastiques*.[76] The libretto leaves us to guess at the nature of these poses, but one might speculate as to their relationship to Doré's celebrated illustrations.[77] The dramatic, gestural pictorialism of the poses would seem to reinforce the scenic historicism of the play, by situating it within the illustrious painterly and monumental history of European Arthurianism. Yet it would seem that their status is more ambivalent than this; for, as Callaway notes, *tableaux vivants* simultaneously honour and burlesque the artworks they recreate.[78] Furthermore, in their very pictorial stasis they have the effect of interrupting the spatio-temporal unfolding of the plays' historical or legendary narrative.

Schoch claims that the pictorial antiquarianism of nineteenth-century historical drama in England was a recuperative gesture reflective of a modern urban society anxious about its alienation from history. He argues that 'a people dispossessed of

[73] William Mower Akhurst, *The Battle of Hastings; Or, the Duke, the Earl, the Witch, the Why & the Wherefore: A Historical Burlesque* (Melbourne: Bell, 1869), p. 7.

[74] This review is quoted by Mimi Colligan in *Canvas Documentaries*, p. 105.

[75] Martin Miesel, *Realizations: Narrative, Pictorial, and Theatrical Arts in Nineteenth-Century England* (Princeton: Princeton University Press, 1983), p. 39.

[76] On *poses plastiques* as a 'sculptural subspecies' of *tableaux vivants*, see Callaway, *Visual Ephemera*, pp. 60–84.

[77] *King Arthur*, p. 17.

[78] Callaway, *Visual Ephemera*, p. 60.

their own history [...] are always already struggling to repossess that history in its former totality and unity by rehabilitating the very material things [...] which are authorized to constitute a national heritage'.[79] We might add to Schoch's argument that this antiquarianism was much more complex and ambivalent not only in burlesque *per se*, with its frank adulteration of the historical by the topical, but most particularly in colonial burlesques, where the desire for historical repossession was shadowed by the anticipation of future separation.

Of course, burlesque audiences did not believe they were viewing history reanimated. Unlike the 'legitimate' drama, of which there was an expectation of accuracy, their striving for pictorial fidelity, and their antiquarian embodiment of the past through costume, gesture, and scenery were significantly and deliberately mitigated by their signature embracing of anachronism. First of all, the Shakespearean idiom that infected the melodramas was strongly evident as a theatrical 'filter' through which medieval history passed in the Australian burlesques: in *King Arthur* Guinevere likens herself to Beatrice in *Much Ado About Nothing*; in *Alfred the Great* the Danish invader Guthrum, who is described in the *Argus* as a 'dyspeptic Hamlet',[80] utters speeches larded with quotations from the Danish prince's most famous speeches; and the Norman minstrel Taillefer in *The Battle of Hastings* is a stage Frenchman in the tradition of Dr Caius in *The Merry Wives of Windsor*, making liberal use of that character's catchphrase 'by gar'. Interestingly, while Schoch claims that Shakespeare's chronicle plays, with their dramatization of key medieval English nationalizing moments, were the most influential on the medievalist theatrical idiom, in the texts of the Australian medievalist burlesques the chronicle plays do not really figure. And yet their visual idiom clearly owed much to the kind of 'upholstered' chronicle productions offered to Melbourne audiences by the Keans and Barry Sullivan only two or three years earlier.

This Shakespearean mediation joined forces with the burlesques' trademark farcical dialogue and comedic performance modes to generate what was at times an extremely distant relationship between the burlesques and their medieval source material.[81] Their irreverent approach to historical personages is marked, for instance, by their pantomimic casting of King Alfred and King Harold Godwinson as breeches roles, and Guinevere and Hecla the Danish Queen as drag roles, as well

[79] Schoch, *Shakespeare's Victorian Stage*, p. 12.

[80] *Argus*, 25 December 1878.

[81] For a discussion of the burlesque acting style of this period, see Barnard Hewitt, 'Mrs. John Wood and the Lost Art of Burlesque Acting', *Educational Theatre Journal*, 13 (1961), 82–85.

as by their inclusion of 'leg-show' ballets, a prurient addition that disgusted both the audience and the Melbourne *Age*'s critic of *King Arthur*.[82] They also, as mentioned earlier, localized their medieval material, as can be seen in Sir Kay's song in *King Arthur* in which he describes himself as 'the cantering cad of Collins street',[83] and traded extensively in deflationary puns, such as the naming of the Knights of the Round Table Sir Cuss, Sir Cumlocution, Sir Pent, Sir Vile, and so on.[84] There is, furthermore, often only the most desultory adherence to the broadest contours of the medieval legend being staged, or, in the case of *Alfred the Great*, significant departure. In this play's conclusion we see historico-political legend mutated into romantic comedy as Alfred marries the poor Saxon girl Bertha, rather than his actual bride Ealhswith. In short, these plays, unlike historical drama, were a determined combination of the monumental and the ephemeral. In this respect they reinforce Veronica Kelly's argument that the response to historical drama in Australia ranged from monumentalism through to modernist irony.[85] Indeed, it could even be said that they extend her thesis by demonstrating that these two apparently incongruous attitudes could in fact function comedically as unexpected bedfellows.

Would audiences have cared about whether the past was presented to them in such a slipshod way? As with the satiric cartoons and poems discussed in the previous chapter, the question of what audiences might have got from these productions must take into account what cultural awareness they might have brought to their viewing of them. According to some critics, the burlesques are notable for their straddling of erudition and popular entertainment. In order for their irreverent treatment to be intelligible, they depended on audiences who were conversant not only with the original texts being burlesqued but also earlier performances and productions, which were also often being lampooned. If the audience has no knowledge of that which is being burlesqued, there is no burlesque. As Fotheringaham says, '[t]he pleasure of viewing in part depended on identifying

[82] *The Age*, 2 November 1868, p. 3.

[83] Akhurst, *King Arthur*, p. 16. Andrew Lynch has demonstrated the extent to which Akhurst also makes allusions to local parliamentary debates in *King Arthur*, in his conference paper 'Arthur, Empire, Australia', delivered at the 'Medievalism, Colonialism, Nationalism' symposium, University of California, Riverside, 7–8 November 2008.

[84] Akhurst, *King Arthur*, p. 3.

[85] Veronica Kelly, 'Julius Knight, Australian Matinee Idol: Costume Drama as Historical Representation', *Australasian Victorian Studies Journal*, 9 (2003), 128–44 (p. 142).

as many witty borrowings and generic inversions as possible'.[86] And yet Schoch also admits that much of the burlesques' humour, especially their torrential punning, would have passed over the original audiences' heads. This raises the question of whether these plays presumed erudition on the part of their audiences or whether, like their print counterparts in the popular press, they traded rather in knowingness, Peter Bailey's 'select conspiracy of meaning that animates [an] audience', giving it a 'flattering sense of membership' that reflects its 'own well-tested cultural and social competence'.[87] While Bailey refers chiefly to music hall, his description could equally describe the mode of appeal the Australian burlesques made to their audience, especially if we take into account Fotheringham's description of colonial Australian audiences:

> [a]nyone who considered themselves worldly [...] had some notion of the characters, the plots, and the key moments in the seminal stories of the times, and could follow (or pretend to follow) the intertextual jokes which both public gossip and stage burlesque exploited to excess.[88]

Reading the libretti, and taking into account that these burlesques generally had a fairly attenuated relationship to their dramatic and literary precedents, it would not seem that their level of satire demanded erudition from their audience. The libretti disclose the dramatists' expectations that their audiences will have a grasp on local news and civic topography, as well as a regular theatre-goers' competency in Shakespeare; but it appears that only a general knowledge of medieval and medievalist works is assumed. This is also borne out in the reviews. These acknowledge the burlesque's logic of wholesale demolition, in which the medieval legends and their grandiloquent contemporary appropriations are rendered equally ridiculous, but nevertheless contain only glancing allusions to medieval legend, and even then such allusions are to such ubiquitous reference-points as Tennyson and Malory. Those audience members with deeper knowledge might have been invited to detect more subtle notes of satire, but those less familiar need not feel left out of the joke. Bailey's incisive characterization of knowingness as 'what everybody knows, but which some know better than others' applies to this satirico-historical theatre as powerfully as it does to Victorian print satire.[89]

[86] Fotheringham, *Australian Plays for the Colonial Stage*, p. xxvii.

[87] Peter Bailey, *Popular Culture and Performance in the Victorian City*, p. 137.

[88] Fotheringham, *Australian Plays for the Colonial Stage*, p. xxvii.

[89] Bailey, *Popular Culture and Performance in the Victorian City*, p. 128.

And yet this should not be taken to mean that the burlesques were devoid of any historical or ideological significance for their audiences. In fact, their concluding scenes in particular support Schoch's contention that in this period '"performing the Middle Ages" was itself a political event because it strove to construct and express a national identity through the display of historical relics and historical bodies'.[90] As spectacular culminations of the historical and pictorial elements of these plays, all three final scenes are the most ideologically charged and hence the most culturally revealing. For instance, *Alfred the Great* concludes with a grand spectacle that, by featuring King Neptune crowning Alfred as monarch of the seas, clearly aligns the medieval hero with modern, naval Britannia; thus he is founder and king not just of England, but of the British Empire.[91] *The Battle of Hastings*, fusing the mythology of medieval nation-formation with that of racial heritage, ends with a song that rehearses the popular nineteenth-century notion that the Norman invasion inaugurated the emergence of a 'naturally selected' imperial race comprised of Saxon, Norman, and Danish:

> The Saxon gave thee liberty,
> Merry land of England.
> The Dane the sceptre of the sea,
> [...] The Norman arms and chivalry,
> [...] And none shall take these gifts from thee,
> Merry land of England.[92]

Finally, *King Arthur*, not content to wait for the monarch's promised return, resurrects him so he can participate in the grand transformation scene that ends the play.[93]

Yet it would be reductive to claim that these plays' conclusions are unproblematic triumphal celebrations of English leadership and ancient nationhood, for the semantic and dramatic instability of burlesque ensures that everything that is celebrated is also simultaneously satirized. It is this instability that renders the burlesque, in Schoch's words, '[l]ess a site of vulgar didacticism than of playful contestation',[94] that is, a vehicle of political imagination rather than of political critique. With the Australian burlesques, it is vital to bear in mind that while they

[90] Schoch, *Shakespeare's Victorian Stage*, p. 116.

[91] Marcus Clarke, *Alfred the Great* (Melbourne: Nicholas and Ascherberg, 1879), p. 12.

[92] Akhurst, *The Battle of Hastings*, p. 32.

[93] Akhurst, *King Arthur*, pp. 30–31.

[94] Schoch, *Not Shakespeare*, p. 152.

were plays about English nationhood, they were also plays about the development of nationhood *per se.* To be sure, any serious federalist movement was still two decades away; but is not unreasonable to speculate that colonial Australian audiences, with their own national sovereignty as yet unrealized, would have responded to these final scenes' spectacular staging of nation-formation in a way that was distinct from English audiences. Their imperial focus means these burlesques do not quite qualify as what Josephine Fantasia has called 'postcolonial' pantomimes, in which '"Australia" is presented in some way as politically separate from "Britannia"'.[95] Yet their unstable dramatizations of medieval English nationhood, although not deliberately critical of England or her Empire, carry nested within them a proleptic evocation of Australian nationhood.

This is perhaps made most explicit in Akhurst's 1867 Christmas burlesque extravaganza *Tom, Tom, the Piper's Son, and Mary Mary, Quite Contrary; Or, Harlequin Piggy Wiggy and the Good Child's History of England.* Despite being set in 'Castle Toorakanruen', a name that satirically medievalizes the Melbourne suburb of Toorak, this was not a specifically medievalist production. But in its libretto we find what the review in *The Argus* described as the extravaganza's 'most noticeable scene': 'The Hall of History, disclosing the Good Child's History of England', in which a 'grand procession of the Sovereigns of England' emerges out of huge onstage book. By beginning with William the Conqueror, and then progressing to Victoria, the scene traces an historical trajectory of conquest and settlement beginning with medieval England itself and concluding with Australia as Britain's imperial apotheosis.[96] But the scene's ideological valency is not straightforward. First of all, the monarchs' procession takes place against a running commentary of deflationary gags. Plus, as discussed at length by the *Argus* reviewer, this spectacle tempered its triumphalist pedagogy with infantilizing satire, by having all of the monarchs played by little children. Having William the Conqueror 'personated by a sturdy little fellow carrying a cross-hilted sword nearly as big as himself',[97] *Tom, Tom* rendered the pomp and pageantry of imperial history mock-

[95] Josephine Vita Fantasia, 'Entrepreneurs, Empires and Pantomimes: J. C. Williamson's Pantomime Productions as a Site from which to Review the Cultural Construction of an Australian Theatre Industry, 1882 to 1914' (unpublished doctoral thesis, University of Sydney, 1996), p. 71.

[96] William Mower Akhurst, *Tom, Tom, the Piper's Son, and Mary, Mary, Quite Contrary; Or, Harlequin Piggy Wiggy and the Good Child's History of England: A Burlesque Extravaganza and Pantomime* (Melbourne: Bell, 1868).

[97] *Argus*, 27 December 1867.

heroic. The play ends, furthermore, on a note that epitomizes perfectly Schoch's notion of 'playful contestation'. Its penultimate stanza is a tribute to the Queen and to Australia's first royal guest, Prince Alfred, who was in Melbourne at the time:

So bless her Royal Majesty
Likewise the Prince of Wales
And the young prince who
In a suit of blue
In the 'Galatea' sails

But this imperial loyalty is, in play's final stanza, humorously destabilized:

And I fancy he says when he gets home
To his own dearest ma, says he, —
I'm a sail-i-or, but Austra-li-a
Is the land, dear ma, for me.[98]

At one level, this is a pure expression of manifest destiny, appearing to suggest that the prince should be the ruler of Australia as an arm of Greater Britain. But these lines also whisper faintly of separation or even abdication, as the sailor prince, who had recently sunk to fifth-in-line to the throne, prefers his prospects in Australia over his life in England. Any faint premonition of separation is immediately dispelled by a chorus of *Rule Britannia*; but this segue is conventional rather than natural, and so does not ultimately settle the question of whether these final lines signal continuity or eventual rupture. This and the other plays discussed here can thus be said to fulfil Schoch's conception that historical burlesque did not so much distort history as proffer 'a true myth of origins for a political reality which had yet to be realized'.[99]

In relation to Australian medievalism more specifically, the burlesques' position is complex. On the one hand, they were an extremely popular local form; and yet their 'Australianness' was less easily located than we might think. It is tempting to locate it within the local allusions; but when Mordred sings a song lampooning the local chief of Railway,[100] or Harold Godwinson marks the rise of the omnibus as a feature of the Melbourne streetscape,[101] what is taking place is simultaneously local and a reiteration of the metropolitan theatrical practices of England, the United

[98] *Tom, Tom, the Piper's Son*, p. 81.

[99] Schoch, *Not Shakespeare*, p. 163.

[100] Akhurst, *King Arthur*, pp. 23–24. The *Age* review of this play (2 November 1868, p. 3) notes that the Chief of Railways, C. E. Jones, was present at the opening performance with his family, and was much amused by the satire aimed at him.

[101] Akhurst, *The Battle of Hastings*, p. 23.

States, Canada, and other sites within the cosmopolitan culture of Victorian popular theatre. Ironically, localization was an international practice, so their local references are more a reflection of what Kelly might call their 'pre-nationalist' participation in transcultural theatrical culture, and their response to 'the economic and discursive currents of nineteenth-century international commercial entertainment'.[102] As a genre, medievalist burlesque was, then, profoundly Australian, not in the sense of producing portraits of local life but insofar as it encapsulated the distinctive ambivalence of Australian medievalism. It both enacted and travestied antiquarian nostalgia; it was both reverential and deflationary; loyal to England yet envisioning separation; and, finally, desirous in equal parts of restoring and preserving, and mutating and destroying, the medieval past.

[102] Veronica Kelly, 'Colonial "Australian" Theatre Writers: Cultural Authorship and the Case of Marcus Clarke's "First" Play', *Australian Literary Studies*, 18 (1997), 31–44.

# BIBLIOGRAPHY

## *Newspapers*

*The Age*
*The Argus*
*Australasian Sketcher*
*Australian News for Home Readers*
*Bell's Life in Sydney and Sporting Reviewer*
*The Bulletin*
*Fremantle Herald*
*The Herald*
*The Lantern*
*London Punch*
*The Lone Hand*
*Melbourne Bulletin*
*Melbourne Punch*
*Quiz*
*The Sketch*
*Sydney Morning Herald*
*Illustrated Sydney News*
*Sydney Punch*

## *Primary Texts: Novels, Poems, Essays, Playscripts*

Adams, Francis, *Australian Essays* (Melbourne: Inglis, 1886)

—, *Songs of the Army of the Night and Mass of Christ* (London: Fifield, 1910)

Akhurst, William Mower, *Tom, Tom, the Piper's Son, and Mary, Mary, Quite Contrary; Or, Harlequin Piggy Wiggy and the Good Child's History of England: A Burlesque Extravaganza and Pantomime* (Melbourne: Bell, 1868)

—, *King Arthur; Or, Launcelot the Loose, Gin-ever the Square, and the Knights of the Round Table and Other Furniture: A Burlesque Extravaganza* (Melbourne: Bell, 1868)

—, *The Battle of Hastings; Or, the Duke, the Earl, the Witch, the Why & the Wherefore: A Historical Burlesque* (Melbourne: Bell, 1869)

Bean, C. E. W., *Flagships Three* (London: Alston Rivers, 1913)

Boldrewood, Rolf, *A Sydney-Side Saxon* (London: Macmillan, 1894; Sydney: Cornstalk, 1925)
—, *The Miner's Right: A Tale of the Australian Goldfields* (London: Macmillan, 1890)
—, *My Run Home* (London: Macmillan, 1897)
—, *Old Melbourne Memories* (London/New York: Macmillan, 1896)
—, A *Romance of Canvas Town and Other Stories* (London: Macmillan, 1901)
—, *Shearing in the Riverina, New South Wales* (London: Smith, Elder, 1873; first published in *Cornhill Magazine*, 1865)
Bulletin Writers, *A Golden Shanty: Australian Stories and Sketches in Prose and Verse* (Sydney: Bulletin Newspaper, Series No. 1, 1890)
Cambridge, Ada, *The Three Miss Kings*, with a new introduction by Audrey Tate (1891; London: Virago, 1987)
—, *A Woman's Friendship*, ed. by Elizabeth Morrison (Kensington: New South Wales University Press, 1988)
—, *The Perversity of Human Nature*, from *The Illustrated Australian News Christmas Supplement* (Melbourne: Syme, 1887)
—, *Thirty Years in Australia*, intro. by Louise Wakeling and Margaret Bradstock (Kensington: New South Wales University Press, 1989)
—, *The Manor House and Other Poems* (London: Daldy, Isbister, 1875)
Clarke, Marcus, *Alfred the Great* (Melbourne: Nicholas and Ascherberg, 1879)
—, *His Natural Life*, ed. by Graham Tulloch, intro. by Michael Meehan (Oxford and New York: Oxford University Press, 1997)
Carlyle, Thomas, *Past and Present*, intro. by Ralph Waldo Emerson (Boston: Little, Brown, 1843)
Daley, Victor J., *Creeve Roe: Poetry by Victor Daley*, ed. by Muir Holburn and Marjorie Pizer, foreword by E. J. Brady, drawings by Roderick Shaw (Sydney: Pinchgut, 1947)
Dilke, Charles, *Greater Britain, A Record of Travel in the English-Speaking Countries During 1866 and 1867*, 2 vols (London: Macmillan, 1868)
Foott, Mary Hannay, *Where the Pelican Builds and Other Poems* (Brisbane: Gordon and Gotch, 1885)
Franklin, Miles, *My Brilliant Career / My Career Goes Bung*, intro. by Elizabeth Webby (Sydney: Harper Perennial, 2004)
Furphy, Joseph, *Such is Life: Being Certain Extracts from the Diary of Tom Collins* (Sydney: Bulletin Newspaper, 1903)
—, *Rigby's Romance: A 'Made in Australia' Novel* (Melbourne: deGaris, 1921)
—, *Bushman and Bookworm: Letters of Joseph Furphy*, ed. by J. Barnes and L. Hoffman (Melbourne: Oxford University Press, 1995)
Gay, William, *The Complete Poetical Works of William Gay* (Melbourne: Lothian, 1911)
Geoghegan, Edward, *The Hibernian Father* [SZ 58] Colonial Secretary CGS 908, *Plays submitted for approval prior to being performed, 1842–52*, New South Wales State Records
Gordon, Adam Lindsay, *Poems* (1893; London and Melbourne: Thompson, Massina, 1920)
Haweis, Mary Eliza, *The Art of Beauty* (New York: Harper, 1878)
Hill, Fidelia S. T., *Poems and Recollections of the Past* (Sydney: Trood, 1840)
Hilhouse Taylor, Rev. T., *Parsifal, or the Redemption of Kundry: A Romantic Mystery Drama* (Sydney: Angus and Robertson, 1906)
Kingsley, Henry, *The Recollections of Geoffry Hamlyn* (Cambridge: Macmillan, 1859)

Knowles, Conrad, *Salathiel, or the Jewish Chieftain,* [SZ 64], Colonial Secretary CGS 908, *Plays submitted for approval prior to being performed, 1842–52,* New South Wales State Records

Lane, William, *The Workingman's Paradise: An Australian Labour Novel* (Sydney, Brisbane, and London: Edwards, Dunlop, 1892)

Lang, John Dunmore, *Poems: Sacred and Secular, Written Chiefly at Sea Within the Last Half Century* (Sydney: Maddock, 1873)

Lowell, James Russell, *The Anti-Slavery Papers of James Russell Lowell,* ed. by William Belmont Parker, 2 vols (Boston: Houghton Mifflin, 1902)

Martin, Catherine, *An Australian Girl* (London: Richard Bentley and Son, 1891)

—, *The Explorers and Other Poems* (Melbourne: Robertson, 1874)

Masterman, C. F. G., *The Heart of the Empire* (London: Unwin, 1901)

Mitchell, Thomas Livingstone, *Journal of an Expedition in the Interior of Tropical Australia in Search of a Route from Sydney to the Gulf of Carpentaria* (London: Longman, Brown, Green, and Longmans, 1848)

Morris, William, 'The Beauty of Life', in *Hopes and Fears for Art: Five Lectures Delivered in Birmingham, London, and Nottingham, 1878–1881* (London: Ellis & White, 1882)

Parkes, Henry, 'Australia and the Imperial Connection', *Nineteenth Century,* 15 (1884), 867–72

—, *The Federal Government of Australasia: Speeches Delivered on Various Occasions (November 1889–May 1890)* (Sydney: Turner and Henderson, 1890)

Pickering, George Ferrers, *Lough Deargh's Shrine, or, The Cave of Penance* [SZ 57] Colonial Secretary CGS 908, *Plays submitted for approval prior to being performed, 1842–52,* New South Wales State Records

Pope, Alexander, 'Peri Bathous, or the Art of Sinking in Poetry', in *Alexander Pope: The Major Works,* ed. by Pat Rogers (Oxford: Oxford University Press, 2006), pp. 195–238

Praed, Rosa, *Policy and Passion: A Novel of Australian Life* (London: Richard Bentley and Son, 1881)

Praed, Rosa, *Australian Life, Black and White* (London: Chapman and Hall, 1885)

Praed, Rosa, *The Romance of a Station: An Australian Story* (London: Chatto and Windus, 1893)

Reeve, Edward, *Raymond, Lord of Milan: A Tragedy in the 13th Century* (Sydney: Hawksley & Cunninghame, 1851)

Richardson, Henry Handel, *The Getting of Wisdom* (London: Heinemann, 1931)

Ruskin, John, *The Stones of Venice,* ed. and intro. by Jan Morris (London: Faber, 1981)

Scott, Sir Walter, *Ivanhoe,* ed. by Graham Tulloch (Edinburgh: Edinburgh University Press, 1998)

Seeley, John Robert, *The Expansion of England: Two Courses of Lectures* (London: Macmillan, 1883)

Stephensen, P. R., 'The Foundations of Culture in Australia' (1935), in *The Writer in Australia: A Collection of Literary Documents, 1856 to 1964,* ed. by John Barnes (Melbourne: Oxford University Press, 1969), pp. 204–44

Tasma (Jessie Couvreur), *Uncle Piper of Piper's Hill* (London: Heinemann, 1892)

—, *A Sydney Sovereign and Other Tales* (London: Trübner, 1890)

Tennyson, Alfred, Lord, *Idylls of the King,* ed. by J. M. Gray (Harmondsworth: Penguin, 1983)

Twain, Mark, *Following the Equator: A Journey around the World* (Mineola, NY: Dover, 1989)

Twain, Mark, *A Connecticut Yankee in King Arthur's Court,* ed. by William Dudley Warner, in *The Writings of Mark Twain* (New York: Harper, 1889)

—, *Life on the Mississippi* (Boston: Osgood, 1883)

Wise, B. R., *The Commonwealth of Australia* (Boston: Little, Brown, 1909)
Woolley, John, 'Schools of Art and Colonial Nationality: A Lecture Delivered at the Inauguration of the Wollongong School of Arts, May 28th 1861' (Sydney: Reading & Wellbank, 1861)
—, *Lectures Delivered in Australia* (Cambridge and London: Macmillan, 1862)

## *Archives*

Coppin Archive, National Library of Australia
New South Wales State Records

## *Secondary Texts*

Ackland, Michael, *That Shining Band: A Study of Australian Colonial Verse Tradition* (St Lucia: University of Queensland Press, 1994)
—, 'Martial Code: Meditation and Action in the Verse of Adam Lindsay Gordon', *Westerly*, 2 (1993), 53–65
Adelaide, Deborah, ed., *A Bright and Fiery Troop: Australian Women Writers of the Nineteenth Century* (Ringwood, Vic.: Penguin, 1988)
Allen, Margaret, 'What Katie Might Have Learnt in Mount Gambier, or Some Early Influences on C. E. M. Martin', *Barcelona University Australian Studies Papers*, 1 (1996), 1–19
Anderson, Warwick, *The Cultivation of Whiteness: Science, Health, and Racial Destiny in Australia* (Carlton: Melbourne University Press, 2005)
Andrew, Brian, *Australian Gothic: The Gothic Revival in Australian Architecture from the 1840s to the 1950s* (Carlton, Vic.: Miegunyah, 2001)
Bagot, Alec, *Coppin the Great: Father of the Australian Theatre* (Carlton: University of Melbourne Press / London and New York: Cambridge University Press, 1965)
Bailey, Peter, *Popular Culture and Performance in the Victorian City* (Cambridge: Cambridge University Press, 1998)
Barnes, Geraldine, *Viking America: The First Millenium* (Cambridge: Brewer, 2001)
Barnes, Geraldine, and Adrian Mitchell, '"Passing Through Customes": William Dampier's Medieval Baggage', in *Medievalism and the Gothic in Australian Culture*, ed. by Stephanie Trigg (Turnhout: Brepols, 2005), pp. 131–45
Barrett, Bernard, 'FitzGibbon, Edmund Gerald (1825–1905)', *Australian Dictionary of Biography*, 18 vols (Carlton: Melbourne University Press, 1966–2007), IV (1972), 181–82
Bell, Duncan, *The Idea of Greater Britain* (Princeton: Princeton University Press, 2007)
Bhabha, Homi K., *The Location of Culture* (London and New York: Routledge, 1994)
Bloch, R. Howard, 'Naturalism, Nationalism, Medievalism', *Romantic Review*, 76 (1985), 341–60
Boucher, Leigh, Jane Carey, and Katherine Ellinghaus, eds, *Historicising Whiteness: Transnational Perspectives on the Construction of an Identity* (Melbourne: RMIT Publishing, in association with the School of Historical Studies, University of Melbourne, 2006)
Braswell, Mary Flowers, 'The Chaucer Scholarship of Mary Eliza Haweis (1582–1898)', *The Chaucer Review*, 39 (2005), 402–19

Brewer, F. C., *The Drama and Music in New South Wales* (Sydney: Charles Potter, Government Printer, 1892)

Briggs, Asa, 'Saxons, Normans and Victorians', in *The Collected Essays of Asa Briggs*, 3 vols (Urbana: University of Illinois Press, 1985–91), II, 215–35

Brisbane, Katherine, *Entertaining Australia: An Illustrated History* (Sydney: Currency, 1991)

Buczkowski, Paul, 'J. R. Planché, Frederick Robson, and the Fairy Extravaganza', *Marvels and Tales: Journal of Fairy-Tale Studies*, 15 (2001), 42–65

Butterss, Philip, 'Fidelia Hill: Finding a Public Voice', in Southwords: Essays on South Australian Writing, ed. by Philip Butterss (Kent Town: Wakefield, 1995), pp. 16–26

Callaway, Anita, *Visual Ephemera: Theatrical Art in Nineteenth-Century Australia* (Sydney: University of New South Wales Press, 2000)

Carens, Timothy L., *Outlandish English Subjects in the Victorian Domestic Novel* (New York: Palgrave, 2005)

Cassidy-Welch, Megan, '"A Place of Horror and Vast Solitude": Medieval Monasticism and the Australian Landscape', in *Medievalism and the Gothic in Australian Culture*, ed. by Stephanie Trigg (Turnhout: Brepols, 2005), pp. 189–204

Chance, Jane, ed., *Women Medievalists and the Academy* (Madison: University of Wisconsin Press, 2005)

Cherry, Deborah, and Griselda Pollock, revised version of 'Woman as Sign in Pre-Raphaelite Literature: The Representation of Elizabeth Siddall', in Griselda Pollock, *Vision and Difference: Feminity, Feminism, and the Histories of Art* (London and New York: Routledge, 1988), pp. 91–115

Clarke, Patricia, 'Two Colonials in London's Bohemia: Rosa Praed and Mortimer Menpes', *National Library of Australia News*, 13.12 (2003) <http://www.nla.gov.au/pub/nlanews/2003/sep03/article4.html>

Cochrane, Peter, 'Anglo-Saxonness: Ancestors and Identity', *Communal/Plural*, 4 (1994), 1–16

Codell, Julie, 'Imperial Difference and Culture Clashes in Victorian Periodicals' Visuals: The Case of *Punch*', *Victorian Periodicals Review*, 39 (2006), 410–28

Cole, Douglas, '"The Crimson Thread of Kinship": Ethnic Ideas in Australia, 1870–1914', *Historical Studies*, 14 (1971), 511–25

Colligan, Mimi, *Canvas Documentaries: Panoramic Entertainments in Nineteenth-Century Australia and New Zealand* (Carlton: Melbourne University Press, 2002)

Corson, James C., 'Scott's Novels: Dramatized Versions', *Notes and Queries*, 189 (1945), 17–18

Croft, Julian, *The Life and Opinions of Tom Collins: A Study of the Works of Joseph Furphy* (St Lucia: University of Queensland Press, 1991)

Crook, Paul, 'Historical Monkey Business: The Myth of a Darwinized British Imperial Discourse', *History*, 84 (1999), 633–57

Dale, Leigh, 'Empire's Proxy: Sheep and the Colonial Environment', in *Five Emus to the King of Siam: Environment and Empire*, ed. by Helen Tiffin (Amsterdam: Rodopi, 2007), pp. 1–14

Dalziell, Tanya, *Settler Romances and the Australian Girl* (Crawley: University of Western Australia Press, 2004)

D'Arcens, Louise, 'Europe in the Antipodes: Australian Medieval Studies', in *Studies in Medievalism, X, Medievalism and the Academy II*, ed. by David Metzger (Cambridge: Brewer, 1998), pp. 13–40

—, 'From Holy War to Border Skirmish: The Colonial Chivalry of Sydney's First Professors', *Journal of Medieval and Early Modern Studies*, 30 (2000), 519–45

—, 'Antipodean Idylls: An Early Australian Translation of Tennyson's Medievalism', in *Postcolonial Moves in Medieval, Early Modern, and Baroque Studies*, ed. by Patricia Ingham and Michelle R. Warren (Basingstoke and New York: Palgrave, 2003), pp. 237–56

—, 'Inverse Invasions: Medievalism and Colonialism in Rolf Boldrewood's *A Sydney-Side Saxon*', *Parergon: Journal of the Australian and New Zealand Association for Medieval and Early Modern Studies*, 22.2 (2005), 159–82

—, '"The Last Thing One Might Expect": The Mediaeval Court at the 1866 Intercolonial Exhibition', *The La Trobe Journal*, 81 (2008), 26–39

Darian-Smith, Kate, and others, eds, *Seize the Day: Exhibitions, Australia and the World* (Melbourne: Monash University ePress, 2008). DOI: 10.2104/sd080000

Deleuze, Gilles, and Félix Guattari, *A Thousand Plateaus: Capitalism and Schizophrenia*, trans. and intro. by Brian Massumi (Minneapolis: University of Minnesota Press, 1987)

Derrida, Jacques, 'Différance', in *Speech and Phenomena: And Other Essays on Husserl's Theory of Signs*, trans. by David B. Allison (Evanston: Northwestern University Press, 1973), pp. 129–60

de Serville, Paul, *Pounds and Pedigrees: The Upper Class in Victoria 1850–80* (Melbourne: Oxford University Press, 1991)

de Serville, Paul, *Rolf Boldrewood: A Life* (Carlton, Vic.: Melbourne University Press, 2000)

Devlin-Glass, Frances, '"Touches of Nature That Make the Whole World Kin": Furphy, Race, and Anxiety', *Australian Literary Studies*, 19 (2000), 355–72

Dixon, Robert, *Writing the Colonial Adventure: Gender, Race, and Nation in Anglo-Australian Popular Fiction 1875–1914* (Cambridge: Cambridge University Press, 1995)

Docker, John, *The Nervous Nineties: Australian Cultural Life in the 1890s* (Oxford: Oxford University Press, 1991)

Dunstone, Bill, 'Dinkum Shakespeare? Perth, Empire and the Bard', in *O Brave New World: Two Centuries of Shakespeare on the Australian Stage*, ed. by John Golder and Richard Madelaine (Sydney: Currency, 2001), pp. 163–79; notes 275–76

Elliott, Brian, *Adam Lindsay Gordon* (Melbourne: Sun Books, 1973)

Fantasia, Josephine Vita, 'Entrepreneurs, Empires and Pantomimes: J. C. Williamson's Pantomime Productions as a Site from which to Review the Cultural Construction of an Australian Theatre Industry, 1882 to 1914' (unpublished doctoral thesis, University of Sydney, 1996)

Fay, Elizabeth, *Romantic Medievalism: History and the Romantic Literary Ideal* (Basingstoke and New York: Palgrave Macmillan, 2002)

Fotheringham, Richard, ed., *Australian Plays for the Colonial Stage 1834–1899* (St Lucia: University of Queensland Press, 2006)

—, 'George Rignold', in *The Companion to Theatre in Australia*, ed. by P. Parsons (Sydney: Currency in association with Cambridge University Press, 1995)

Frantzen, Allen J., *Bloody Good: Chivalry, Sacrifice, and the Great War* (Chicago: University of Chicago Press, 2004)

Frantzen, Allan J., and John D. Niles, eds, *Anglo-Saxonism and the Construction of Social Identity* (Gainesville: University Press of Florida, 1997)

Freedman, Paul, and Gabrielle Spiegel, 'Medievalisms Old and New: The Rediscovery of Alterity in North American Medieval Studies', *American Historical Review*, 103 (1998), 677–704

Fulton, Helen, 'Medieval Studies in Australia', *AUMLA: Journal of the Australasian Universities Language and Literature Association*, 100 (2003), 1–12

Gagnier, Regenia, 'Women in British Aestheticism and the Decadence', in *The New Woman in Fiction and Fact: Fin-de-Siècle Feminisms*, ed. by Angelique Richardson and Chris Willis (Basingstoke: Palgrave Macmillan, 2001), pp. 239–49

Gascoigne, John, *The Enlightenment and the Origins of European Australia* (Cambridge: Cambridge University Press, 2002)

Gilmartin, Sophie, *Ancestry and Narrative in Nineteenth-Century British Literature: Blood Relations from Edgeworth to Hardy* (Cambridge: Cambridge University Press, 1998)

Girouard, Mark, *The Return to Camelot: Chivalry and the English Gentleman* (New Haven: Yale University Press, 1981)

Golder, John, and Richard Madelaine, eds, *O Brave New World: Two Centuries of Shakespeare on the Australian Stage* (Sydney: Currency, 2001)

Graham, John, 'National Identity and the Politics of Publishing the Troubadours', in *Medievalism and the Modernist Temper*, ed. by R. Howard Bloch and Stephen G. Nichols (Baltimore: Johns Hopkins University Press, 1996), pp. 57–94

Griffiths, Tom, *Hunters and Collectors: The Antiquarian Imagination in Australia* (Cambridge: Cambridge University Press, 1996)

Gumbrecht, Hans Ulrich, '"Un Souffle d'Allemagne ayant passé": Friedrich Diez, Gaston Paris, and the Genesis of National Philologies', *Romance Philology*, 40 (1986), 1–37

Hanawalt, Barbara A., 'Golden Ages for the History of Medieval English Women', in *Women in Medieval History and Historiography*, ed. by Susan Mosher Stuard (Philadelphia: University of Pennsylvania Press, 1987), pp. 1–24

Hardwick, J. M. D., *Emigrant in Motley: The Journey of Charles and Ellen Kean in quest of theatrical fortune in Australia and America, as told in their hitherto unpublished letters* (London: Rockliff, 1954)

Hewitt, Barnard, 'Mrs. John Wood and the Lost Art of Burlesque Acting', *Educational Theatre Journal*, 13 (1961), 82–85

Hill, Christopher, 'The Norman Yoke', in *Democracy and the Labour Movement: Essays in Honour of Dona Torr*, ed. by J. Saville (London: Lawrence and Wishart, 1954), pp. 11–66

Hoffenberg, Peter, *An Empire on Display: English, Indian, and Australian Exhibitions from the Crystal Palace to the Great War* (Berkeley: University of California Press, 2001)

Horsman, Reginald, *Race and Manifest Destiny: The Origins of American Racial Anglo-Saxonism* (Cambridge, MA: Harvard University Press, 1981)

Houghton, Walter E., 'Periodical Literature and the Articulate Classes', in *The Victorian Periodical Press*, ed. by Joanne Shattock and Michael Wolff (Toronto: University of Toronto Press / Leicester University Press, 1982), pp. 3–27

Hutton, Geoffrey, *Adam Lindsay Gordon: The Man and the Myth* (London: Faber, 1978)

Hutchison, David, ed., *A Place like No Other: The Living Tradition of New Norcia* (South Fremantle: Fremantle Arts Centre, 1995)

Inglis, Alison, 'Aestheticism and Empire: The Grosvenor Gallery Intercolonial Exhibition in Melbourne, 1887', in *Seize the Day: Exhibitions, Australia and the World*, ed. by Kate Darian-Smith and others (Melbourne: Monash University ePress, 2008), pp. 16.1–16.17. DOI: 10.2104/sd080016

Irvin, Eric, *Australian Melodrama: Eighty Years of Popular Theatre* (Sydney: Hale & Iremonger, 1981)

Jauss, Hans Robert, 'The Alterity and Modernity of Medieval Literature', *New Literary History*, 10.2 (1979), 181–229

Johnston, Anna, and Alan Lawson, 'Settler Colonies', in *A Companion to Postcolonial Studies*, ed. by Sangeeta Ray (Maldon, MA, and Oxford: Blackwell, 2000), pp. 360–76

Johnston, Judith, *George Eliot and the Discourses of Medievalism* (Turnhout: Brepols, 2006)

Jones, Joseph, *Radical Cousins: Nineteenth Century American & Australian Writers* (St Lucia: University of Queensland Press, 1976)

—, 'Mark Twain's Connecticut Yankee and Australian Nationalist Thought', *American Literature*, 40 (1968), 227–31

Jordan, Richard D., 'Adam Lindsay Gordon: The Australian Poet', *Westerly*, 2 (1985), 45–56

Jordens, Ann-Mari, *The Stenhouse Circle: Literary Life in Mid-Nineteenth-Century Sydney* (Carlton: Melbourne University Press, 1979)

—, 'Shakespeare in Settler-built Spaces: Oscar Asche's 'Recitals' of Julius Caesar in the Melbourne and Sydney Town Halls', *Contemporary Theatre Review*, 19 (2009), 353–66

—, 'J. C. Williamson Produces *Parsifal, or the Redemption of Kundry:* Wagnerism, Religion, and Sexuality', *Theatre History Studies*, 15 (1995), 161–81

—, 'Julius Knight, Australian Matinee Idol: Costume Drama as Historical Re-presentation', *Australasian Victorian Studies Journal*, 9 (2003), 128–44

—, 'Colonial "Australian" Theatre Writers: Cultural Authorship and the Case of Marcus Clarke's "First" Play', *Australian Literary Studies*, 18 (1997), 31–44

—, 'Burlesque', in *The Companion to Theatre in Australia*, ed. by P. Parsons (Sydney: Currency in association with Cambridge University Press, 1995), p. 147

—, with Mary Ann Hunter and Sue Cullen, *Annotated Calendar of Plays Premiered in Australia, 1850–1869*, 4 files (School of English, Media Studies, and Art History, University of Queensland: ePrints@UQ, 1995 and 2004)

Kramer, Leonie, 'The Literary Reputation of Adam Lindsay Gordon', *Australian Literary Studies*, 1 (1963), 42–56

Kreyling, Michael, 'The Hero in Antebellum Southern Narrative', *Southern Literary Journal*, 16 (1984), 3–21

Ledger, Sally, 'The New Woman and the Crisis of Victorianism', in *Cultural Politics at the Fin de Siècle*, ed. by Sally Ledger and Scott McCracken (Cambridge, London, and Melbourne: Cambridge University Press, 1995), pp. 22–44

Lee, Christopher, 'Strategies of Power and Catherine Martin's *An Australian Girl*', *Southerly*, 51 (1991), 189–206

Love, Harold, *The Golden Age of Australian Opera: W. S. Lyster and his Companies 1861–1880* (Sydney: Currency, 1981)

—, ed., *The Australian Stage: A Documentary History* (Kensington: University of New South Wales Press, 1984)

Lupack, Alan, ed., *Arthurian Drama: An Anthology* (New York: Garland, 1991)

Lynch, Andrew, 'C. J. Brennan's A Chant of Doom: Australia's Medieval War', *Australian Literary Studies*, 23 (2007), 49–62

—, '"Thingless Names"? The St George Legend in Australia', *The La Trobe Journal*, 81 (2008), 40–52

MacRae, C. F., *Adam Lindsay Gordon* (New York: Twayne, 1968)

McCann, Andrew, 'Romanticism, Nationalism and the Myth of the Popular in William Lane's *The Workingman's Paradise*', *Journal of Australian Studies*, 70 (2001), 1–12

—, 'Colonial Nature-Inscription: On Haunted Landscapes', in *Five Emus to the King of Siam: Environment and Empire*, ed. by Helen Tiffin (Amsterdam and New York: Rodopi, 2007), pp. 71–84

McGregor, Russell, 'The Necessity of Britishness: Ethno-Cultural Roots of Australian Nationalism', *Nations and Nationalism*, 12 (2006), 493–511

Madelaine, Richard, 'Substantial Pageant: Oscar Asche, Latter-Day Pictorialism, and Australian Audiences, 1909–24', in *O Brave New World: Two Centuries of Shakespeare on the Australian Stage*, ed. by John Golder and Richard Madelaine (Sydney: Currency, 2001), pp. 103–20

Magarey, Susan, 'History, Cultural Studies, and Another Look at First Wave Feminism in Australia', in *Debutante Nation: Feminism Contests of the 1890s*, ed. by Susan Magarey, Sue Rowley, and Susan Sheridan (St Leonards, NSW: Allen and Unwin, 1993), pp. 96–110

Mahood, Marguerite, *The Loaded Line: Australian Political Caricature 1788–1901* (Carlton: Melbourne University Press, 1973)

Mangum, Teresa, *Married, Middebrow, and Militant: Sarah Grand and the New Woman Novel* (Ann Arbor: University of Michigan Press, 1998)

Mansfield, B., 'The Socialism of William Morris: England and Australia', *Historical Studies*, 7 (1956), pp. 271–90

Martin, A. W., 'Parkes, Sir Henry (1815–1896)', *Australian Dictionary of Biography*, 18 vols (Carlton: Melbourne University Press, 1966–2007), V (1974), 399–406

Martin, Susan K., '"Surmounted by Stuffed Sheep": Exhibitions and Empire in Nineteenth-Century Australian Women's Fiction', in *Seize the Day: Exhibitions, Australia and the World*, ed. by Kate Darian-Smith and others (Melbourne: Monash University ePress, 2008), pp. 13.1–13.11. DOI: 10.2104/sd080013

Matthews, David, 'Marcus Clarke, Gothic, Romance', in *Medievalism and the Gothic in Australian Culture*, ed. by Stephanie Trigg (Turnhout: Brepols, 2005), pp. 3–18

Mead, Jenna, 'Medievalism and Memory Work: Archer's Folly and the Gothic Revival Pile', in *Medievalism and the Gothic in Australian Culture*, ed. by Stephanie Trigg (Turnhout: Brepols, 2005), pp. 99–118

Melman, Billie, 'Claiming the Nation's Past: The Invention of an Anglo-Saxon Tradition', *Journal of Contemporary History*, 26 (1991), 575–95

Menz, Christopher, *Morris & Co.* (Adelaide: Art Gallery of South Australia, 2002)

Miesel, Martin, *Realizations: Narrative, Pictorial, and Theatrical Arts in Nineteenth-Century England* (Princeton: Princeton University Press, 1983)

Montana, Andrew, *The Art Movement in Australia: Design, Taste and Society 1875–1900* (Carlton, Vic.: Miegunyah, 2000)

Murphy, Patricia, *Time is of the Essence: Temporality, Gender, and the New Woman* (Albany: State University of New York Press, 2001)

Nairn, Bede, 'Robertson, Sir John (1816–1891)', *Australian Dictionary of Biography*, 18 vols (Carlton: Melbourne University Press, 1966–2007), VI (1976), 38–46

Nikolopoulou, Anastasia, 'Medievalism and Historicity in the English Gothic Melodrama: Maturin's *Bertram: or, The Castle of St Aldobran*', *Poetica: An International Journal of Linguistic Literary Studies*, 39–40 (1994), 139–53

'Osric' (Humphrey Hall and Alred John Cripps), *The Romance of the Sydney Stage* (Sydney: Currency in association with National Library of Australia, 1996)

Osterweis, Rollin G., *Romanticism and Nationalism in the Old South* (New Haven: Yale University Press, 1949)

Otto, Peter, 'Romantic Medievalism and Gothic Horror', in *Medievalism and the Gothic in Australian Culture*, ed. by Stephanie Trigg (Turnhout: Brepols, 2005), pp. 19–40

Parsons, P., ed., *The Companion to Theatre in Australia* (Sydney: Currency in association with Cambridge University Press, 1995)

Pelosi, Janette, 'Colonial Drama Revealed, or Plays Submitted for Approval', *MARGIN: Life and Letters in Early Australia*, 60 (2003), 21–34

Platt, Len, '"Altogether Better-bred Looking": Race and Romance in the Australian Novels of Rosa Praed', *JASAL*, 8 (2008), 31–44

Playford, John, 'Playford, Thomas (1837–1915)', *Australian Dictionary of Biography*, 18 vols (Carlton: Melbourne University Press, 1966–2007), XI (1988), 245–47

Randles, Sarah, 'Rebuilding the Middle Ages: Medievalism in Australian Architecture', in *Medievalism and the Gothic in Australian Culture*, ed. by Stephanie Trigg (Turnhout: Brepols, 2005), pp. 147–69

Reel, Jerome V. Jr, 'The Music of Arthur: A Listing', on the *Arthuriana* website: <http://www.lib.rochester.edu/camelot/acpbibs/reel.htm>

Reynolds, Henry, *Dispossession: Black Australians and White Invaders* (St Leonards, NSW: Allen and Unwin, 1989)

Riede, David G., *Dante Gabriel Rossetti Revisited* (New York: Twayne, 1992)

Robb, Frank Maldon, 'Introduction', in *Poems of Adam Lindsay Gordon*, ed., intro., notes, and appendices by Frank Maldon Robb (London: Oxford University Press, 1912), pp. xiii–cxxvii

Roe, Jill, *Stella Miles Franklin* (London: Fourth Estate, 2008)

—, '"The Scope of Women's is Necessarily Less": The Case of Ada Cambridge', *Australian Literary Studies*, 5 (1972), 388–403

Rogerson, Margaret, 'Australian "Everymans": Post-Medieval Spiritual Adventurers', in *Medievalism and the Gothic in Australian Culture*, ed. by Stephanie Trigg (Turnhout: Brepols, 2005), pp. 81–97

Rutledge, Martha, 'Buchanan, David (1823?–1890)', *Australian Dictionary of Biography*, 18 vols (Carlton: Melbourne University Press, 1966–2007), III (1969), 281–83

Saunders, Clare Broome, '"Judge No More What Ladies Do": Elizabeth Barrett Browning's Active Medievalism, the Female Troubadour, and Joan of Arc', *Victorian Poetry*, 44 (2006), 585–97

—, *Women Writers and Nineteenth-Century Medievalism* (Basingstoke: Palgrave Macmillan, 2009)

Scates, Bruce, *A New Australia: Citizenship, Radicalism and the First Republic* (Cambridge: Cambridge University Press, 1997)

Schaffer, Talia, and Kathy Alexis Psomaidis, eds, *Women and British Aestheticism* (Charlottesville: University Press of Virginia, 1999)

Schech, Susanne, and Jane Haggis, 'Migrancy, Whiteness, and the Settler Self in Contemporary Australia', in *Race, Colour, and Identity in Australia and New Zealand*, ed. by John Docker and Gerhard Fischer (Sydney: University of New South Wales Press, 2000), pp. 231–39

Schlegel, A. W. von, *Observations sur la langue et la littérature provençales* (Paris: Librarie Grecque-latine-allemande, 1818)

Schmidt, Peter, 'Walter Scott, Postcolonial Theory, and New South Literature', *Mississippi Quarterly*, 56 (2003), 545–54

Schoch, Richard, *Not Shakespeare: Bardolatry and Burlesque in the Nineteenth Century* (Cambridge: Cambridge University Press, 2002)

—, *Shakespeare's Victorian Stage: Performing History in the Theatre of Charles Kean* (Cambridge: Cambridge University Press, 1998)

—, *Victorian Theatrical Burlesques* (Cambridge: Cambridge University Press, 2003)

Scragg, Donald, and Carole Weinberg, eds, *Literary Appropriations of the Anglo-Saxons from the Thirteenth to the Twentieth Centuries* (Cambridge: Cambridge University Press, 2000)

Scragg, Donald, 'Introduction: The Anglo-Saxons, Fact and Fiction', in *Literary Appropriations of the Anglo-Saxons from the Thirteenth to the Twentieth Centuries*, ed. by Donald Scragg and Carole Weinberg (Cambridge: Cambridge University Press, 2000), pp. 1–21

Shattock, Joanne, and Michael Wolff, eds, *The Victorian Periodical Press: Samplings and Soundings* (Toronto: University of Toronto Press / Leicester University Press, 1982)

Siberry, Elizabeth, *The New Crusaders: Images of the Crusades in the Nineteenth and Early Twentieth Centuries* (Aldershot and Burlington, VT: Ashgate, 2000)

Simmons, Clare A., *Reversing the Conquest: History and Myth in Nineteenth-Century British Literature* (New Brunswick: Rutgers University Press, 1990)

Slemon, Stephen, 'Unsettling the Empire: Resistance Theory for the Second World', in *Contemporary Postcolonial Theory: A Reader*, ed. by Padmini Mongia (London: Arnold, 1996), pp. 72–83

Smith, Andrew, and William Hughes, eds, *Empire and the Gothic: The Politics of Genre* (New York: Palgrave Macmillan, 2003)

Spring, John R., *A Frequency List of Dramatic Performances Advertised in the Melbourne* Argus *between January 1860 and December 1869* (Melbourne: Monash University, English Dept., 1977)

Sutherland, Kathryn, 'Elizabeth Elstob', in *Medieval Scholarship: Biographical Studies on the Formation of a Discipline*, ed. by Helen Damico, 2 vols (New York: Garland, 1998), II, 59–74

Tate, Audrey, *Ada Cambridge: Her Life and Work 1844–1926* (Carlton: University of Melbourne Press, 1991)

Trigg, Stephanie, ed., *Medievalism and the Gothic in Australian Culture* (Turnhout: Brepols, 2005)

van den Hoorn, Rob, 'Chinner, John Henry (1865–1933)', *Australian Dictionary of Biography*, 18 vols (Carlton: Melbourne University Press, 1966–2007), Supplementary Volume (2005), p. 67

van der Poorten, Helen M., 'Rignall, George Richard (1839–1912)', *Australian Dictionary of Biography*, 18 vols (Carlton: Melbourne University Press, 1976), VI, 30

Vann, J. Don, and Rosemary T. VanArsdel, eds, *Periodicals of Queen Victoria's Empire: An Exploration* (Toronto: University of Toronto Press, 1996)

Voskuil, Lynn M., 'Feeling Public: Sensation Theater, Commodity Culture, and the Victorian Public Sphere', *Victorian Studies*, 44 (2002), 245–74

Wakefield, Sarah R., 'Charlotte Yonge's Victorian Normans in *The Little Duke*', in *Beyond Arthurian Romances: The Reach of Victorian Medievalism*, ed. by Jennifer Palmgren and Lorretta Holloway (Basingstoke: Palgrave Macmillan, 2005), pp. 53–72

Wawn, Andrew, *The Vikings and the Victorians: Inventing the Old North in 19th-Century Britain* (Cambridge: Brewer, 2000)

Webby, Elizabeth, *Early Australian Poetry: An Annotated Bibliography of Original Poems Published in Australian Newspapers, Magazines & Almanacks Before 1850* (Sydney: Hale and Iremonger, 1982)

—, 'Australia', in *Periodicals of Queen Victoria's Empire: An Exploration*, ed. by J. Don Vann and Rosemary T. VanArsdel (Toronto: University of Toronto Press, 1996), pp. 19–58

—, '"Born to Blush Unseen": Some Nineteenth-Century Women Poets', in *A Bright and Fiery Troop: Australian Women Writers of the Nineteenth Century*, ed. by Debra Adelaide (Ringwood, Vic.: Penguin, 1988), pp. 41–52

Wilde, W. H., *Adam Lindsay Gordon* (Melbourne: Oxford University Press, 1972)

Williams, Margaret, *Australia on the Popular Stage 1829–1929: An Historical Entertainment in Six Acts* (Melbourne: Oxford University Press, 1983)

Wilson, Elizabeth, *Adorned in Dreams: Fashion and Modernity*, rev. edn (New Brunswick, NJ: Rutgers University Press, 2003)

Wood, George Arnold, 'Australia and Imperial Politics', in *Australia: Economic and Political Studies*, ed. by Meredith Atkinson (Melbourne: Macmillan, 1920), pp. 330–415

Zumthor, Paul, 'Comments on H. R. Jauss's Article', *New Literary History*, 10.2 (1979), 367–76

# INDEX

# Making the Middle Ages

All volumes in this series are evaluated by an Editorial Board, strictly on academic grounds, based on reports prepared by referees who have been commissioned by virtue of their specialism in the appropriate field. The Board ensures that the screening is done independently and without conflicts of interest. The definitive texts supplied by authors are also subject to review by the Board before being approved for publication. Further, the volumes are copyedited to conform to the publisher's stylebooks and to the best international academic standards in the field.

**Titles in Series**

*Medievalism in the Modern World: Essays in Honour of Leslie Workman*, ed. by Richard Utz and Tom Shippey (1998)

David Matthews, *The Invention of Middle English: An Anthology of Primary Sources* (2000)

Richard J. Utz, *Chaucer and the Discourse of German Philology: A History of Reception and an Annotated Bibliography of Studies, 1793–1948* (2002)

Margaret Clunies Ross, *The Old Norse Poetic Translations of Thomas Percy: A New Edition and Commentary* (2001)

John Kennedy, *Translating the Sagas: Two Hundred Years of Challenge and Response* (2007)

Judith Johnston, *George Eliot and the Discourses of Medievalism* (2006)

*Maistresse of My Wit: Medieval Women, Modern Scholars*, ed. by Louise D'Arcens and Juanita Feros Ruys (2004)

*Medievalism and the Gothic in Australian Culture*, ed. by Stephanie Trigg (2005)

*Constructing Nations, Reconstructing Myth: Essays in Honour of T. A. Shippey*, ed. by Andrew Wawn, Graham Johnson, and John Walter (2007)